To: Colonel Collard
In his 25th year of most loyal
Service to Blairmae

From: The Governas

THE MOUNTED TROOPS
OF THE BRITISH ARMY
1066–1945

PRIVATE, LIGHT TROOP, 11TH DRAGOONS, *circa* 1760.

(By kind permission, from the original oil painting by David Morier, in the possession of the Earl of Pembroke.)

Note the method of supporting the carbine with the belt swivel when firing.

THE IMPERIAL SERVICES LIBRARY
VOLUME III

THE MOUNTED TROOPS

OF THE

BRITISH ARMY

1066-1945

By

Colonel H. C. B. Rogers, O.B.E.

LONDON
Seeley Service & Co.
Limited

©

Colonel H. C. B. Rogers, O.B.E.
Seeley Service & Co Ltd.
1959

New Edition
1967

Printed in Great Britain

TO MY WIFE
who followed
Trumpet and Saddle
from Catterick Camp to the
Khyber Pass

CONTENTS

PREFACE . . . . *page* 13

Chapter   I. THE MEDIAEVAL PERIOD . . . 17

II. BETWEEN THE CIVIL WARS . . 33

III. FROM KING TO COMMONWEALTH . 49

IV. FROM RESTORATION TO REVOLUTION . 59

V. THE RIVAL KINGS 69

VI. QUEEN ANNE 83

VII. HANOVER & STUART . . . 93

VIII. BEFORE THE FRENCH REVOLUTION . 115

IX. THE NAPOLEONIC WARS—THE FIRST
PHASE 145

X. THE PENINSULA & WATERLOO . . 165

XI. THE GOLDEN AGE OF HORSES . . 183

XII. EARLY VICTORIAN 195

XIII. THE END OF AN ERA . . . 213

XIV. THE LAST OF THE HORSE SOLDIER . 233

INDEX 249

LIST OF PLATES

Plate

I Private, Light Troop, 11th Dragoons, *circa* 1760

[*In colour*] FRONTISPIECE

OPPOSITE PAGE

II Major-General Randolph Egerton, *circa* 1672 . . . 50

III Duke of Cumberland's Dragoons 110

IV 1st Troop, Horse Grenadier Guards 112

V The 4th Queen's Own Dragoons, 1802 . . . [*In colour*] 122

VI Lieutenant-General Sir Thomas Dallas, G.C.B.
(1758–1839) . . . . [*In colour*] 134

VII The 4th Royal Irish Dragoon Guards, 1849 . . [*In colour*] 136

VIII A Sergeant, 10th Light Dragoons, 1793 138

IX Privates, Scots Greys, 1807 166

X Officer, The 6th (Inniskilling) Dragoons, 1811 . [*In colour*] 172

XI Trooper, 6th (Inniskilling) Dragoons, *circa* 1815 . . . 178

XII Officer, 8th The King's Royal Irish Hussars, *circa* 1823

[*In colour*] 180

XIII An Officer, 15th Hussars, *circa* 1827 . . [*In colour*] 184

XIV First Life Guards, 1833 186

XV 8th Hussars, 1833 188

XVI 14th Light Dragoons, 1833 190

XVII Trumpeters and Drummers, 1st King's Dragoon
Guards, 1927 . . . . . . [*In colour*] 192

XVIII 6th and 7th Dragoons, 1833 196

XIX The Royal Horse Guards, 1833 198

XX The Royal Horse Artillery, 1833 200

XXI Officer of the 12th Royal Lancers, 1820 . . [*In colour*] 202

XXII Trooper, Review Order, 9th Lancers, 1841 . . [*In colour*] 204

List of Plates

Plate   OPPOSITE PAGE

XXIII   The 12th Royal Lancers, 1844   .   .   .   . [*In colour*] 208

XXIV   The Royal Dragoons, 1848   .   .   .   . [*In colour*] 210

XXV   1st Middlesex Light Horse (Metropolitan
         Light Horse), 1861–67 .   .   .   .   . [*In colour*] 214

XXVI   Officers of 11th Hussars, *circa* 1865   .   . [*In colour*] 216

XXVII   The Band of the Royal Dragoons, 1890   . [*In colour*] 218

XXVIII   The Charge of General French's Cavalry Division
         at Klip Drift   230

XXIX   A Trooper of the 17th Lancers, 1918 234

XXX   The Gloucester Yeomanry, 1918   242

XXXI   Cavalry in Reserve, 17th September, 1918 .   .   . 242

XXXII   Royal Signals Cable Laying in the Field   .   . [*In colour*] 244

XXXIII   The Cheshire Yeomanry in Palestine, 1941 .   .   . 246

FIGURES IN THE TEXT

Figure   Page

1   Knights, from 'The Lives of the Two Offas', thirteenth century .   22

2   Knights, *circa* 1327   27

3   The Departure of King Henry VIII from Calais, 15th July, 1544 .   38

4   The Encampment of King Henry VIII at Marquison, July, 1544 .   40

5   A Battle between the Irish and the English   45

6   From Ufano's 'Treatise on Artillery', Brussels, 1613 .   .   .   47

7   'The Life Guards' in the Procession at the Opening of the First Parliament of James the Seventh and Second in Edinburgh, 1685 .   62

8   An Officer, 'Queen's Regiment of Horse', 1689   70

9   Light Troop. From 'The Discipline of the Light-Horse' by Captain R. Hinde, 1778   118

10   Form of the New Saddle. From 'The Discipline of the Light-Horse' by Captain R. Hinde, 1778   120

11   A Troop of Light-Dragoons, drawn up. From 'The Discipline of the Light-Horse' by Captain R. Hinde, 1778   .   .   .   122

12   Light Dragoon. From 'The Discipline of the Light-Horse' by Captain R. Hinde, 1778   124

13   The Encampment of a Regiment of Light Dragoons. From 'The Discipline of the Light-Horse' by Captain R. Hinde, 1778   130 & 131

14   A Regiment of Light-Dragoons, drawn up in 3 Squadrons, to be reviewed. From 'The Discipline of the Light-Horse' by Captain R. Hinde, 1778   139

15   A Regiment of Light-Dragoons marching in 3 Squadrons by the King or the Reviewing General. From 'The Discipline of the Light-Horse' by Captain R. Hinde, 1778   142

Figures in the Text

Figure   Page

16 Cut Two against Infantry. From 'Rules & Regulations for the Sword
    Exercise of the Cavalry', 1796   150

17 The Six Cuts. From 'Rules & Regulations for the Sword Exercise of
    the Cavalry', 1796   151

18 Guard. From 'Rules & Regulations for the Sword Exercise of the
    Cavalry', 1796   152

19 The Introduction to 'Rules & Regulations for the Sword Exercise of
    the Cavalry', 1796   154

20 Sword Exercises. Guards. From 'Rules & Regulations for the Sword
    Exercise of the Cavalry', 1796   156

PREFACE

The greater part of a book about the horse soldier must, of necessity, be devoted to the cavalryman; for it was not until the eighteenth century that there was any other mounted arm, and until the virtual disappearance of the horse from the Army it was only in the cavalry that all ranks were employed on mounted duties. Nevertheless, in addition to the Mounted Arms of the Service (Cavalry, Royal Artillery, Royal Engineers and Royal Signals) horses were used to a varying extent in practically every corps, regiment and department of the Army; and in the South African War the Mounted Infantry assumed the cavalry rôle of the original Dragoons. Officers of all arms were expected to be able to ride, and to have a thorough knowledge of horse management.

Association with horses seemed to produce a type of individual who was to be found in all units of the Army where 'stables' formed part of the day's routine. He was a simple soul; slow of speech and movement (when dismounted), and inclined to some richness of language. When reasonably contented he grumbled incessantly, and especially when engaged in the care of the horses he loved. Mechanization seems to have found no place for him. At any rate he has gone, and the Army is the poorer for his departure.

This, then is his biography. The tale of his service from the days when the Normans brought the war horse to England, till garages replaced stables in military barracks. It deals with his uniform and equipment, his weapons and horses, and his life in peace and war. It is not a military history, and no attempt has been made to describe campaigns or battles, except to provide such background as is required to show the conditions under which the horse soldier fought and the methods he used.

In the writing of this book I have received most generous

help from many sources. I would mention firstly the Society for Army Historical Research, of which I have the honour to be a member. Without the wealth of military information contained in its Journals, which have been published by the Society from 1922 onwards, I doubt whether it would have been possible to write the book at all. In addition, I have had the generous permission of the Society to reproduce a number of the colour and other plates from the Journal and to make use of their blocks for this purpose. I am particularly indebted to Mr. R. T. Eldridge, F.L.A., the Honorary Secretary of the Society, for the great trouble he has gone to in helping with the illustrations, which entailed considerable research. I am indebted, too, to Mr. T. H. McGuffie, M.A., Honorary Editor of the Society's Journal for his assistance, and for his kind permission to quote from his book *Peninsular Cavalry General*. I am also most grateful to that great military historian Mr. C. T. Atkinson for allowing me to make use of the invaluable material which he has contributed to the Journal, and which is the result of his expert researches.

Secondly I must mention the Military Society of Ireland, to which I am also honoured to belong, and their great generosity in allowing me to make use of the many excellent articles and other contributions which have been published in the Society's journal, *The Irish Sword*. In particular I owe my gratitude to Professor G. A. Hayes-McCoy, Vice-President of the Society, for his assistance.

My third main source of information (by no means in that order) has been the Royal United Service Institution, to which I have been privileged to belong for more years than I care to remember. Brigadier J. Stephenson, O.B.E., the librarian, has gone to considerable trouble to find me suitable references in the Institution's incomparable military library.

Through the kindness of the Right Honourable Sir Winston Churchill, K.G., P.C., O.M., C.H., F.R.S., M.P., and Messrs. Eyre and Spottiswoode (Publishers) Ltd., I have been permitted to reproduce Sir Winston Churchill's account of the cavalry charge at the Battle of Omdurman from his book, *The*

River War. To Messrs. Macmillan and Co. Ltd. I am indebted for permission to make use of passages from the late Field-Marshal Lord Roberts' book, *Forty-One Years in India*, and to Messrs. Edward Arnold (Publishers) Ltd. for permission to quote part of Lord Roberts' foreword to Erskine Childers' book, *War and the Arme Blanche.*

I owe much to the generosity of Brigadier-General Sir Ernest Makins, K.B.E., C.B., D.S.O., who has lent me the blocks for three beautiful colour plates of his Regiment, the Royal Dragoons. Major-General Sir Robert Hinde, K.B.E., C.B., D.S.O., Colonel of the 15th/19th The King's Royal Hussars, Brigadier C. H. M. Peto, D.S.O., D.L., Colonel of the 9th Queen's Royal Lancers, and Lieutenant-Colonel A. T. Smail, D.S.O., Colonel of the 11th Hussars (Prince Albert's Own), have all kindly given me permission to reproduce colour plates belonging to their Regiments. Major-General Sir Robert Hinde's association with the book is particularly interesting. I have quoted extensively from *The Discipline of the Light-Horse*, written by his ancestor, Captain Robert Hinde. Captain Hinde, although serving with the 2nd Troop of Horse Guards at the time, rode with the 15th Hussars at the battle of Emsdorf. Sir Robert Hinde's great-grandfather, Charles Hinde, and grandfather, Jacob William Hinde, both served in the 15th Hussars.

For other colour plates I owe the kind permission of the Earl of Pembroke, M.V.O., Lady Victoria Wemyss, Brigadier T. J. F. Collins, C.B.E., and Captain Russel V. Steele.

For the reproduction of the painting of the Cheshire Yeomanry in 1941, and for his own personal account of the campaign in Syria, I am indebted to Lieutenant-Colonel D. E. Williams, M.B.E.

I owe much to Mr. A. L. Kipling of Messrs. Gale and Polden for the trouble he has taken to assist me with the illustrations.

Lastly, I would express my gratitude to the President of the Headquarters Mess of my own Corps, the Royal Signals, for his permission to reproduce the painting of the Cable Wagon.

THE MEDIAEVAL PERIOD

The history of the British horse soldier begins on 28th September, 1066; for it was on that date that the army of William the Conqueror landed in England.

There had, it is true, been cavalry in England in earlier times. The Roman Army depended mainly on auxiliary troops to provide the cavalry regiments which were attached to the Legions; and the cavalry stationed in Roman Britain was probably composed principally of Celtic Britons. Certainly their cousins the Gauls on the other side of the channel were noted for the quality of their cavalry and the standard of their horses. When the Romans left Britain, this British cavalry probably remained to take part in the struggle against the barbarian invaders. Lt.-Colonel Burne, in his excellent book *The Battlefields of England*, considers that King Arthur finally smashed the Saxon Army at the decisive battle of Mount Badon by a charge at dawn with his heavy cavalry.

But the Saxons were not horsemen, and after the collapse of British resistance it is likely that the horse soldier was seen no more on British battlefields until, some 400 years later, a largely cavalry army destroyed the last of the Saxon kings.

Some ninety years after the battle of Hastings, Robert Wace wrote a poem, the *Roman de Rou*, which includes a vivid description of the Norman army:

'The barons and knights and lancemen were all now armed, the men on foot well equipped, each bearing bow and sword; on their heads were caps, and to their feet were bound buskins. Some had good hides which they bound round their bodies, and many were clad in frocks, and had quivers and bows hung to their girdles. The knights had hauberks and swords, boots

B   17

of steel, and shining helmets; shields at their necks, and in their hands lances. And all had their cognisances, so that each might know his fellow, and Norman might not strike Norman nor Frenchman kill his countryman by mistake. Those on foot led the way with serried ranks and bearing bows. The knights rode next supporting the archers from behind. Thus both horse and foot kept their course and order of march as they began, in close ranks, at a gentle pace, that the one might not pass or separate from the other. All went firmly and compactly, bearing themselves gallantly . . .'

Of Duke William's final cavalry charge Wace says:

'Then those who kept close guard by him, and rode where he rode, being about a thousand armed men, came and rushed with closed ranks upon the English; and with the weight of their good horses, and the blows the knights gave, broke the press of the enemy, and scattered the crowd before them, the good Duke leading them on in front. Many pursued and many fled, many were the Englishmen who fell around and were trampled under the horses, crawling upon the earth, and not able to rise. Many of the richest and noblest men fell in the rout, but still the English rallied in places, smote down those whom they reached, and maintained the combat the best they could, beating down the men and killing the horses.'

The famous Bayeux Tapestry gives a nearly contemporary illustration of the battle, and of the dress and equipment of the Norman soldier. All the horsemen are clad in a form of armour which consisted of a tunic, or hauberk, covered with metal rings and having a cowl over the head. They wear a conical helm with a nose-piece, or nasal. The cavalry appear to be divided into two types. Some are armed with a javelin, which is either thrown or used as an overarm stabbing weapon; others carry a heavy lance which is couched under the arm and frequently ornamented with a pennon. Swords and maces appear to be used at close quarters by those men who have hurled their javelins. The shields are long and are pointed at the foot. The spurs are of the simple prick pattern. The Norman horse furniture included saddle and stirrups, which would provide a firm seat in the charge. At this period the horses used by the Saxons were equipped with little more than a pad for the rider to sit on; and if King Harold's army had included mounted troops, therefore, they would have been of little use for shock action.

The horses appear to be small, probably about 14 hands, and all stallions. Duke William is said to have ridden a Spanish horse which was given to him by his friend Alfonso of Spain, and the horses of his followers are of a similar size and type. Armour at this time was still comparatively light, and there would have been no requirement for the heavy horse which was used in the later days of armour.

The type of army which followed William was the result of a fairly recent movement which had swept Western Europe, but which had not yet reached England. In the year 919, Henry, a Saxon prince known as the 'Fowler', was elected Emperor of Germany. At that time much of Germany was being overrun and ravaged by the Hungarian light cavalry. As part of his military measures against the Hungarians, Henry decided to raise a force of cavalry from the feudal aristocracy. To make such service popular amongst these proud nobles, he devised a form of mounted order with a code of honour to which it would be a privilege to belong. From this beginning there gradually arose the order of chivalry, or mounted knights, pledged to honour, courtesy, charity, justice and the service of God. The civilizing influence of the order was immense. Militarily, it produced a formidable force of heavy cavalry. Although this new order had spread all over the western part of the continent of Europe, it had not, at the time of the Norman invasion, reached England. Had it done so it seems unlikely that William's expedition could have succeeded.

One result of Norman rule was, of course, that the horse became a much more important factor in the military and sporting life of the nation. William brought many horses from Normandy, and these are supposed to have been the ancestors of the Anglo-Norman draught and saddle horses which are still bred in Normandy to-day. The first real efforts to improve the

British breed of horses seem to have been made during the reign of the Conqueror's son, William Rufus. Robert de Belesme, who owned property in Powysland, central Wales, is recorded by Giraldus Cambrensis as having imported Spanish stallions; with the result that the district became noted for the quality of its horses. Some 200 years later 'a Powys horse' occurs amongst those purchased by Edward II. The reputation of the Spanish horse was due to the cross between the native breed and the Barbs and Arabs which had been brought to Spain by the Moors. The result was the horse known as the Spanish Jennet, which became famous throughout Europe for its docility and appearance.

The first pure Arabs arrived in England during the reign of Henry I. These were a gift from Eastern Europe and were accompanied by sets of Turkish armour. One of these Arabs was sent by King Henry as a present to King Alexander I of Scotland, who, in turn, gave it to the church of St. Andrews. The Arab is the oldest breed in the world, and it had already, at this period, been long famous for its beauty, speed and endurance. Drawings nearly 5000 years old have been found of named Arab horses.

During the reign of Henry II mounted military sports took place at Smithfield. According to William Stephanides, a monk of Canterbury: 'Every Sunday in Lent after dinner young men ride out into the fields on horses which are fit for war and excellent for their speed. The citizens' sons issue out through the gates by troops, furnished with lances and shields, and make representation of battle and exercise and skirmish. To this performance many young courtiers yet uninitiated in arms resort, and great persons to train and practice. They begin by dividing into troops; some labour to outstrip their leaders without being able to reach them; others unhorse their antagonists without being able to get beyond them. At times two or three boys are set on horseback to ride a race and push their horses to their utmost speed, sparing neither whip nor spur.'

There was little change in the type of armour worn for the first 150 years after the Conquest. The most popular wear was the hauberk, covered with overlapping metal rings called 'single mail'. A tunic was generally worn under the hauberk and a surcoat over it. This latter was a long linen garment which served to give some protection both against rust and the heat of the sun. Many different types of helm were worn. Greater protection was sought until eventually the features were completely obscured, the minimum apertures being left to see through. The barrel helm, introduced at the end of the twelfth century, was a heavy inverted pot with slits for the eyes and perforations for breathing. It was made in a number of different shapes and was constructed either of boiled leather (*cuirbouilli*) or metal.

In the first half of the twelfth century the remarkable and colourful system of personal symbols, which we know as heraldry, swept over Europe, and the shields, surcoats and flags of knights and barons became emblazoned with their armorial devices. These same devices, too, were later embroidered on the great cloth bardings, or coverings, which were worn by the horses. Personal arms served a useful military purpose, for they enabled soldiers to recognize their leaders, whose faces were hidden by their helms.

The increased weight of the armour worn by the knights and mounted men-at-arms led to the introduction of a heavier type of horse. This was the so-called English 'Great Horse', a native breed which had been used for draught rather than the saddle. Even the Great Horse, however, soon proved insufficiently powerful for the ever-growing weight of armour, and King John made great efforts to increase its size. The largest and most powerful horses were bred in the Low Countries, and King John imported 100 of the Flemish stallions. These were probably the ancestors of the present great Brabançon breed, which stands between 16 and 17 hands. John also purchased some large stallions from Spain. This may have been the native breed previously referred to. They are described as Spanish *dextrarii*, or Great Horses. The war horse of the Middle Ages was commonly called a *dextrarius*. The result of John's breeding policy was the forerunner of the

21

great Shire horse of to-day which was well able to carry the 30-odd stone of the armoured knights and men-at-arms.

As a result of the Crusades a new type of mail armour was adopted early in the thirteenth century. It had been worn by the Saracens and consisted of interlocking rings, forming a complete garment without any foundation. It was based on a five-ring construction; that is to say, each ring was a connecting link for four others. This armour was known as chain mail.

Fig. 1.

From 'The Lives of the Two Offas', thirteenth century.

Towards the end of the century an enormous helmet made its appearance. This was the Great Helm, which rested on the shoulders and was only put on for actual combat. At other times it was hung from the saddle by a chain.

All men, from youths to old age, were liable to service in the Middle Ages. The cavalry was provided by the more wealthy of the population, and the equipment which a man was required to produce was governed by the value of his possessions. The Statute of Winchester of 8th October, 1285, and the thirteenth year of King Edward I's reign, contains the following regulations:

'And further it is commanded, that every man have in his

house harness for to keep the peace after the ancient Assise; that is to say,

'2. Every man between fifteen years of age and sixty years shall be assessed and sworn to armour according to the quantity of their lands and goods;

'3. That is to wit, from fifteen pounds lands, and goods forty marks, an hauberke, a breast-plate of iron, a sword, a knife, and a horse.'

A man with land worth ten pounds and goods twenty marks had to produce the same armour and weapons, but not the horse. Less wealthy men were required to provide a more modest scale of equipment.

The mounted knights and men-at-arms provided a force of heavy cavalry which was the predominant arm on the battle-fields of the early Middle Ages. It was, however, an unwieldy and cumbersome force. It is unlikely that the Great Horses with their heavy mounts ever moved faster than a trot, and their cross-country capacity must have been limited.

The first experiment in supplementing the heavy cavalry with light horse seems to have been made in 1296; when 260 Irish Hobelars were included in Edward I's army in Scotland. The Hobelars were so called from the small horse which they rode known as a 'hobin' (hobby horse). The hobin was the native horse of Ireland, and only stood between 12 and 14 hands. Its descendant is probably the Connemara pony of to-day, which was still found in a wild state in western Connaught until fairly recent times. The hobin could not, of course, carry a heavily armoured man and was too small for shock action. At reconnaissance and patrol work, however, the hobelar excelled. He rode his small mount without saddle, stirrups or bridle, and was far too mobile across country ever to be caught by the men-at-arms. Hobelars were used in each of the next two reigns, and Edward II raised a large number of hobelars in England. The English hobelars were bound to keep 'a little nag', and some of them were stationed at Portsmouth and other maritime places to form a covering screen and to give notice of invasion. They were armed with a sword, a knife and a lance.

23

In 1333 Edward III formed a body of mounted archers. These were really the first dragoons. As light horsemen they were far more effective than the hobelars, and the latter disappeared from the English armies.

Edward I's expedition against Scotland in 1300 and his siege of the castle of Caerlaverock are commemorated by a contemporary poem which is of particular interest in showing the type of work which the heavy cavalry were expected to undertake. Infantry at this time were largely untrained levies who were relegated to comparatively minor rôles, and the major part of the fighting was done by the knights and men-at-arms, either mounted or dismounted.

Edward's army assembled at Carlisle, and was divided into three divisions, of which the first was temporarily split into two for the advance. The army seems to have consisted of 85 barons and knights-banneret, about 600 knights-bachelor, 3000 men-at-arms (all mounted) and an unspecified number of infantry. The method of raising this army was fairly simple. When he was required to do so, every holder of one knight's fee had to present himself for military service, or he had to provide a substitute in the form of a fully equipped man-at-arms. If a knight held more than one fee he had to produce, in addition to himself, one man-at-arms for each extra fee of his estate. The contingent provided by a knight possessing four fees, for instance, would normally consist of himself and three mounted men-at-arms. Furthermore, the Statute of Winchester, already mentioned, required the richer freemen to serve as mounted men-at-arms, and others to serve on foot with equipment according to their wealth. Most of the knights, with their men-at-arms, followed one of the barons in whose domains they held their fees.

The Caerlaverock poem gives an interesting picture of the army on the march:

> And the King with his great force
> Set forth immediately against the Scots,—
> Not lightly clad and on palfreys,—
> But on costly Great Horses,

> And well and fully armed,
> In order that they might not be taken by surprise.
> There was many a rich caparison
> Embroidered on silks and satins;
> Many a beautiful pennon fixed to lance,
> And many a banner displayed.
> And one could hear the noise from afar
> Of the neighing of horses;
> Mountains and valleys were everywhere
> Covered with sumpter horses and wagons
> Carrying provisions, and with the train
> Of tents and pavilions.

The first half-division was the vanguard of the army, and in it the poem says:

> There were fully a hundred good bachelors
>   [*i.e.* knights-bachelor],
> Not one of whom would dismount into his lodgings,
> Until they have all
> Reconnoitred the vulnerable approaches.

After the arrival in front of Caerlaverock Castle, the quartering of the troops is described as follows:

> And as soon as we were drawn up
> And the Marshals had allotted the camp sites
> And divided up the area,
> One could see houses arise
> Without carpenters or masons,
> Of many different fashions,
> Of white and coloured cloth;
> Many a rope was pulled tight,
> Many a peg driven into the ground,
> Many a large tree cut down
> To make huts; and leaves,
> Herbs and flowers gathered in the woods,
> With which they were strewed within.
> And then our people dismounted.

The preliminary assault on the castle was launched by infantry, of whom probably no great things were expected, for the attack and its subsequent repulse are dismissed in a few lines. The main assault was then conducted by the dismounted knights and men-at-arms. The preliminary attack and the start of the main attack are described as follows:

And then the footmen began
To march against the castle;
And one could see flying amongst them
Stones, arrows and quarrels.
And so effectually were the weapons served
By both attack and defence,
That in a short time many bodies
Were wounded and maimed,
And I know not how many killed.
When the men-at-arms saw
How much the footmen had suffered
Who had begun the attack,
Many ran to the attack in one direction, and
    many in another,
And many were so anxious to advance
That they had no time for speech.
Then again one could see
Stones falling as thickly
As if it were raining them.
Hats and helms were crushed,
Shields and targets broken in pieces;
For the game they played
Was to kill and wound;
And they shouted savagely at each other,
As they saw the carnage inflicted.

There is no mention of the hobelars at the siege of Caerlaverock, but there may well have been a detachment with the vanguard of the army and as part of the protective screen during the attack on the castle.

The replacement of the hobelars by mounted archers led to a far more effective employment of the cavalry. The battle of Auberoche in 1345 affords a classic example. The castle of Auberoche was besieged by a French army 7000 strong; and the Earl of Derby, who had only a small mounted force of 400 men-at-arms and 800 archers, decided to attempt its relief. Marching under cover of the woods, he reached a point about two miles from Auberoche and close to the French camp without being discovered. A reconnaissance disclosed that the French were cooking their evening meal. Derby decided on a surprise attack. He sent his archers through the woods to a position overlooking and in range of the French camp. The men-at-arms then moved forward to an assault position. As soon as

FIG. 2.
Knights, circa *1327*.

they were ready, they gave a prearranged signal and charged the camp. The archers gave covering fire from the flank. The surprise was complete and the result decisive.

Towards the end of the thirteenth century steel plates were commonly worn over the shins to give better protection than was afforded by the mail alone; and during the fourteenth century more and more plates were added until complete plate armour made its appearance in about 1410. A bascinet, or conical steel helmet, replaced the mail coif as a head covering.

27

The great helm was worn over the bascinet for actual combat; but later, with the improvement of the bascinet, the great helm was only worn at tournaments.

Edward II made great efforts to improve the breed of English horses by purchasing stallions from the Continent. There are records of horse-buying commissions sent by him to the Champagne district of France, to Italy and to other places described as 'beyond seas'. One commission brought back from Lombardy thirty war horses and twelve others which were also of a heavy type. Edward III bought large numbers of Great Horses from the Low Countries. These, however, were not only for stud but to meet the demands of his forces for the Scottish wars. His purchases were so extensive, indeed, that at one time he owed the Count of Hainault 25,000 florins for horses. The cost of this influx of Great Horses into England so horrified the Archbishop of Canterbury in 1310 that he included the excessive expense of their upkeep amongst the worst abuses in the country. He said that each Great Horse cost 2s. 7d. a week, 'which would keep four or five poor people'. In addition a groom was paid, apparently, the unnecessarily lavish sum of three halfpence a day. The Wardrobe Accounts of Edward III's reign mention a number of other horses which were required for military purposes. These were known as palfreys, hackneys, hengests, somers, coursers, trotters, hobbies, nags and genets. A palfrey was a light saddle horse which had been taught the comfortable ambling pace. It was the normal mount for knights and their ladies; and it accompanied knights on campaigns, for more comfortable riding than was afforded by the Great Horse, when armour could be temporarily laid aside. The hackney was another saddle horse, but with a trotting gait. It was also taken to war as a light charger. The trotter was probably very similar, but a cheaper breed. Hengests and somers appear to have been the pack and draught horses used for baggage and supplies. Courser seems to have denoted a fast and good jumping horse. It might have been required for light cavalry. Hobbies (*i.e.* hobins) were the small horses as ridden by the hobelars, and were probably for mounted

28

archers. Genets, or Jennets, were the Spanish horses already mentioned. The jennet was a valuable and famous animal, and these were probably also intended for use by the knights. Nags were very likely cheap saddle horses used by servants and camp followers.

By the reign of King Henry V hobelars, as a light cavalry distinct from the mounted archers, had been reintroduced into the army. The force which Henry V took to France comprised men-at-arms (heavy cavalry), hobelars (light cavalry), horse archers, foot archers and pikemen.

A description of the Agincourt campaign is given in the narrative of a priest who accompanied the expedition. The organization and activities of the mounted troops get only brief mention, but the information given is of considerable interest.

The landing of the army in France was preceded by a reconnaissance:

'And when the following day dawned, that is on Wednesday, the Vigil of the Assumption of the Blessed Virgin, the sun shining and the morning beautiful, between the hours of six and seven, the noble Knight, Sir John Holland, Earl of Huntingdon, the King's cousin, having been sent by his desire before daybreak, in the stillness of the night, with certain horsemen as scouts to explore the country and place, the King, with the greater part of his army, landed in small vessels, boats, and skiffs.'

After the fall of Harfleur the King started his advance to Calais. The army reached Abbeville, 'hoping on the following day to cross the Somme: but it was suddenly told us by our scouts and advanced guard of horse, that the bridges with the causeways were broken down and that a great part of the French army was on the opposite side of the bank to prevent our crossing'.

The army moved upstream trying to find a crossing place; the French keeping pace with it on the opposite bank. Eventually a suitable crossing place was found. 'In the meantime a report was circulated through the army, upon the information of certain prisoners, that the enemy had appointed many companies of horsemen, in hundreds, on armed horse, to break through the battle and strength of our archers, when they should come to an engagement with us. Therefore the King gave orders through the whole army, that each archer should provide himself with a square or round pole or staff, six feet in length, and of sufficient thickness, and sharp at each end; directing that whenever the French army should approach to battle, and begin breaking through their ranks with troops of horse of that sort, each one should fix his pole before him in front, and those who were behind, other poles intermediately; one end being fixed in the ground towards them, and the other sloping towards the enemy, higher than a man's waist from the ground, so that when a horseman came to the charge, they would either retreat affrighted at the sight of the stakes, or regardless of their own safety, both horses and horsemen be in danger of being thrown on them.'

The French order of battle before the battle of Agincourt is described:

'On the morrow, viz. Friday, the feasts of Saints Crispin and Crispinian, the xxvth of October, the French at break of day, arrayed themselves in battalions, troops, and squadrons, and took their position in terrific numbers below us in the said plain named AGINCOURT, through which lay our road towards Calais; and they placed many companies of horse in hundreds at each side of their van-guard to break up the line and strength of our archers. The van being a line of infantry, all selected from the nobles and choicest of them, forming a forest of lances, with a great multitude of helmets shining among them, and the horse in the flanks. . . . But the troops and squadrons composing their rear-guard and wings were all on horse-back.'

The King gave the signal to the English army to advance, and the priest, who surely qualifies as a horse soldier, continues, 'I who write this, sitting on horse-back among the baggage in the rear of the battle, and the other priests who were there, did then, and whilst the conflict lasted, humble our souls before God'. One has a mental picture of this gallant priest, seated on his quiet palfrey, with writing materials balanced precariously, scribbling down his impressions of the fierce struggle which was taking place in front of him.

Under the strain of the Hundred Years War the French feudal military system broke down, and the first European standing army was formed in its stead. In 1445 the bands of heavily armed knights and men-at-arms (*gendarmes*) and light horse (*chevaux-légers*) who had followed the great vassals were replaced by a force of professional cavalry.

Charles VII's new cavalry units were a combination of heavy and light cavalry. He raised fifteen *Compagnies d'Ordonnance*, in each of which there were 100 *gendarmes*, 100 *coutiliers*, 300 mounted archers and 100 pages. The basic sub-unit was the 'lance', which consisted of one *gendarme*, one *coutilier*, three archers and one page. The *gendarme* was the commander of the lance. The *coutilier*, so called from the type of sword with which he was armed, was the *gendarme's* valet, but was also a heavily armed soldier. The page carried the *gendarme's* lance, and probably acted as horse holder when the unit was fighting on foot. The archers were the light cavalry element and were armed with a small lance and a crossbow. All the men in the *Compagnie d'Ordonnance* were of noble birth. The senior company of the force was the Scottish, known as the *Cent Lances Écossaises*. It was formed from the Scottish Gendarmes, who had been organized in 1440 from the Scottish troops brought into the French service by John Stuart, Earl of Buchan and Constable of France.

The English Army met the *Compagnies d'Ordonnance* in the final stages of the Hundred Years War, and their experiences against these formidable troops almost certainly led to a similar reorganization being applied to some of the English horse. The lance organization was, in fact, widely adopted in Western Europe, and it became customary to assess the strength of cavalry in lances. It is likely that lances of professional cavalry were used on both sides in the Wars of the Roses.

The lance had a large establishment of horses. A typical allotment seems to have been four for the man-at-arms, two each for the archers and the *coutilier* and one for the page.

CHAPTER II

BETWEEN THE CIVIL WARS

The prolonged Wars of the Roses did severe injury to the horse stock of England. Not only were large numbers lost during the wars, but, since horses in private use were liable to seizure by either side, there was little incentive to breed them. The number of horses, in fact, had been so reduced and prices had risen to such an extent, that, in 1495, Henry VII passed an Act which prohibited the export of any horse without royal permission and of any mare of which the value exceeded six shillings and eightpence or which was under three years old. Henry VIII went even further. He forbade the export of any horses, and directed all prelates and all nobles, of a degree of wealth assessed by the richness of their wives' dresses, to maintain stallions of a given standard.

The effect of the shortage of powerful horses on the military strength of the country is shown by the following extract from a report written in 1519 by the Venetian Ambassador to England:

'In England they did not make use of men-at-arms, so that they could not raise 100 in the whole island. The real military force of the country consisted in its infantry, which was supposed to amount to 150,000 men, whose peculiar weapon was the long bow.'

Henry VII raised a small mounted force of fifty men entitled the Yeomen of the Crown. They each had two horses and the services of a mounted groom. In peace they were principally employed as royal messengers. In war it was intended that they should form the nucleus of the mounted levies.

There is an old record, which was started in 1512, called *The Regulations of Algernon Percy, Fifth Earl of Northumberland,* which contains a detailed list of the horses maintained for the Earl's household. It is of interest in showing the types of horse which were in use at the start of the reign of Henry VIII. The horses are said to be those 'that are appointed to be in the charge of the house yearly, as to say, gentell horseys, palfreys, hobys, naggis, cloth-sek hors, male hors'. The horses are then listed as follows:

'First, gentell horsys, to stand in my lordis stable, six. Item, palfreys of my ladis, to wit, oone for my lady and two for her gentell-women, and oone for her chamberer. Four hobys and nags for my lordis oone [*i.e.* own] saddill, viz., oone for my lord, and oone to stay at home for my lord.

'Item, chariot hors to stand in my lordis stable yerely.

'Seven great trottynge horsys to draw in the chariot and a nag for the chariott man to ride—eight. Again, hors for Lord Lerey, his lordship's son and heir. A gret doble trottynge hors called a curtal, for his lordship to ride out on out of towns. Another trottynge gambaldyn hors for his lordship to ride on when he comes into towns. An amblynge hors for his lordship to journeye on daily. A proper amblynge little nag for his lordship when he goeth on hunting and hawking. A gret amblynge gelding, or trottinge gelding, to carry his male.'

Of the above classifications: gentle horse was a general term applied to any horse of good breeding; a great trotting horse was a powerful draught horse; a curtal was a docked great horse; a trotting 'gambaldyn' horse was one with a high showy action; a 'cloth sek' horse carried personal baggage; and a 'male' horse carried armour.

The first permanent mounted unit was raised by Henry VIII on his accession to the throne in 1509. This was the royal body-guard, still in existence, which was known at various times as the 'Men of Arms', 'Speres', 'Gentlemen Pensioners' or 'Gentlemen-at-Arms'. The order instituting the force appeared as 'Certain ordinances devised and signed by the King's Majesty for a Retinue of Speres or Men of Arms, to be chosen of Gentlemen that be commen and extracte of Noble Blod'. A gentleman of blood was defined in the Statutes of the Order of the Garter, as revised by Henry VIII, as one who was 'descended of three descents of noblesse; *i.e.*, of name and of arms, both on his father's side and also of his mother's side'.

Hall's *Chronicle* for the year 1509 shows that the new guard was formed on the lance organization. It says: 'This year the King ordered fiftie Gentlemenne to be Speeres, every one of them to have an archer, a demi-launce, and a custrell, and every speere to have three greate horses, to be attendaunt on his persone, of the which bende the Erle of Essex was Lieutenant, and Sir John Pechie Captain, who endured but a while, the apparell and charges were so greate, for there was none of theim but they and their horses were appareled and trapped in clothe of golde, siluer and golde smithes' worke, and their seruantes richely appareled also'. The chronicler has reversed the rôles of Essex and Pechie, and is in error in thinking that expense caused the dissolution of the guard, though it may have been responsible for some temporary trouble.

The custrell is, of course, the English equivalent of *coutilier*. A demi-lance was a lancer who was known as such because he was not so heavily armed as a man-at-arms. Together with the mounted archer he constituted the light cavalry element. Hall does not mention the page, but he was probably included.

The ordinary bands of cavalry, which were raised as required, were also organized in lances. An interesting, but rather long-winded description of the tactical employment of cavalry on the lance organization is contained in Thomas Audley's *Treatise on the Art of Warre*, which was written in 1550. Audley was Provost Marshal of Guisnes under King Henry VIII, and later Lieutenant of the Lower Town of Boulogne in 1544. The following are extracts from his book:

'. . . For your standard on horsebacke cause every standard to have so many men Atarmes unbarbed And so many lyght-horsemen. . . . And if you have light horses to every standard as me thinkethye necessarie Then must you have for your light horses a Gwydon, for if you send out your horsemen to do any enterprise and send not forth your wholse band then maye you in no wise send forth your standard. For if a Standard be overthrown it is accompted to a great dishonor. But if a Gwydon be overthrown it is accompted in manner no dishonor at all. For commonlie the Gwydon goeth forthe with small numbers. But if the standard be present, if he have but XXti horses wythe hym yet thenymes will reporte the whole band was there And receive no less honor then although the whole band had been present. It hathe been used of olde tyme, that if one hundred men Atarmes were furnished with V horses [*i.e. 5* horses each] then they had a standard a Gwydon *&* a cornet or penon. And if the band were to fewe for the Gwdon to go forthe withall Then the cornet or penon should go forthe. For it is less honore to losse a penon then a Gwydon for because commonlie the cornet goeth forthe with less than a Gwydon.

'. . . And now in the latter ende of the last warre, thoughte it best to have no light horses but men Atarmes and did experiment the same bothe at the deathe of Sir Raufe Eldercar and at the taking of Monsr. de Tree. But Monsr. de Tree wished and said to me that woulde they had light horses as well as man Atarmes for thei be necessarie as well both for the skirmishe and also to be van-carriers. And as me thinketh good I would have at the least the one half of the band light horses, that is to say the men Atarmes *&* his dimilance.

'. . . And some will saie you must have horses to give the chase. But I would never wish That a man Atarmes should follow fast in the chase, But that the men Atarmes should follow softly in a Troup together kepeing their horses in Breath for the succour of the light horses if any nede should happen. And otherwise peradventure bothe light horsemen and men Atarmes also might be overthrown. Also I would that the main Battaile of footmen with a band of horsemen, should never break order, But kepe the felde. And the Artillarie to be newly charged, and set in good order for doubt of any chance that might happen And if you have three horses to the furniture of a man Atarmes, his dimilaunce his hargabusseere armed on horseback Or else a bores spere and a Dage which is a shorte gonne, to hang at the Saddle bow and if there be V horses to the furniture of a man Atarmes Then some use the man Atarmes with all thes peces Two dymilaunces or Hargabusseeers on horseback with a bores spere with a Dagg, and a page to carrie his Masteres hed pece and his staffe.

'. . . Also alwaies at the first arrival to a campe give in commandement to the Bandes of the horsemen of everye warde that no man dismount from his horse untill such tyme as all the footemen be quietly lodged and that alwaies at suche tymes good and sure scoutes be put forthe towardes there enymes, for upon those scoutes at such tyme depends the wealthe of anye Campe, for when footemen be making their lodging, then be they out of order and strengthe.

'. . . The broad square is very good for horsemen to fight in & I would desier to have horsemen in dyvers and several Bandes to thentent that if one Bande were repulsed or disordered that then thother Bande might be readie to reskew at hand; I would wishe there were for every Battell of footemen, two wings of horsemen which is a strength for the flankes of every Battell of footemen and an occasion to take thadvantage of the flankes of the enemyes, when tyme is.'

The lance organization, however, was becoming obsolete. In France, in 1530, gendarmes and light horsemen were formed into separate bodies of heavy and light cavalry; confirming what was already the normal tactical practice.

A diary of King Henry VIII's siege of Boulogne in 1544, probably written by a member of the expedition, gives some information on the composition and employment of the cavalry. The order of march of the army from Calais is described as follows:

'The Ordre howe the KINGES MAJESTIE departed out of the Toune of Calleys on Fridaye the xxvth of July.

'*Furst* the *Drommes* and *Viffleurs*, then the *Trompets*, then *thofficers of armes*, then the *Barons*, then *Mr. Gartier* next before the Kings banner displayed, then the *Kings Ma^te* armed at all Peces upon a great courser, then the *lorde Harberde* bering the Kings Hedpece and Speare, then the *Henchemen* well horsed and well appoincted; and when the *Kings Majestie* came wt out the Gates, there met wt him the *Duke of Alberquercks* company

37

FIG. 3. THE DEPARTURE OF KING HENRY VIII FROM CALAIS. 15TH JULY, 1544.

Engraved from a contemporary painting.

to the nombre of a *Hundred Hors*, whereof vj of them were barbed wt clothe of Golde, also *therle of Essex* chief captaine of the men of arms, and Sir *Thomas Darcy* petie Captaine, accompanyed with a great nombre of Horsmen and theare set themselfes in their best Order; Furst the *Light Horses* and *Demy Lances*, then the Garde on Fote, that is to say, twenty five *Archers* on the right side, and as many Gunners on the left side, *Chestre Gentylman Huissier* had the leading of the Archers, and *Harman Gentylman Huissier* had the leading of the Gonners, the Kyngs Ma^te in the myds of his *pikmen*, then followed the *men of armes*, Also aloof off there went *fyfftie archers on Horsbacke* on the right syde who were ledde by *Mr. Willoughbye*, And on the left syde as many *Gonners* on Horsbake who were ledde by *John Uprychards*. And thus Marched forwards, And at Sandingfelde stood embattelyd the *captaine of the garde* wt all the garde and other in good ordre tyll the *Kynge* ws past, And so marched after the Kinge, evry bande in ordre havyng his banner displayed, and the *bands of Horsmen* wt their Guydons metinge the *Kinges Ma^te* all the Wayes, and camped that nyght at Marguysen; being a very greate tempestious nyght of Raine and thondre.'

This expedition was commemorated by a series of paintings executed at Cowdray House, in Sussex, the home of Sir Anthony Brown. Sir Anthony, who probably supervised the paintings, was standard-bearer to King Henry VIII and was present throughout the operations in France. The paintings were unfortunately destroyed in 1793 when Cowdray House was burnt down; but facsimiles of the originals had been engraved in 1788. Two of these (Figs. 3 & 4) show the departure from Calais and the arrival at Marquison. These pictures provide a vivid illustration of the military life of the time.

In 1550 there was a royal review of the King's levies; some ten thousand men taking part. The notice of the review in the royal diary says of the horses that they were 'all fair and great, none under fourteen hands full, and a half the most part, and all horses'; and that 'the worst would not have been given for twenty pounds'. The height of the horses is not very impressive, and it would seem that there can have been no very

FIG. 4. THE ENCAMPMENT OF KING HENRY VIII AT MARQUISON.
JULY, 1544.
Engraved from a contemporary painting.

high standard for the horses of the light cavalry. This impression receives some confirmation from a report by one

Daniel Barbaro in 1551, which is contained in the Venetian State Papers. He says:

'The villages, castles and all other places send the whole of their male population capable of bearing arms, from the age of 15 years to 40, and from 16 to 60, who are all mustered on a spacious place where they perform their military exercises with such arms as they possess, in the presence of the commanders appointed for this purpose. The stoutest and most robust are then selected, and England has, in fact, men of strength and well proportioned; and were they equally able to endure a long run of fatigue and privations believes that no militia could equal that of England.

'Of these able bodied men, some serve on foot, others on horse-back. Those who are neither tall nor short, but of agile frame, are mounted, and divided into two classes, one of light horse, the other of men-at-arms, consisting for the most part of gentlemen rather than of others, as they are better able to bear the expense and to provide themselves with good horses.

'Of the light cavalry, part are armed in the Albanian fashion and the others with a shirt of mail and a sallet and a light long spear, and they use any sort of horse, as they never charge, save in flank, and they are called demi-lances.

'... The infantry is divided into companies of 100 men, who have their captain, lieutenant, ensign and serjeant.

'The cavalry is also divided into squadrons of 100, and officered in a like manner. The cavalry use trumpets, the infantry use drums.'

Another Venetian, Giovanni Michele, writing on 13th May, 1557, has a very poor opinion of English horses:

'As to the cavalry (I speak of light cavalry) if it were but a good description it might be very numerous as that island produces a greater number of horses than any other region of Europe; but the horses being weak and of bad wind, fed merely on grass, being like sheep and all other cattle kept in field or pasture at all seasons, the mildness of the climate admitting of this, they cannot stand much work, nor are they held in much account, but nevertheless as they are mettlesome and high couraged, most especially if they chance to be Welch, when, in the field, they are said to do fairly (according to their small strength) for reconnoitring and foraging, and to harass the enemy, and they would do much better were they better fed. With regard to heavy horse, good for men-at-arms, the island does not produce any, except a few in Wales, and an equally small amount from the Crown stud; so the country cannot have any considerable quantity of heavy horse. The heavy horses, therefore, now seem all are foreign, imported from Flanders, the Queen having chosen all persons to provide the amount assigned them, lest from want of horses the thing should fall into disuse, as it was doing.'

The 'thing', as a matter of fact, shortly did 'fall into disuse', as with the increase in the effectiveness of firearms the heavily armoured man-at-arms was rapidly becoming obsolete.

If the above report is accurate the number of Great Horses must have been sadly diminished. That the standard of English horses was deplorably low seems to have been endorsed by Sir Thomas Challoner, in a Latin poem written in 1579, when he was ambassador at Madrid. He claimed that England had none but 'vile and ordinary horses', which were allowed to run at large with the mares; but that if Englishmen would attend to horse breeding, they could, with the advantages the country afforded, raise better horses than they could import.

Nevertheless, from the first year of her reign, Queen Elizabeth I took urgent steps to improve matters. She renewed her father's act forbidding the export of horses to Scotland; and later issued a Proclamation enforcing the previous laws which had been enacted by Henry VIII and Philip and Mary. These included the keeping of a stallion by nobles of a prescribed degree; regulations concerning the height of mares in parks and enclosed lands; the rounding up and destruction of worthless mares, fillies and geldings; and the obligation on certain people to keep horses or geldings for national defence. One of Henry VIII's laws concerned the stature of horses in certain shires, and applied, amongst others, to Cambridgeshire, Huntingdon-shire, Northamptonshire, Lincolnshire, Norfolk and Suffolk. In 1566 the Isle of Ely and 'other moors, marshes and fens of Cambridgeshire', and the above-mentioned counties, were exempted from the provisions of the Act, because 'the said moors, of their unfirmness, moysture and wateryshness', could not carry the weight of big horses without danger of their 'mireyng, drowning and peryshinge'.

In spite of its depleted numbers, interest in the Great Horse continued, and it was probably bred in a number of places in England in addition to the Crown stud. In 1566 Thomas Blundeville, of Newton Hotman in Norfolk, wrote a book entitled *The Art of Ryding and Breaking Great Horses*, which was sold by one William Seres at 'The Sygne of the Hedgehogge' in St. Paul's Churchyard. Blundeville was the first writer on veterinary subjects in this country, and he was the author of another work, produced in the same year, which condemned the practice of docking horses. Blundeville said that Italians were ashamed to ride horses so mutilated and provided them with false tails; but that in England and France, on the other hand, 'so much has custom prevailed against nature' that it was considered no shame to be seen riding a 'curtail'. Docking had been forbidden by ecclesiastical law as far back as A.D. 747; but despite Blundeville's protest, the practice was destined to continue until our own day. Markham, another veterinary writer, stated in 1610 that the public believed that the back was strengthened by the amputation of the tail, and, in fact, he believed this himself! In Markham's time and for nearly a century afterwards it was frequently cut off at the third bone below the croup, leaving only a very short stump.

During the reign of Queen Elizabeth I the principal military feature was the long series of campaigns in Ireland. Heavy horse were not required, for the Irish cavalry were still mounted and equipped very much as the mediaeval hobelars; and they fought in much the same way. The Irish horseman rode without stirrups, and his saddle was nothing more than a kind of pillow, secured by a surcingle and straps round the horse's breast and hindquarters. His chief weapon was a light lance which was used overarm. Against such a foe the English light horseman, or demi-lance, was a heavy cavalryman. But although only demi-lances were used in Ireland, the small Irish horses were not powerful enough to carry their weight, and all English cavalry horses had to be shipped across the Irish Sea. The dress of the demi-lances varied considerably during the course of the Irish campaigns. They generally, however, seemed to have worn a steel helmet and cuirass, with some armoured protection for the forearm. Some were armed as lancers and some as swordsmen. The former carried two small pistols, and the latter one large horse pistol, or petronel, and a dagger.

The cavalry unit was the band of fifty, commanded by a captain. In Ireland, though, in addition to the normal strength of the band, each cavalry soldier was attended by an Irish horse boy, whom he had to keep out of his pay. The horse boy was mounted on a native horse known as a garran, and was responsible for foraging for his master and for cleaning his equipment.

Fig. 5 from a contemporary illustration shows English and Irish cavalry in action.

By the end of the sixteenth century the man-at-arms in his heavy armour had completely disappeared. The erstwhile light horse, the demi-lances, had now become heavy cavalry, and the light element of the cavalry arm was provided by the 'shot on horse-back', who fought as mounted infantry, and were the forerunners of the later dragoons.

A list of cavalry trumpet-calls is contained in the *Soldiers Accidence*, second edition of 1635, by Gervase Markham. They are described as follows:

'The fifth and last lesson belonging unto the horse troop is to teach the soldier the sounds and commands of the trumpet, and to make him understand the notes and language of the trumpet, as also in due time to perform all those duties and commands which are required by the trumpet. And of these soundings (which we generally call the *Points of War*)

44

FIG. 5. A BATTLE BETWEEN THE IRISH AND THE ENGLISH.
From Derricke's 'Image of Ireland', 1581.

there are six which are most necessary for the soldier's knowledge. The first is:

'1. *Butte Sella,* or Clap on your saddles.

'Which as soon as the soldier heareth (in the morning or at other times) he shall presently make readie his horse and his own person, truss up his sack of necessaries, and make all things fitting for his journey. The second is:

'2. *Mounte Cavallo,* or Mount on horseback.

'At which summons the soldier shall bridle up his horse, bring him forth and mount on his back. The third is:

'3. *Al'a Standardo,* or Go to your colours.

'Whether it be *Standard, Cornet* or *Guidon,* upon which sound the soldier with those of his fellowship shall trot forth to the place where the cornet is lodged, and there attend till it be dislodged. Also this sound in the field and in service, when men are disbanded, is a retreat for the horseman, and brings him off being engaged, for as oft as he hears it he must retire and go back to his colour. The fourth is:

'4. *Tucquet,* or March.

'Which being heard simplie of itself without addition, commands nothing but a marching after the leader. The fifth is:

'5. *Carga, Carga,* or An alarm, Charge, Charge.

'Which sounded, every man (like lightning) flies upon his enemy and gives proof of his valour. The sixth and last is:

'6. *Auquet,* or The Watch.

'Which sounded at night, commands all that are out of duty to their rest, and sounded in the morning, commands those to rest that have done their duty, and those that have rested to awake and do duty. And in those sounds you shall make the soldier so perfect, that as a song he may lauquet or sing them, and know when they are sounded unto him.

'Other soundings there are; as *Tend Ho* for listening, *Call*

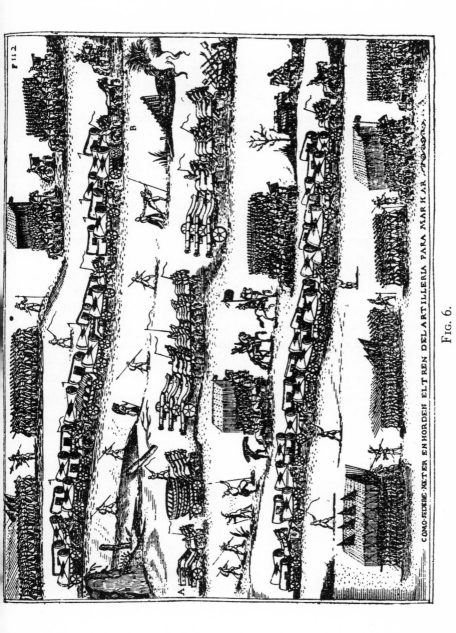

COMO-SE-DE:VTER EN HORDEN EL TREN DEL ARTILLERIA PARA MARHAR

F 112

Fig. 6.

From Ufano's 'Treatise on Artillery', Brussels, 1613.

for summons, a *Senet* for state, and the like. But they have reference to the greater officers, and those have no need of my instructions.'

With regard to the last sentence, it is conceivable that at least some of the 'greater officers' might have implored Gervase Markham to continue with his instructions.

It is an interesting speculation as to whether the sixth *Point of War* could be yet another possible origin of the colloquialism 'O.K.'

In 1624 King James I repealed Henry VIII's delightful law which required every person to keep a stallion whose wealth was such that his wife wore 'any French hood or bonnet of velvet'. However, the horse population cannot have been in a satisfactory position, for Sir Edward Harwood presented a memorial to Charles I, drawing his attention to the serious deficiency of horses of a useful type. Interest in racing had grown rapidly under James I, and was now so general that excessive attention was being paid to the breeding of race horses. As a result King Charles, in 1641, granted licences for the importation of horses, with the injunction that these should be coach horses, mares and geldings not under 14 hands, and between the ages of three and seven years. Owing to the state of the roads at this time the majority of these horses would have been of a heavy draught type.

CHAPTER III

FROM KING TO COMMONWEALTH

At the start of the civil war between King and Parliament the troops raised by each side were largely untrained levies. Troops of Horse, and later Dragoons, were raised independently at first and then grouped into regiments. In the early days of the war, however, the troop was the basic unit.

The principal weapon of the Horse was the sword, but each trooper was armed in addition with a pair of pistols. The horse pistols of the period were generally snaphances, that is, ordinary flintlocks. The more expensive firelock (*i.e.* wheel-lock flint-lock) pistols were widely used by officers, and others, such as gentlemen serving as troopers and foreign mercenaries, who provided their own weapons. (In 1631 the price of a pair of firelock pistols was £3 and a pair of snaphance pistols £2.) Carbines were sometimes issued to Horse, but were unpopular as they were an encumbrance in the charge. Officers sometimes carried petronels, a two-handed weapon which was a cross between a pistol and a carbine.

Dragoons were armed with carbines, otherwise called musketoons. They varied in length and shape but were all snaphances. When mounted, the dragoon carried his carbine hooked to a shoulder belt, and either the muzzle or the butt was sometimes supported in a leather bucket. There was little change in the method of carrying muzzle-loading carbines until they passed out of the Army. Though the musket was nominally a 12-bore weapon, there were $14\frac{1}{2}$ balls to the pound. The carbine was nominally 16-bore, and actually had 20 balls to the pound. The nominal bore of the pistol was 20-24, and the weight of bullet 34 to the pound.

Cavalry charged at a sharp trot, firing their pistols when

they reached a close range, and without halting, and then closed with the sword. Pistol fire was also often used in the pursuit.

The first major cavalry action of the war was at the battle of Edgehill. Sir Richard Bulstrode, who rode in the ranks of *The Prince of Wales's Regiment of Horse*, took part in the great cavalry charge on the right wing of the Royalist army under Prince Rupert. In his *Memoirs* he gives an interesting account of Prince Rupert's orders before the charge. He says:

'Just before we began our march, Prince Rupert passed from one wing to the other, giving positive orders to the horse, to march as close as possible, keeping their ranks with sword in hand, to receive the enemy's shot without firing either carbine or pistol till we broke in amongst the enemy, and then to make use of our firearms as need should require; which order was punctually observed.'

The Royalist newspaper, *Mercurius Aulicus*, relates an incident in an action at Middleton Cheney, on 6th May, 1643, affecting the same regiment, which shows the penalty exacted for losing a standard:

'Sergeant Major Legg's courage having ingaged him too farre among the Rebells so long, became their Prisoner, till themselves were Routed. The same mischance (and some slight wounds) had Sergeant Major Daniel, by the fall of his Horse; but being remounted, he in pursuit requited it upon his adversaries, he having before that shot dead a Cornet of the Rebells, recovered the honour to the Prince of Wales His Troope, henceforth again to bear a Cornet which (having heretofore in fight at Hopton Heath lost their own) it seems by the Law of Arms they might not beare, till some of theirs again in fight had wonne a Colour from the Rebells.'

The *Prince of Wales's Regiment* took part in the last action in Cornwall, on 7th March, 1646, before the Royalist surrender in the West. There are two accounts of this action, one by the Parliamentarian historian, Joshua Sprigge, and the other by Major H. Puckering of the *Prince of Wales's Regiment*.

The former says that Fairfax 'sent out Colonel Rich with a thousand horse and Dragoons to beat up their quarters, which

MAJOR-GENERAL RANDOLPH EGERTON, *circa* 1672.

(*From the painting by John Wyck, by kind permission of Brigadier T. F. S. Collins.*)

he did near St. Collombe, forcing the Out-Guards up to the Main-Guard, which consisting of about 600, most of them his Highness's the Prince of Wales's Life Guard, and brave Gentlemen, then commanded by Major [actually Major-General] Pert, a proper stout Gallant Man, who drew out to meet them, and gave a most brisk home-Charge, the Major himself Charging quite through the first Division, but being shot was taken Prisoner, (and afterwards died of his wounds) upon which his troops retired in disorder, and were pursued two or three miles by Quartermaster-General Fincher, who led the Van, wherein many were Slain and Wounded, near an hundred taken Prisoners, and about 300 Horses taken, their Riders deserting them to facilitate their Escape'.

Major Puckering's account differs in several particulars: 'At last was sent a party of about 700 commanded horse with Collonel Rich, to discover what wee were doeing. Six troopes of our regiment were to come upon the out guard that night, who, when they came to relieve a like number of my Lord Goreing's horse, they found the Major that was over that party asleep in a barn, and not able to give any account of the enemy whose body lay within 5 miles of them, but were glad to be relieved and marched off. These men were not gone out of sight, when drawing towards night a body of the enemy was seen to move. Their strength or number could not at that distance be judged. But the alarum was thereupon sent to the quarters, and that party newly gone off, sent to and desired to return and joyne, but they would not. It happened that Colonel Rich came so quick upon ours that wee had but just time to withdraw two parties of about 40 horse a peece, sent to two churches a mile off, as out guards to our main guards; and a corporal sent out with a patrole of a dozen horse for discovery, was forced to fight his way through the enemy to come home to us. Not knowing but this might be the van of their whole army Collonel Trevor drew off my Lord's with 3 other troopes in orderly retreat, Sir Thomas Corbet's and Major General Pert's two troopes giveing the enemy a very brisk charge before the mouth of the lane, wither they alsoe were to follow in

51

retreat, which charge I believe the enemy did not like because he followed not our party further. In this charge only 5 or 6 lost, besides Coronet Coe taken prisoner, and Major General Pert—a very brave person—who 10 dayes after dyed at Bodmin of his wounds.' General Pert had voluntarily organized all that was left of his own regiment as a troop of the *Prince of Wales's Regiment*, and himself served as a troop commander.

A week later the Royalist army in the West surrendered, the men being disbanded and sent to their homes, and the officers being allowed to return to the King. Puckering comments: 'So that no hopes being left to get in a body to the King, or to keep with the Prince, who was by this time taking shipp for Scilly, wee fairly saved a bloody nose, and carried most of the officers—with a convoy—to the King to Oxford. The troopers goeing with passes and convoys to their several homes.'

On the side of Parliament Sir Thomas Fairfax wrote a *Short Memorial* of the actions in the North during the years 1642 and 1643. Of an incident in January, 1642/3, he wrote:

'After some time we found that our men must either have more room or more action. Therefore Captain Hotham and I took a resolution early in the morning to beat up a quarter of the enemy that lay at Fenton. But they being gone, we marched towards Sherborne, intending only to give an alarm there. But they might see us a mile or two march over a plain common which lay by the town, and therefore had sent about 20 or 30 horse to guard a passage near the town. I having the van, (for at this time we commanded our troops distinct one from the other, both making 5 troops of horse and 2 of dragoons), I told him if he would second me I would charge those horse and if they did flee I would pursue them so close as to get in the town with them. He promised to second me. I went to the head of my troop and presently charged them, who fled, and we pursued close to the barricado, but they got in and shut it upon us, where my horse was shot in the breast. We so filled the lane, being strait, that we could not retreat without confusion and danger of their falling in our rear; so we stood to it and stormed the work with pistol and sword. At the end of the barricado there was a strait passage for one single horse to go in. I entered there and others followed one by one. Close at one side of the entrance stood a troop of horse, but so soon as 8 or 10 of us got in they fled; and by this time the rest of our men had beaten them off from their barricado and entered the town which soon cleared the streets, and pursued those that fled. And now my horse that was shot in the lane, fell down dead under me, but I was presently mounted again.'

At the battle of Marston Moor, on 2nd July, 1644, Fairfax was commanding the cavalry of the right wing.

'The place was Marston Fields (which afterwards gave the name to the battle). Here we drew up our army. The enemy was drawn up in battalia on the moor a little below us. The day being for the most part spent in preparation, we now began to descend toward them. Lt.-Gen. Cromwell commanded the left wing of the horse, seconded by Major Gen. Leslie. I had the right wing with some Scots horse and lances for my reserves. The three generals were with the foot. Our left wing charged first the enemy's right wing, which was performed a while with much resolution on both sides; but the enemy at length was put to the worst. Our right wing had not all so good success by reason of the whins and ditches which we were to pass over before we could get to the enemy, which put us into great disorder. Notwithstanding, I drew up a body of 400 horse. But because the intervals of horse in this wing only was lined with musketeers (which did much hurt with their shot) I was necessitated to charge them. We were a long time engaged one with another till at last we routed that part of their wing. We charged and pursued them a good way toward York. Myself only returned presently to get to the men I left behind me; but that part of the enemy which stood (perceiving the disorder they were in) had charged and routed them before I could get to them, so that the good success we had at first was eclipsed much by this bad conclusion. But the other wing and most of the foot went on prosperously till they had cleared the field. But I must not forget to remember with thankfulness God's goodness to me this day, for having charged through the enemy, and my men going after the pursuit, returning back to go to my other troops, I was gotten in among the enemy, which stood up and down the field in several bodies of horse. So taking the signal [*i.e.* distinguishing badge] out of my hat, I passed through them for one of their own commanders, and so got to my Lord Manchester's Horse in the other wing; only with a cut in my cheek, which was given me in the first charge, and a shot which my horse received. In which charge also many of my officers and soldiers were slain and hurt. The captain of my own troop was shot in the arm. My cornet had both hands cut, which rendered him ever after unserviceable. Captain Micklethwayt, an honest stout man, was slain; and scarce any officer which was in this charge did not receive hurt. But Colonel Lambert who should have seconded us, but could not get to us, charged in another place.'

There is affection and sorrow in that brief mention of Captain Micklethwayt; and the name and description, one feels, convey the image and character of a stolid and gallant East Anglian Yeoman.

In the *Depositions from the Castle of York*, edited by James Raine and published by the Surtees Society in 1861, there is a very interesting account of a, doubtless, thorough rascal who had served as an officer in the army of Parliament. This Mr. Peter de Beauvoir was arrested as a dangerous person. His plausible account of his career and movements probably gives a typical picture of the life of a Parliamentarian officer. His story is as follows:

'That, on the 14th day of December, 1650, as I was travellinge from the town of Doncaster, on my march to Scottland, to repaire to Collonell Whaley's owne troope (whom by God's blessinge I did hope to have gone in), I was seiszed upon in my inne as if I had beene somme common malefactor or dangerous person against this state or common whealth. That I had served this nine yeares in severall qualifications; first, at the very beginning of these wars I have ingaged for the Parlement case with my owne horses and armes from time to time, as my little abylity did innable mee to doe; first as a horseman-reformadoe under Collonell John Fiennes, and afterwardes was preferde to bee c^t of foote to Captn Douty, ant c^t of horse twisce under the saide Collonell Fiennes, to Captain John Hunt and Barnarde at Nazeby fight, untill wee were disbanded by order, havinge been taken before by the enemy Prince Robertt att Bristoll, and was prefferd to bee cornet to Collonell Nazzares, under the Earle of Manchester, where at our disbandinge I rid reformadoe under Captain Fulke Grevill's troope with my men and my tow horses in Sir William Waller's army untill the said John Fiennes preferd me to be l^t of horse as abovesaide; and afterwardes have beene of my Lord Fairfax his liffe guarde, untill the disbanding thereof at London. Where, by a speciall order from General Fairfax, given to Doctor Stanes for my entertainmen in Collonell Wheeley's owne troope, for the space of tow years an a halfe, with my servant and tow horses and armes at my own cost and charges, where the said Collonell did chuze mee to bee a conductor for Irelande, where I shipt neer or above height score souldiers as recreutes a twelve months agon at King's Roade at Bristoll. And sinsce I have ride in Captn Jinkin's troope untill I was put out of the muster rolle, in regarde I was to goe for Scottlande in the above saide Collonell Whaley's owne troope. I did mett Captn John Cresset foote company belonging to Boaston garrison in the regiment of Colonell Liliarde upon their march from London towards Boaston, quarteringe with them all along our march as farre as it lie in my way towards Scottland, officiatinge for that present time as quartermaester in the towne of Upton, foure miles of Stillton in Huntingdonshire. Where I tooke my leave of him, he being goeinge to quarter to Peterborough that night, where I did lie in the inne or alehouse in Crocksom in my roade northwardes . . . the which things I doe certifie to be the plaine truth att my perill. Peter de Beauvoir, Captn.'

Captain de Beauvoir was suspected, however, of intending to attack Judge Francis Thorpe, a Baron of the Exchequer, whom he had encountered on the road. He was armed with no less than 'fower pistolls, a carbine, a raper and a pockett dagger'. It also appeared that he was no longer a soldier, having been 'putt out of the rolle, for some misdemeanor'.

General Monk, the future Colonel of the *Coldstream Regiment*, wrote his *Observations on Military and Political Affairs* when he was a prisoner in the Tower in 1646. His book embodies, no doubt, the ideas which he had formulated during the Civil War. As regards cavalry equipment he says:

'I will now show you how Horsemen, Footmen and Dragooners ought to be armed with offensive and defensive arms.

'A Horseman's offensive arms are these: A carbine, or a musquet barrel of the length of a carbine barrel, well stockt with a snapance; the which I hold to be better than a carbine for service. Also a case of pistols, and a good stiff long tuck [a thrusting sword], and a belt.

'A Horseman's defensive arms are: An head piece with three small iron bars to defend the face, back and breast, all three pistol proof: a gauntlet for his left hand, or a good long buff glove. A girdle of double buff about eight inches broad, which is to be worn under the skirts of his doublet, and to be hooked unto his doublet, and made so that it may be fastened together before. If you find buff to be scarce and dear, you may make those girdles of buff before spoken of with bull hides, or good oxes hides dressed like buff.

'The furniture that belongeth to an horseman's horse is as followeth: He ought to have a very good horse, and a good pad saddle made, so that it may well carry a case of pistols, three good girts, a pair of good stirrups and stirrup leathers; with a crupper and a forepattern [a piece of breast armour]; also a good bitt, rains, and head-stall, with a good leathern halter.

'I have omitted here to speak anything of the armour of a good cuirassier, because there are not many countries that do afford horses fit for the service of cuirassiers: but where horses are to be had fit for that service, there a General ought to have two thousand of them in his army.

'The offensive arms of a Dragoon are these: A musquet, or a good snapance to a musquet barrel; which I hold much better for Dragoon service, being upon occasion they may be able to make use of their snapances on horse back, and upon any service in the night they may go undiscovered [the snapance would not give away a position like the continually burning match of the matchlock]. He must have also a belt to hang his musquet in, with a pair of bandaliers, and a good long tuck, with a belt. And all your dragoons ought to have swine-feathers.

'Of a Dragoon horse and furniture: He ought to have a good ordinary horse, saddle, snaffle, rains, stirrups, and stirrup leathers, an halter, and two girts.'

The cuirassiers of this period were the successors to the earlier men-at-arms. They wore heavy armour and were dependent on horses of the Great Horse type to carry them.

A swine-feather was a pointed stake used as a weapon of defence against cavalry. It was either fixed in the ground as a palisade or carried in a musket rest like a bayonet. It was sometimes called a Swedish feather.

Although not the Great Horse, the charger for the Horse was a very heavy animal. Dragoons were normally mounted on stout cobs. With a view to breeding a type of horse more suited to the lighter weight of the cavalry, Cromwell imported a number of Arabs and Barbs. He also encouraged the breeding of horses for hunting and hawking.

The roads at this time were still appalling, and most of them continued so until late in the following century. The average vehicle, therefore, of any type, was still hauled by heavy draught horses. Nevertheless, there is in the diary of a Yorkshire clergyman of 1659 the first recorded mention of stage-coaches. In that year stage-coaches and waggons were then running between London and Aylesbury, London and Coventry, London and Bedford and on a few other routes. It may be that these roads were already good enough for a trotting carriage horse. The time when such horses could be used to haul the guns and supply waggons of the Army, however, was still far ahead.

The traditional red coat of the British Army was first adopted for the New Model Army of the Commonwealth. An attractive picture of the Royalist forces on the Continent, after their expulsion from England, is contained in *Memoirs and Correspondence of Prince Rupert and the Cavaliers*:

'Prince Rupert, after defeating the garrison of Rheims, which he had wantonly provoked, resumed his march: a picturesque array, accoutred in the old chivalric fashion, with plumed helmet and bright armour, over a leathern doublet, steel cuisses to the knee, and huge gambadoes with the large knightly spur. Tall powerful horses . . . stepped proudly under their caparisons; and the small cornet . . . that fluttered over each troop gave a liveliness to the glaring column.'

CHAPTER IV

FROM RESTORATION TO REVOLUTION

The restoration to the throne of King Charles II was followed by the formation in England, for the first time in its history, of a permanent standing army. A manuscript book of January, 1660/1, gives the first known recorded establishment of the Army. The only mounted units on this establishment were the three Troops of *Horse Guards* (now *The Life Guards*) and *The Royal Regiment of Horse* (now *The Royal Horse Guards*). They consisted of the following officers and other ranks:

The King's Troop of Horse Guards: Captain, 4 Lieutenants, Cornet, Quartermaster, Chaplain, Surgeon, 4 Corporals, 4 Trumpeters, Kettle Drummer, 200 Soldiers.

The Duke of York's Troop and the Duke of Albemarle's Troop, each: Captain, Lieutenant, Cornet, Quartermaster, Chaplain, Surgeon, 4 Corporals, 4 Trumpeters, Kettle Drummer, 150 Soldiers.

The Royal Regiment of Horse:

Regimental Headquarters—

Colonel as Colonel; Major as Major; Chaplain, Surgeon, Quartermaster.

King's Troop—

Captain and 2 horses; Lieutenant and 2 horses; Cornet and 2 horses; Quartermaster and 1 horse; 3 Corporals, 3 Trumpeters, Kettle Drummer, 80 Soldiers.

Colonel's Troop—

Colonel as Captain and 2 horses; Lieutenant and 2 horses; Cornet and 2 horses; Quartermaster and 1 horse; 3 Corporals, 2 Trumpeters, 60 Soldiers.

Six other troops each with the same establishment as the Colonel's Troop.

The Surgeon in each unit is shown as having 'one Horse to carry his Chest'.

As regards armour and weapons, it was laid down that, 'Each Horsman to have for defensive Armes Back, Brest, and Pott, and the Brest and Pott to bee Pistoll proofe, the offensive to bee a sword, a case of Pistolls, the Barrells whereof to bee not under fourteene inches length, and each Trooper of the Horse Guards is allso to have a carbine'. The 'Pott' was a steel skull-cap worn under the hat.

The Troops of *Horse Guards* of the King and the Duke of York had both been formed in exile from the loyal followers of Charles II. The Duke of Albemarle (the peerage conferred on General Monk) had formed his Troop in 1659 when he was commander-in-chief of the Commonwealth Army. *The Royal Regiment of Horse*, or *Lord Oxford's Regiment*, had originally been *Colonel Unton Crook's Regiment* of the Commonwealth Army. It was re-formed in 1661 under the colonelcy of the Earl of Oxford. Both Royalist and Commonwealth troops were therefore incorporated in the first regular cavalry, with the latter in the majority.

At the coronation of Charles II *The King's Troop of Horse Guards* wore white armour, red scarves and plumes of red and white feathers. The Duke of York's Troop had black armour, red scarves and plumes of red, white and black feathers.

In Cosmo's *Travels* there is a description of the uniform worn by the Troops of *Horse Guards* in about 1669. All three Troops wore red jackets faced with blue, but those of the First Troop only were ornamented with gold lace. The First and Second Troops had white feathers in their hats, and the Third Troop crimson ribbons.

After the death of the Duke of Albemarle in 1670 his Troop became the Queen's, and replaced the Duke of York's Troop as second in seniority.

Plate II is a reproduction of the painting of Major-General Egerton by John Wyck. The battle scene in the background of the picture may represent the 1672–3 campaign in the Low Countries. General Egerton wears the uniform of *The King's*, or *First, Troop of Horse Guards*. In the right background is a trooper of the King's Troop using his carbine from the saddle. By 1677 all Horse were armed with carbines, and this was also the practice on the Continent. In the French and other continental armies it was becoming customary to fire the carbine from the saddle. An enemy charge was received at the halt with fire; and, in the charge, the squadrons normally halted at close range, fired their carbines, and then closed with the sword. In the British Army, however, it was usual to fire pistols only from the saddle.

In their early years the *Horse Guards* incurred some criticism from the extravagance of their dress. Anthony à Wood, the Oxford antiquary, wrote of them in 1663: 'A strang effeminate age when men strive to imitate women in their apparell, viz. long periwigs, patches on their faces, painting, short wide breeches like petticoats, muffs, and their clothes highly scented, bedecked with ribbons of all colours. And this apparell was not only used by gentlemen, and others of inferior quality, but by soldiers especially those of the Life Guard to the King, who would have spanners [for adjusting firearms] hanging on one side and a muff on the other, and when dirty weather some of them would relieve their gards in pattens [*i.e.* clogs].'

A Scottish Troop of *Horse Guards* was raised in 1661 'for the honour of his Majesties service and the grandeur of the hie court of Parliament'. It held its first parade on the links of Leith on 2nd April, 1661. It consisted of a Captain, a Lieutenant, an under-Lieutenant, a Cornet, a Quartermaster, 4 Brigadiers, a Surgeon, a Clerk, 3 Trumpeters, a Kettle Drummer, and 120 Private Gentlemen. The majority of all ranks had served as officers on the Royalist side during the Civil War. Officers and other ranks wore long scarlet coats, lined with white serge, a blue waistcoat and blue breeches. They were armed with weapons of types similar to those of the English *Horse Guards*. Trumpets and kettle drum were silver. They were probably mounted on black horses of the heavy native Lanarkshire breed. From this Lanarkshire horse, by the use of imported Flemish stallions, was evolved the present Clydesdale (Fig. 7).

FIG. 7. 'THE LIFE GUARDS' IN THE PROCESSION AT THE OPENING OF THE FIRST PARLIAMENT
OF JAMES THE SEVENTH AND SECOND IN EDINBURGH, 1685.

From a contemporary engraving by Thos. Summers.

It would seem that at this early period in their history the chargers of the English *Horse Guards* were not always of very high quality or uniform in their appearance. The following advertisement appeared in the *London Gazette* of 4th–7th June, 1677:

'Stolen out of the grounds of *Mr. Barrett* near *Paddington*, on Monday night, the 4th instant, three Geldings belonging to His Majesties Guards, all betwixt 15 and 16 hands. One an old dark bay, with cropt ears, blind of his off-eye, flat footed, long leg'd, and some white of his off-foot behind. Another of a dark iron gray, with crop ears also, shorn mane, branded on his near buttock with a C. The other of a darkish brown with a star in his forehead, and one foot behind. Whosoever discovers the said Geldings to the said Mr. *Barrett* or to Mr. *Griffith* at the *Bull* Inn in *St. James's* Market, shall have 5£ Reward.'

In 1679 a troop of *Horse Grenadiers* was added to each troop of *Horse Guards*. Their function seems to have been very similar to the earlier custrells. They were servants to the gentlemen of the *Horse Guards*, and they fought as Dragoons.

The first permanent Dragoon units of the Army were raised in Scotland. These were two independent companies of Dragoons which were formed in 1678. They were clad in grey coats and bonnets and carried broad swords. A third company was raised later in the same year. In 1681 a regiment was formed by raising three new companies and grouping the six under one command. This was the origin of the present *Royal Scots Greys*. Grey appears to have been adopted as the uniform of the regiment, for, in 1683, leave was granted for 2436 ells of stone-grey cloth for clothing to be imported from England.

During most of the seventeenth century Dragoons were essentially foot soldiers, who used their horses to provide mobility but who dismounted for actual fighting. By about 1680, however, Dragoons were being gradually transformed into cavalry. Finally, by the Royal Warrant of 1684 it was directed that regiments of Dragoons in the field should be classed as Horse, and in garrison should be reckoned as Foot. The Dragoons' weapons were sword, pistols and musket; and they were expected to be as proficient as the infantry in the use of their firearms. By virtue of their rôle, Dragoons had to be able to mount and dismount quickly, but they were also required to ride as well and with as much dash as the Horse. They became such a generally useful arm that they were employed on a wide range of duties, including patrols and outposts, escorts to the Artillery and dismounted assault on fortifications.

In 1683 the *Tangiers Horse*, which had been formed in 1661 from troops of Horse engaged in the defence of Tangier, was converted into a Dragoon regiment as *The King's Own Royal Regiment of Dragoons*, or *Lord Churchill's Regiment*. It is now *1st The Royal Dragoons*.

In 1684 Nathan Brooks compiled an Army List, and included an account of the royal review which had been held on Putney Heath that year. Of the mounted troops which took part in the parade he says:

'The Horse that day consisted of the three Troops of Guards, and of their three of Granadiers, of the Earl of Oxford's Regiment of Horse-Guards, and the Lord Churchil's Regiment of Dragoons.

'The Horse at their usual depth made four Squadrons upon the Right Wing, of which the Troops of Guards made three, and their Granadiers one. The Left Wing of Horse in the like manner made four Squadrons, whereof my Lord of Oxford's Regiment formed two, and my Lord Churchil's Dragoons the other. The three Troops of Guards flanking in that Figure upon the Right of the main Body. My Lord of Oxford's, and my Lord Churchil's Regiments flanking it on the Left: in all of Horse eight Squadrons, each consisting of two Hundred.'

The Army List gives some interesting details of the regiments. *The Royal Regiment of Horse Guards* is described as follows:

'This Regiment of Horse-Guards consists of eight Troops, each of them having, besides those commissioned officers above-named, three Corporals, two Trumpets, forty five private Men, distinguish't by their Carbine-Belts laced with Gold upon Buff with a red edging, Hooses and Holdster-Caps with the Royal Cypher, embroidered upon Blew, Coated and Cloaked Blew, lined Red. The Colonels pay *per diem*, as Col. and Capt. £1 14s. The Majors, as Major and Captain 17s. A Captains 11s. A Lieutenants 10s. Cornets 9s. Quarter-masters 6s. Corporals 3s. Trumpets 3s. A private mans pay 2s. 6d. The King's Troop has only a kettle Drum, which none of the other Troops have, with a Standard, Crimson, and the Imperial Crown embroidered; The Colonel's Colours flyes the Royal Cypher, Crimson: The Major's Gold Streams, Crimson. The First Troop, the Rose Crown'd; The second a Thistle Crown'd; The third, the Flower-Deluces Crown'd; The fourth, the Harp Crown'd; The fifth, the Royal Oak, embroidered upon their Crimson Colours.'

In the same year the establishment of the *Royal Dragoons* was fixed at a Colonel, Lieutenant-Colonel, Major, Chaplain, Surgeon, Adjutant, Quartermaster, Gunsmith; and six troops each of a Captain, Lieutenant, Cornet, Quartermaster, 2 Serjeants, 3 Corporals, 2 Drummers, 2 Hautboys and 50 Soldiers. From the Tower of London were issued to the regiment 316 muskets and bayonets, 12 halberds, 12 partisans, 316 cartouche boxes and belts, 318 waist belts and bayonet frogs, 358 saddles and bridles, 388 sets of housings and holster caps. The muskets were of the same bore as those of the Foot Guards, but they were four inches shorter in the barrel.

The swords carried by private soldiers of both Horse and Dragoons were straight-bladed with steel full basket-hilts. The length of the blade was generally about 38 inches, and it was often double-edged.

There was an increase in the number of stage-coaches and waggons during the reign of Charles II. The coaches must have been hauled by light carriage horses, for the writer of a tract in 1673 cited the type of horse used on the stage-coaches as the prime reason for their suppression. He urged that all coaches should be withdrawn, 'especially those within 40, 50, or 60 miles of London'. He pleaded that harm would be done 'by destroying the breed of good horses, the strength of the

E

nation, and making men careless of attaining to good horse-manship, a thing so useful and commendable in a gentleman'. However, the anonymous writer of the tract found out, as others are still doing nearly 300 years later, that technical progress is not to be halted by doubts as to the benefits it brings. In 1677 the dawn of a new era in transport was signalized by King Charles's foundation of the Company of Coach and Coach Harness Makers.

There was a great expansion of the Army during the reign of King James II. Many new regiments were raised owing to the threats to the throne occasioned by Monmouth's rebellion and the subsequent invasion plans of William of Orange. A number of these new units did not outlive James's departure from his kingdom; but six regiments of Horse and two of Dragoons survived to be incorporated into the regular establishment of the Army.

King James was a great organizer and administrator, with a passion for detail. He took a great interest in his Army, and few matters of any importance escaped his attention. The following letters written by William Blathwayt, Secretary at War, illustrate the thoroughness of the King's attention to the Army's affairs:

'WHITEHALL 11th Jan. 1686/7
'To Coll. Berkeley or the Officer
    in Chief &c at Glocester

'His Majesty being informed that upon a quarrell between Sir John Guise and Cornett Gashion a Guard of Severall Dragoons had been put upon the house or lodging of the said Sir John Guise; His Majesty being informed at the placing of such a Guard, commands me to signify His Pleasure that it be immediately taken off, wherein you are forthwith to give effectual Orders. I am &c.'

'WHITEHALL 25 October 1688
'To Colonell Butler

'I have acquainted his Majesty with what you write in your letter to me, in answer to which I am to let you know his

Pleasure, that those houses that have in that manner pulled down their Signes to avoid the quartering of the Dragoons under your Command [an Irish Dragoon regiment] are nevertheless to bear their equall proportions least others might follow their example at this time, when every one ought to be assisting in his Majesty's Service.

'His Majesty has withall given Orders thet the Quarters of your Regiment be enlarged to Colebrook and Places adjacent, which will conveniently hold five Troops, and may immediately receive such a proportion, as you shall think according to the enclosed Order.

'As to your entering into English Pay, his Majesty has ordered My Lord Ranelagh Pay Master of the Forces, to pay you what shall be necessary upon your account, untill his Majesty shall know from the Earl of Terconnell what has been received in Ireland.'

'WHITEHALL 6th November 1688

'To Mr. Phill Musgrave

'His Majesty having ordered severall Regiments of horse to leave their Armour at the places from whence they are next to march; I sent you the enclosed Lists of those Regiments, and of the Places and days when and where they have left, or are to leave their Armour, and am commanded by his Majesty to signify his Pleasure, That the Principall Officers of the Ordinance, send forthwith fit persons to receive the Armour so left from the Mayor or Chief Magistrates of the severall Towns, in whose hands it will be found, and to bring it away from thence to the Tower of London.'

All mounted regiments in King James's Army wore red coats (actually crimson), which had an enormous number of buttons. Those of the *Scots Greys*, for instance, in 1687 had '10 dozen tin buttons'. Over their coats regiments of Horse wore steel cuirasses, or 'backs and breasts', and under their hats they had steel skull-caps, or 'pots'. Pots were also worn by some Dragoon regiments. Cuirasses were discontinued during the reign of William III, but were resumed under

67

Marlborough. The Horse wore leather breeches as a rule, but those of the Dragoons were generally of cloth. Mounted troops had an advantage over the foot soldiers, as cloaks were generally carried rolled on the saddle, whereas the latter had no such protection from the weather. Both Horse and Dragoons frequently wore buff (*i.e.* leather) waistcoats, which were very useful garments against sword-cuts and also cold winds. In Horse regiments sword and carbine were secured to two broad belts of buff leather which crossed each other on the chest.

The Horse were the best-paid men in the Army. A trooper got 2s. 6d. a day, out of which he had to maintain his horse. A Dragoon got 1s. 6d. a day, also to include the maintenance of his horse. A Captain of Horse received 10s. a day pay and 11s. 6d. a day allowances. A Captain of Dragoons got 8s. pay and 7s. 6d. allowances.

When James II came to the throne a series of new firearms was produced which was a great improvement on previous issues. All carbines and pistols were flintlocks; the pistol barrel being 14 inches in length. Dragoons were still armed with snaphance muskets, and these had bright barrels 3 feet 8 inches long. They also carried grenades, bayonets and hammer-hatchets.

The great Irish camp of the Curragh, that paradise for horse soldiers, was established by Richard Talbot, Duke of Tyrconnell; and a proclamation of his of 1st June, 1688, said that, 'three regiments of horse, one regiment of dragoons and seven regiments of foot . . . shall encamp at the Curragh of Kildare on the first day of July next and shall continue there till the last day of the said month'.

CHAPTER V

THE RIVAL KINGS

Following the revolution and the installation of William of Orange as King, there came the struggle for the throne between the rival monarchs. Most of this took place in Ireland; the contending forces being, on the Williamite side mainly English and Dutch, and on the Jacobite side mainly Irish and Anglo-Irish.

In the Sloane MS. in the British Museum is the pocket-book diary of one Gédéon Bonnivert, a volunteer trooper in an English regiment of Horse, who served in the Irish campaign. When the diary starts he was probably on the way as part of a draft or reinforcements for his regiment in Ireland. His story is as follows:

'I came out of London the 6th of June 1690 and layn at St. Albans. We were to guard 5 carriadges loaded with two hundred and fifty thousand pounds for the pay of the army in Ireland.

'Saturday the 7th we went to Newport Pagnell where a troop of dragons relieved us. Wee tarri'd there till Monday following then we went to Daventry. Tuesday we went to Coissel.

'Wednesday to Stafford the party went, but I left 'em by the way and went to meet a friend of mine at Lichfield. About foure miles this side of Cosswell there is a stone bridge full of the plant call'd maiden hair.

'Thursday I met the party at Namptwytch. Within three miles of that place is a very fine house belonging to Sir Thomas Delf with a very fine pool full of all wild fowls. You may take notice of a carp that was taken there three quarters of a yard and odd inches long which is set up as a weather cock at the top of yᵉ house. Friday we came to Chester, the chief town of the county. Generally Cheshire is a very fine country for corn and grass which being intermix'd with fine woods render it very pleasant to the eyes. Chester is a very large town of great trade it being the sea port town though the ships come no

FIG. 8. AN OFFICER, 'QUEEN'S REGIMENT OF HORSE', 1689.
Drawn by P. Sumner from several contemporary sources.

nearer on't than 16 miles at a place call'd High-Lake, there's the River Dee runs by its walls, and it has a pretty strong though but small castle.

'Sir . . . Morgan is now Governour of that place. The two main streets of Chester have cover'd walks where you may walke at the hottest sun free from heat, and in the wett weather shelter'd from rain; their shopps are underneath these walks. Round about the walls of the citty you may walk upon large stones, and have a prospect of the town and country. High Lake is the sea port and has but two houses besides the Kings store house. Wee stay'd there from monday in the evening ye 16th till tuesday at 8 in the morning, then we embark'd our horses and us selves we hauss'd our saile about three in the afternoon, with the tide, but with a contrary wind, which made us ply to and fro all that day. About ten in ye night no wind stirring we cast anchor till two in the morning.

'All the day after we had no wind and our ship was only carried by the tyde.

'Thursday we fish'd most of ye day and tooke great many gornetts and whitings, the sea being in a great calm. That day we left Cumberland behind us and endeavour'd to reach the Ile of Man but could not. In the night time the wind arising, and pretty favourable for our voyage we left the Ile of Man at our left hand and we discover'd the coasts of Scotland at our right hand, which they call Galloway, and Friday being the 19th we came between three Islands and a town call'd Donahadee which is a markett town and seems a good pretty one. Wee left it at our right and Copplen Ilands at our left. Wee saw after that at our left the village call'd Bangar, which is but a small one but very fitt for vessels to come to the very sides of it, both sides are very rocky. That small village is famous for Duke Schomberg landing there with the forces under his command. Upon your right you see the Castle of Carickfergus which is a strong place; we took it last yeare and lost no great quantity of men. We landed at the White house, where we saw on our arrival great nomber of poor people, the women are not very shy of exposing to men's eyes those parts which are usuall for the sexe to hide. We went that night to Belfast which is a large and pretty town and all along the road you see an arm of the sea upon your left, and on the right great

71

high rocky mountains which tops are often hidden by the clouds, and at the bottom a very pleasant wood and very full of simples of all sorts.

'The town is a sea port. There is in it the kings Custom House, and you see hard by it a very long stone bridge which is not yett finished. The town is compass'd round about it with hills. The people very civill, and there is also a great house belonging to my L⁴ Donnegall L⁴ chief J with very fine gardens and groves of ash trees. The inhabitants speak very good English, wee stay'd there two days and three nights and we went from thence on tuesday being the 23th of June to Lisbourn, where there is a great house and good gardens belonging now to my Lady Mulgrave; it was left her with the whole estate which amounts to 14000 lb per annū by my L⁴ Canaway, the house is out of repair. There's a markett kept there on that day. Wednesday the 24th wee sett forth betimes in yᵉ morning, resolv'd to joyn our army which was then encamp'd at Loughprickland. We pass'd by Hillsborough, a great house belonging to the King standing on a hill on the left hand of yᵉ road, and frō thence we went to Druamore— hard by that place is the Bishops house. The succes answer'd our expectation tho' we had a very hard and troublesome day's work. At our arrivall our friends shew'd joy in their faces to see us come amongst them, and each of us went to his respective tent. Thursday yᵉ 28th of June we marched at two of yᵉ clock in the morning and went over the high hills to Newry. Tis not to be imagin'd how strong naturally many passages are that way; and besides that many strong tho' small forts made by King James, which made me admire many times what should have made him quitt those passages, which might have ruin'd most part of our army with the loss but of few of his own. That day was the first of my seeing the King riding in Irish land, and he had then on an orange colour sash. We cross'd the river at Newry which was formerly a strong place but now burnt and destroy'd, and encamp'd upon yᵉ side of a hill, where watter was very scarce. We left Dundalk on our left hand, it stands by yᵉ sea, and we encamp'd in very rugg'd ground. There as soon as we had order to dismount I left my horse to shift for himself, and I tir'd with heat and want of drink fell fast asleep for the space of 4 houres. Awaked as I was afterwards, I look'd for my horse, but no horse to be found, in short I went upon down for about 4 houres longer ere I could heare any tidings of him, night was approaching, we were nigh the ennemy, and were looking every minutt to be commanded to horse, but being in this agony, as God would have it, I spied upon the side of a banck my saddle all in pieces. I soon after found my Gentleman too, but however 'twas not without great trouble. Therefore I advise all horsemen in such case never to part with his horse but if he falls a sleep tye yᵉ reyns fast to his arm. The Inniskilling Dragoons came there to us. They are but middle siz'd men, but they ar never the less brave fellows. I have seen 'em like masty dogs runn against bullets.

'Saturday yᵉ 28th we were taken 15 men out of each squadron to go with a detachment of 1200 to Ardagh; where we heard the late king's army was, the rest of our army stayed behind till the Sunday following. Just as we came within sight of yᵉ town, we saw the dust rise like a cloud upon the highway beyond it. It was the enemy's arriere garde scowreing away with all speed. Some dragoons were detach'd to follow them who brought back two or three prisoners and many heads of cattle. We encamp'd this side of the town the Saturday and the Sunday after our Army coming to us, we marched on the other side of the river where we encamp'd by a corn field by a small ruin'd village. The town of Ardagh is seated in a very pleasant soil, and has been a fine and strong borrough, as one may see by yᵉ great towrs still extant. King James made ther very strong works, as if he would have made it a place to withstand our Army, and indeed it is a strong seated town, being in a plain having a river of one side and boggy of yᵉ other. Monday the last of June we marched towards Drogheda where the Enemy were, and we came within sight of the town at 9 in yᵉ morning. There we drew up our horse in three lines and came in order of Battle upon the brow of a long hill. There we

73

saw the enemy and were so neare them that we could heare one another speak, there being nothing but the river between us. As we were drawn up we had order to dismount and every man stand by his horse's head. We had not been there long but some of the King's Regiment of Dragoons were detached and sent to line the river side. So they began to shutt at the enemy and those of King James's army at ''em. They had not been long at that sport, when the King passing by the first Troop of his Guards, the enemy fir'd two small gunns at him one of the bulletts greas'd the kings coat: then they play'd on till three of the clock upon us, and shott often men and horses. One Mr. William of the 3rd Troop of Guard had his arm shott. Some of yᵉ Dutch Troop were kill'd and wounded. Indeed 'twas a madness to expose so many good men to the slaughter without neede, for we had no artillery yet come to answer theirs. Ours not commeing till 3 in the afternoon. We did retire confusedly behind the hill at the sight of the Ennemy, when it might hav bin better manadged. King James made that day a Review of his Army. We had a great mind to force a passadge through the river to go to them, but we left it till next morning. At three in the afternoon our Artillery came up and begunn to play upon theirs stoutly, then the ennemy shew'd they had many other batteries besides the first. They play'd upon one another till night then we retired about a mile sideways. Next morning we were up at two of the clock and we march'd to gain a passage two miles of about 5 in the morning. The passage was a very steep hill and a shallow river at the bottom. That leaded into a very fine plain, as we came there we found a party of the Ennemy with four or five pieces of Artillery ready to receive us, but that did not daunt our men, they went doun briskly, not with standing their continuall fire upon us. The Grenadiers and Dragoons were first of the other side, and we soon followed them, but the ennemy made haste away with their Cannon. We drew up in battle as we came in the Plain, and marched directly toward the place appointed for the Battle. After some houres we saw the ennemy comming down a turneing between two Hills, which we knew by the rising of yᵉ dust, and by and by they shew themselves in their best colours, for they drew up upon a line only, and our Army was upon three. We look'd upon one another who should come first, but at last we seeing that their foot and baggage was running away, and that their king had engaged their right way, we marched towards them over ditches and tranches. They presently retir'd upon a mountain behind a little Town call'd Dulick—where they fir'd three or foure peeces at us, we killed abondance of their men, and pursued the rest till nine of the clock, that we overtaking them, and having too hotly pursued them were almost upon them when they faceing about made as if they had been willing to receive us, but we haveing left our foot and cannon behind, and considering how late it was, made halte. They fir'd for an houre and half small shott very thick upon us, for they had hid partly in bushes. That day we had all some green on our hatts to know one from the other. At last our cannon came and play'd very smartly upon them till the night comming they retir'd, and so did we, we laying in the plow'd lands and had no tents. That day we lost Duke Schomberg and Dr. Walker Governour of Londonderry. They were kill'd in forcing the passage. The king himself pass'd that way. Next day we stay'd encamped by that place, and there was a popish gentleman's house plundred by us. Thursday being the 3rd of July we came neare a fine house belonging to a papist where we encampid and where I fell sick of a violent feavour and an extream fitt of ye gout in ye same time. I was sent to Dublin where I stay'd till Saturday ye 12th. that I went in the company of ye Ajutant gñall of the Danish forces to rejoyn our army. That day I went to Kerkollenbridge 16 long miles from Dublin. I passed through the Ness, a good big burrough. At Kerkollenbridge I found our army encamp'd, and there we stay'd one night and the next day we marched but eight mile. There my sickness continueing, or indeed rather encreaseing I was forced to go to Castle-dermatt; it has bin the seat of some of the kings of Lyster, but now is a poore beggarly town, though in a very pretty plain. Eight miles beyond it upon the high way, is the burying place of the kings of Lyster and there you may see the vaults still full of bones and some old inscriptions upon large stones. Our army went before Watterford and after the town was surrendred the king went to lay the siege before Limerick, whilst gnall Douglas was gone to endeavour with part of our army to take Athlone, but he had no better success there than our men at Limerick where through the ill manadgement of Capt. Poultney, who haveing had the conduct of eight bigg pieces of artillery and several other provisions, unadvisedly order'd his detachment to unbridle and turn the horses to grass, for Sashfield haveing notice of this fell upon 'em with a very considerable party and cut most of the men to pieces, took the canon, nail'd them, burnt the carriadges and all the amonitions, and so caus'd by so long a delay and the weather growing bad to raise the siege. The king haveing left that place, with the loss of many men, took shipping for England. Not long after my Ld Marlborough came from England with 8000 men and besiedged Cork, he was not long before it for it was soon taken but we had a great loss by the Duke of Grafton who died few days after, of a wound in his side, before Kingsale. After the raising of the siege of Lymerick, I came along with our troop, thinking (as the order was then) to have gone for England, but after my staying the matter of three months, I went to Lurgan in the north of Ireland, and was quarter'd between Litsenagaroy and Lurgan in the parish of Ballandery.'

Bonnivert's regiment, at the battle of the Boyne, took part in the wide flanking movement on the right; but, unknown to him, disaster had nearly overtaken the Williamite forces.

Opposite William's centre was the Jacobite cavalry of the right wing. It consisted of the *Duke of Berwick's Troop of the Irish Life Guards* and *Tyrconnell's*, *Parker's* and *Sutherland's Regiments of Horse*. These troops were the cream of King James's Army. Most of the officers and a large proportion of the troopers were descendants of the Anglo-Norman settlers of the Pale. They rode, therefore, with the English hunting seat; and their fondness for all mounted sports made them as at home in the saddle as on their feet. Their horses were very different from the native Irish stock which had so limited the

76

Irish cavalry of the past. Stallions had been imported from England, with the result that a type of horse was produced which has become famous as a hunter and cavalry charger, both in England and on the continent of Europe.

This brigade of some thousand superbly mounted troopers was under the command of Major-General Dominick Sheldon, a cavalry leader in the Prince Rupert tradition.

As the regiments of King William's centre pushed southwards from the crossings about Oldbridge, Sheldon launched his cavalry to the attack. The second battalion of the *Dutch Guards* had just cleared the Boyne ford when the Duke of Tyrconnell, at the head of his regiment, crashed into it. In a few minutes the Dutch battalion was utterly destroyed, and the remnants were reeling back across the river. Wheeling, Tyrconnell struck Wolsey's *Inniskilling Regiment of Horse* and drove it in disorder. Sutherland's regiment fell on the *Danish Horse*, who dispersed in flight. Duke Schomberg, William's commander in the centre, was killed in the onslaught of the *Irish Life Guards*; and in the charge by Parker's regiment, Walker, the Governor of Londonderry, was slain. Sheldon's regiments, wheeling and re-forming, delivered charge after charge. The *Life Guards* alone charged ten times. The whole Williamite centre was thrown into confusion, and had there been a few infantry battalions at this juncture to support the cavalry the result of the battle might have been an overwhelming victory for the Jacobite army. A dynasty trembled in the balance. But the infantry was not there. At this stage of the war the bulk of the Irish infantry was a half-trained rabble, quite incapable of offensive action. Sheldon withdrew.

Later in the battle, when the Jacobite infantry were broken and fleeing in disorder, Sheldon intervened again. From Plattin Hall his cavalry charged again with the same fire, and for half an hour held odds of ten or twelve to one at bay to save the beaten infantry.

The pursuit was not pressed. William's army, moving cautiously forward, encountered the fresh cavalry regiments of the Jacobite left wing, together with the French infantry. At the prospect of another encounter with that formidable cavalry William halted.

Supporters who were anxiously awaiting the arrival of the Williamite army in Dublin heard music and the clatter of many hoofs on the cobbles. They rushed out to welcome the victors of the Boyne; but, as one of them said, in what one suspects is something of an under-statement, 'We were greatly surprised when . . . we heard the whole of the Irish horse coming in, in very good order, with kettle-drums, haut-boys, and trumpets'. And so did Sheldon's troopers withdraw from one of the most gallant cavalry actions in the annals of war.

Before the Revolution James had increased his army in Ireland as well as in England, and some of the Irish regiments had been sent over to England. After the successful seizure of the English throne by William of Orange, there remained in Ireland three regiments of horse of the old army who were loyal to King James. These were the regiments of Tyrconnell, Galmoy and Sarsfield. Each of them had nine troops of a nominal strength of 58 all ranks. The Colonel and Lieutenant-Colonel each commanded a troop, but the Major was available for regimental duties. Four more regiments were raised and commanded by Abercorn, Luttrell, Sutherland and Parker. A fifth regiment of Horse was formed by Colonel Purcell on the remnants of his Dragoon regiment of the old army. The bulk of this regiment had been sent to Scotland to reinforce Dundee. Each of these five regiments had six troops. In addition two Troops of *Horse*, or *Life*, *Guards* were raised of 200 private gentlemen each, and commanded by the Duke of Berwick and Colonel Patrick Sarsfield respectively. The junior N.C.O.'s of these troops, the brigadiers and sub-brigadiers, ranked as officers. There was also a troop of *Horse Grenadiers*, commanded by Colonel Butler. The organization was thus the same as that of the English Troops of *Horse Guards*.

In William's army two Inniskilling cavalry regiments have been mentioned. There were in fact three, two of Horse and one of Dragoons. Of these only the Dragoons, of whom Bonnivert gives such a good account, remained to be permanently

78

incorporated in the Army. It may be that the battle of the Boyne had shown the existing Dragoon sword to be unsatisfactory, for on 16th March, 1691, Sir Albert Cunningham, Colonel of the *Inniskilling Dragoons,* wrote to the Secretary at War: 'We want good broad cutting swords with three-barred hilts'.

Some of the problems and difficulties of the Jacobite cavalry, as the war progressed, are shown from the following extracts from two letters written by Major-General Patrick Sarsfield, Earl of Lucan, in February and March 1691, to Lieutenant-General Justin MacCarthy, Lord Mountcashel; and translated by Mr. Henry Mangan from copies in the French archives:

'As to the state of our affairs here, it is true that a good many things are wanting, but if they would have the kindness to send them to us we shall have this summer a more numerous army and better soldiers than those who were at the river Boyne. We shall have at least as many cavalry and dragoons as we had then, provided they send us from France enough oats to keep them before the end of the spring, for by then our forage will be consumed. We have not much in truth, this country which we hold producing hardly any grain. That is the greatest difficulty we shall have to surmount. If we could preserve our horses until the grass grows (which could be done with ten thousand barrels of oats) we propose to have seven thousand horse and dragoons and as many infantry as the King wishes, provided they have the necessary accoutrements. If we are not sent a great deal of corn I fear we shall have a great scarcity here.'

'Our mountaineers take horses from them [that is the enemy] every day, and if we had a little money to reward them, our cavalry would be very well mounted at the enemy's expense, which would be a double advantage for us, for while accommodating ourselves, there would be as many dismounted men for them. We have already had more than a thousand this winter, and they have brought me thirty seven from Lanier's [Major-General Lanier] quarters, of which twenty two were

79

out of his stable. If we had only a hundred pistoles per company, and arms, we would have all our regiments complete.'

When the war with France was terminated by the Treaty of Ryswick, in 1697, the cavalry under William III's command consisted of:

Horse—British, 86 troops; Dutch, Danes and Hanoverians, 76 troops. Dragoons—British, 64 troops; Huguenots, 18 troops. From the above figures it would appear that Dragoons were far more popular in the British Army than in the armies of the other Allies.

As soon as the treaty was signed a start was made on a drastic reduction of the British Army. Many cavalry regiments disappeared altogether; others were reduced in strength by cutting down the number of troops, and reducing the establishment of those which were left.

With regard to the disposal of horses, an order of 13th August, 1697, said: 'And if it should happen that any of the troop should be disbanded, the several horses of such troops are hereby declared to belong to the troopers that ride them, and not to the Captain, and each trooper shall carry off the horse on which he served'.

Nevertheless, it seems that horses of disbanded men were frequently retained by the regiments to which they belonged. Colonel Poultney, in fact, speaking on behalf of the Duke of Ormonde in the House of Commons, admitted that horses and accoutrements were taken from troopers when they were discharged from the *Horse Guards*, although they had provided their own horses on enlistment and had paid 2s. 6d. a month for remounts. He pleaded, however, that as soon as they entered their troop, their horses were the King's; and if any, on discharge, were given their horses 'it was a favour, and more than they could of right demand'.

In response to a complaint about their horses from some discharged men of Ross's Dragoons, Colonel Ross produced an order from the King to the effect that horses of reduced men were to be exchanged for any inferior horses of men who were remaining in the regiment, and the horses so discarded were to

80

be sold for the benefit of the regiment. The House of Commons apparently agreed that there was nothing wrong in this procedure.

Whether a trooper left the Army with his own horse, or, in fact, any horse, seems to have depended on the practice obtaining in his regiment. There was another order of 1697, however, which may have been an attempt to regularize the position. According to this, troopers of Horse and privates of Dragoons were to be allowed to take away cloak, clothes, and accoutrements; and horse if they had served a whole year. If they had served for less than a year they were to be given a share of the purchase money for the horse.

In 1693 two Scottish regiments of Dragoons crossed the border into England. These were Levington's (now *The Royal Scots Greys*) and Cunningham's (now the *7th Hussars*). The former regiment is mentioned in two letters from Hugh James, of Levens Hall, near Kendal, to James Graham:

1st June, 1693. 'On Tuesday last Captain Leveston's regiment of dragoons came into Kendal.'

5th June, 1693. 'Major William commands the dragoons at Kendal. They are yet very civil. I hope they will not offer any ill thing in the park.'

There is mention of these regiments in the diary of John Evelyn:

'22 April 1694: Some Regiments of Highland Dragoons were on their march through England; they were of large stature, well appointed and disciplined. One of them having reproch'd a Dutchman for cowardice in our late fight, was attack'd by two Dutchmen, when with his sword he struck off the head of one, and cleft the skull of the other down to his chin.'

Their arrival in London is noted by Narcissus Luttrell in his *Brief Relation of State Affairs*:

'Thurs., 19 April 1694. This day the king took a view of colonel Cunningham's and sir Thomas Levingtons dragoons in Hide Park, being too regiments lately come from Scotland; they made a fine show, especially the latter, who were all

F
81

mounted on gray and white horses, and new clothed, and are more like troopers than dragoons.'

Two notices of deserters in the *London Gazette* of 1700 and one in 1702 throw some light on troop horses of the period. The first of these, 30th May–3rd June, 1700, refers to a deserter from the *Earl of Arran's Regiment of Horse* 'in new Regimental Clothes lined with large Pewter Buttons and took with him a cole-black Gelding'. The next of 11th–15th July, 1700, mentions 'Deserters from the Royal Regiment of Dragoons, commanded by Lord Raby, Edward Nash, . . . on a thick black Gelding, . . . and George Wiggons on a black Gelding. . . . They had new Crimson Clothes lined with Blue, and Hats with broad Gold Lace.' Finally, lest one should think that all except the *Scots Greys* had black horses, the *Gazette* of 5th–9th March, 1702, records a deserter of the *Queen's Regiment of Horse* (now *The King's Dragoon Guards*), who took with him a bright-bay troop gelding.

The population of black horses was, however, increased considerably by William III. In about 1690 he imported a large number of Dutch cart horses; very big and heavy animals, standing up to 18 hands, black in colour, and so slow and ponderous in their movements that they became known as the 'snail breed'. In later years the type was referred to (somewhat erroneously) as the 'Old English Black Horse', and was associated with the Fens where it was predominantly bred. At the end of the eighteenth century a well-known sheep and cattle breeder, called Bakewell, set about producing a lighter and more active animal by crossing this large black horse with others, the type of which he kept secret. He apparently succeeded, at least to some extent, and certainly got rid of their heavy hairy legs. It may well be that Bakewell's crosses, and others by earlier breeders, produced the heavily built black troop horse which was so popular in the cavalry of the eighteenth century, and which can be seen in so many contemporary pictures.

CHAPTER VI

QUEEN ANNE

At the beginning of the eighteenth century there was some danger that the breeding of riding horses would suffer from the enormous increase in the national enthusiasm for racing. Most of the races were becoming short sprints, which encouraged the breeding of horses purely for speed without any staying power. Early in the reign of Queen Anne this practice was discouraged by the institution of new Royal Plates, awarded for races which demanded considerable endurance. The introduction of these Plates is described by a writer in the *Sporting Magazine* of 1819:

'. . . Gentlemen went on breeding their horses so fine for the sake of shape and speed only. Those animals which were only second, third or fourth rates in speed were considered to be quite useless. This custom continued until the reign of Queen Anne, when a public spirited gentleman (observing inconveniences arising from this exclusiveness) left thirteen plates or purses to be run for at such places as the Crown should appoint. Hence they are called the King's or Queen's Plates or Guineas. They were given upon the condition that each horse, mare or gelding should carry twelve stone weight, the best of three heats over a four-mile course. By this method a stronger and more useful breed was soon raised; and if the horse did not win the guineas, he was yet strong enough to make a good hunter. By these crossings—as the jockeys term it—we have horses of full blood, three-quarters blood, or half bred, suitable to carry burthens; by which means the English breed of horses is allowed to be the best and is greatly esteemed by foreigners.'

On the roads of England the task of coach horses had been made easier by the introduction about 1700 of steel springs.

83

Before this, leather straps had been used to ease the jolting of the cumbersome vehicles. With the steel springs came a lighter carriage; but most coaches were still very unwieldy, and the heavier ones were still pulled by the Great, or Shire, Horses. In the Army the Shire horse was used almost universally for heavy draught purposes.

Cavalry tactics underwent considerable change at the direction of the great Duke of Marlborough. It may be that Marlborough was influenced by Sheldon's devastating charges at the Boyne. In any case, the pace of the charge was increased from the trot to the gallop, and cavalry were not allowed to use pistols between the start of a mounted attack and the crash into the ranks of the enemy. To remove any temptation from commanders to indulge in the old habit of halting and firing, Marlborough restricted the pistol ammunition to three charges of powder and ball for a campaign, and this was intended only for the protection of horses when at grass. Writing of Marlborough's cavalry in his *Discipline of Horse*, Brigadier-General Richard Kane says that they were required to 'handle their swords well, which is the only Weapon our *British* Horse makes use of when they charge the Enemy; more than this is superfluous'. As regards Dragoons he adds, 'Dragoons should be well instructed in the use of arms, having often occasion to make use of them on foot; but when on horseback they are to fight as the Horse do'. Dragoons, in fact, were rapidly becoming indistinguishable from the Horse; and their original function as a form of mounted infantry had practically ceased. In a letter of 6th April, 1706, Captain George Benson of the *Royal Dragoons* said, 'Good swords are the only things necessary for us, especially in Catalonia, where upon all occasions we are made use of as Horse'.

There were seven cavalry regiments which served under Marlborough through all his campaigns. Five of these were Horse (the regiments which later became *The King's Dragoon Guards*, and the *3rd, 5th, 6th* and *7th Dragoon Guards*) and two Dragoons (the *Greys* and the *5th Royal Irish*).

Lord Charles Cathcart, the eighth of the title, served in the

Greys in Marlborough's army, and has left some interesting records of life in the cavalry, which are preserved in the Cathcart MSS. In the *Greys* there were separate messes for captains and subalterns. Field officers appear to have lived apart, but to have dined quite frequently in both officers' messes.

Cathcart was Brigade Major in the brigade of British Dragoons commanded by Lord Stair, during the campaigns of 1707–09, and much information is contained in the order books which he kept. Strict regulations were laid down to govern the activities of foraging parties. Regiments had to detail regular foraging parties, and commanding officers were held responsible that only these parties were used for foraging. A regimental party normally included representatives from each troop, to ensure that the forage was fairly distributed throughout the regiment.

The protection of these parties received considerable attention. Covering patrols watched all approaches to the area, the foragers themselves were armed, and parties were forbidden to scatter.

In camp, cavalry had to 'smooth the ground' in front of their lines in order that they could form up easily.

On the march galled and weak horses and dismounted cavalrymen had to march in the rear of the column.

Charles Cathcart had an active time at the battle of Oudenarde. His brigade was formed up and ready to move, when news was received that a detachment of French troops was attacking the village where the Generals had been quartered and plundering their 'equipages'. Stair despatched a squadron from the *Greys* and one from the *Royal Irish* to drive off the enemy. The French retired but the British Dragoons had to settle with some of the 'friendly' population who were engaged in pillaging the sutlers. In the meantime the Army had marched. Cathcart rode on ahead to report to the General of the Day, and caught up with the main body as 'the lines were galloping', and 'clearly there was something to be done in the front'. By the time he reached the river Scheldt the Allied advanced guard under Cadogan had apparently already crossed and were in action. Cathcart joined some German cavalry, with whom was the Electoral Prince of Hanover, who was later to become King George II. The Prince had his share of misadventure; for, first of all, when the leading squadron, with which he was riding, had to dismount to cross a marshy stream, George fell into the marsh; and secondly, when the squadron remounted and charged a French rearguard, he had his horse shot under him.

Cathcart found Lord Stair with the cavalry Quartermasters and their escorts, whom he had 'formed into a squadron'. With this improvised unit he charged the enemy. Some foreign Dragoons who should have supported him, however, 'broke'.

Marlborough and Eugene were up with these forward troops; and Cathcart now seems to have been employed as 'galloper' to take messages back to the commanders of the various components of the force, which were hastening towards the battlefield.

Of the fierce cavalry action at the battle of Malplaquet, Cathcart says that the charge of the *Greys*, *King's Dragoon Guards*, *3rd Dragoon Guards* and *7th Dragoon Guards* against the French, 'that stood in three lines upon the hill', broke the enemy cavalry; but that the Hanoverian and Prussian squadrons who should have supported the British cavalry 'did not show a proper forwardness'.

At the opening of the campaign of 1710 Cathcart speaks appreciatively of the condition of his own regiment, which was in good order; and the horses, though not fat, were quite fit. His own troop, he thought, was by no means the worst. He considered the British Horse, however, to be below the standard of the Dragoons.

James Cathcart, brother of Charles, would have liked to buy a troop of the *Greys*, but the price, £1720, was more than he could afford.

In 1711 James Campbell, Lieutenant-Colonel of the *Greys*, who was at home recruiting, wrote a letter in which he apologized for having to buy a bay horse for Cathcart's troop, as he was unable to obtain any greys 'to please me'.

The Mounted Troops of the British Army

It seems to have been a regimental custom in the *Greys* to 'present' a new officer to the men of his troop. This practice may, however, have been common to all British cavalry regiments at this time.

Lord Cadogan, who was Marlborough's Quartermaster-General in the Low Countries, was responsible for directing that the tails of cavalry horses should be docked very short. This 'Cadogan' tail was frequently only two inches long.

Marlborough's unbroken series of successes were not reflected in the campaign in the Peninsula. The greatest battle in Spain, in fact, was the disastrous defeat which Marlborough's nephew, the Duke of Berwick, inflicted on the British–Dutch–Portuguese army at Almanza.

A well-known eighteenth-century cavalry general, Hawley, then a Captain in the *4th Dragoons*, has left three separate accounts of the battle, of which the following are extracts:

During the retreat, 'The Captain [*i.e.* Hawley] . . . seeing about 70 horsemen on a rising ground and some yellow liveries among them, which he took to be Major General Pearce by the liveries, he passed near several French squadrons in his way to that hill, he being accidentally clothed that day in grey faced with red and laced with gold, by which he also came up very near these people on the hill. Then he perceived the white papers [*i.e.* as hat-distinguishing badges or cockades]. This was the Duke of Berwick with some officers and aids de camps and the rest were orderly men. When he was within 100 yards he also saw the Duke's star, who was upon a little English bay nag. He then turned off but three of the orderly men pushed out after him and chased him and turned him once and shot his horse through the neck, but he being a better horse than theirs' he got off. . . .

'At last he found the Lt. General alone at the head of two Dutch squadrons of Trimburn's Horse, persuading them to charge some foot before them but in vain.'

Another account describes the arrival of the Lt.-General [Erle] on the left flank and gives some more detail of this incident:

87

'A little beyond this battery where he [Erle] supposed our left wing had been, he found Hill's and Mark Kerr's battalions pretty entire, and two squadrons of Trimburn's Dutch Horse and Harvey's [now the *Bays*] two squadrons a little further to the left, who had not engaged all day, by reason of a hollow mill dam that was just before them in the beginning of the day, which they at last had passed. The enemy's squadrons were coming up to these people every way, and the two battalions coming up to the front of these two English battalions and the Duke of Berwick's own battalion coming down upon their left flank, the French squadrons were at some distance coming up the ascent behind their two battalions in front. The Lieut.-General went up to Trimburn's two squadrons and ordered them to charge those two battalions in flank that were going to attack the two English battalions. The two squadrons upon that order moved very handsomely about 50 yards, sword in hand, in order to charge the Foot, but then at once made a sudden wheel to the left about, and came to their ground a full trot, wheeled again and faced as before. The Lieut.-General went up to the commanding officer a second time and gave him the same orders, he marched again both squadrons very handsomely, but did the very same thing, only wheeled to the right about, and came back and wheeled upon his ground. All this while there was not a shot hardly fired in this part. The Lieut.-General spoke no more to Trimburn's people, but went to Harvey's two squadrons who had no orders that day.'

The following paragraphs are an amalgamation of two separate accounts: 'The enemy were all this time drawing down both Horse and Foot, upon this little body, upon which one of the battalions went off and a little too fast to last. 'Twas Hill's battalion [later *11th Foot* or *Devonshire Regiment*] that remained, commanded by Colonel Clayton, who had taken post at a pond with the water in their front. The General sent his Aid de Camp [Hawley] to order Mr. Clayton to keep that ground and his fire as long as he could, for he would go and charge the Foot (who were coming upon his flanks) with the Horse and that was the last thing he could do for him. As the

Captain was giving these orders at the head of the Colours to Colonel Clayton, a French battalion came up to the tail of the pond and gave them their whole fire at once. Colonel Clayton was shot through the body and dropped; a good many officers dropped at the same time, but the Captain escaped and having no more business there he was coming away to go back to his General, when he met Major Collingwood upon the left flank of the battalion, as he was ordering the files to be completed again after that fire. He told him Col. Clayton was killed, as he concluded, and advised him to go to the head of the regiment, telling him the orders he had given Colonel Clayton. The Major had dismounted whilst he was talking to him and had just given his horse to a drummer when there came another fire which killed him and the drummer both. The Captain and his horse both escaped again.

'He then made what haste he could to find the General again, which he soon did at the head of Harvey's two squadrons. While he was making his report that Col. Clayton and the Major were both killed, the General saw the two Dutch squadrons (who had refused to charge) wheel and go off but at the same time that poor battalion of Hill's keep its ground. The Duke of Berwick's own regiment of Irish of two battalions was now coming both in front to attack the left flank of that poor single regiment but as they would not go on without giving their right flank to the two squadrons of Harvey's, they halted to keep the squadrons in check.

'The General then said to Colonel Roper of the Horse "as you have had no share of this day's work, let us do what we can to save those brave men there". He ordered Colonel Roper to wheel to the left and he himself went to the head of the second squadron and then both squadrons at once attacked Berwick's two battalions, sword in hand in front: they at the same time the squadrons were coming up to them, calling every officer of Harvey's by their names as well as many of the men, asking them if they were mad and crying out they would give them good quarter, but finding no notice taken of their offers they began to fire. At the same time the enemy's Horse were come up pretty near, and they let go or broke two squadrons of theirs like Hussars and came up full trot with two more, and took that first or right squadron of Harvey's in flank just upon the wheel, which of course with the fire of the battalion soon broke them and the other squadron too. Then everybody shifted for themselves as well as they could, happy those who were best mounted.'

Three years after Almanza, in 1710, Harvey's had their revenge. The battle of Almenara was a cavalry action in which the Allied vanguard, under the command of Lord Stanhope, drove the enemy army from the field. Harvey's (*Queen's Bays*) were in the leading line, with Stanhope at the head of one of the squadrons. In an epic encounter, worthy of the romances of mediaeval chivalry, Stanhope slew the opposing Spanish cavalry commander in single combat.

In its account of this battle the *Evening Post* said, 'Though this may be looked upon as but an engagement of horse, yet it was so sharp and considerable an action that the enemy's whole cavalry being routed and their foot flying in the utmost disorder and confusion, many throwing down their arms, several of their cannon and ammunition wagons and their baggage being left behind, it is certainly an advantage gained very little inferior to an entire defeat'.

The enemy were pursued to the walls of Lerida, and the triumph of the troopers was expressed in their shouts, 'Almanza, ye dogs! Remember Almanza!'

One of the regiments to fight at Almenara was *Rochford's Dragoons*, which had come out from Ireland the previous year. They had embarked without horses, having handed theirs over to *Pearce's Dragoons*, when that regiment had relieved them at Belfast. On arrival in the Peninsula, Rochford's had to be sent to Italy to be equipped with horses, and thus became, incidentally, the first British regiment to serve in that country.

Pearce's Dragoons had an unusual history. Owing to the shortage of cavalry in the Peninsula, on 7th January, 1706, *Lord Barrymore's Regiment of Foot* (later the *13th* and now *The Somerset Light Infantry*) was converted into a Dragoon Regiment under the colonelcy of Pearce. Barrymore, together with twenty-two of his officers and a few N.C.O.'s, was sent home to re-raise his Regiment of Foot. Pearce's distinguished itself in action; and then, at the end of 1707, it was itself reduced as a result of its losses at Almanza. The men were incorporated into other regiments and the officers were sent home to recruit the new Dragoon regiment again up to its establishment of 589 all ranks. It was at this stage that Pearce's took over from Rochford's in Belfast. After the Peace of Utrecht the regiment was disbanded.

Colonel St. Pierre, commanding the *Royal Dragoons* in the Peninsula, appears to have held strong views on the subject of swords. A letter written by him on 13th June, 1707, says, 'The swords are good, but a handful too short, there is no dealing with the French but with good swords, they having excellent ones. We are all resolved, whatever it cost, if we come to Barcelona and can find German blades, to buy them and put them upon our handles, which are large enough.'

On 17th September, 1707, he wrote another letter in which he said, 'My Lord [Lord Stanhope] hath ordered new swords for all the Horse and Dragoons. It is really true that the swords sent out of England were good for nothing, ours were the best, and I have made the hilts which are good and large serve for these blades, which are extraordinarily good, pretty broad, and as long as any. I have got ledges of tin to the scabbards, and each blade and scabbard cometh to above 8/-.

'My Lord hath got also skull iron caps made for all the Dragoons.'

The *8th Dragoons* acquired the unusual distinction, by their gallantry in the field, of wearing the two broad belts crossing the chest which were normally part of the equipment peculiar to the Horse. According to General Severne, who was Colonel of the regiment from 1760 until his death in 1787, this distinction owed its origin to the feat of the regiment at the battle of Almenara, where the *8th Dragoons* 'defeated and took a regiment of Spanish Horse prisoners, when the men exulting in victory took from their prisoners their cross-belts and wore them, which as a mark of the honour they had thereby gained in battle Marshal Staremberg permitted them to wear, which they continued to do from that time'. As a result of this peculiarity in their dress the regiment acquired the name of the 'Cross-Belt Dragoons'.

The end of war seems to have been celebrated by military parades. According to *The Post Boy* of 23rd/25th March, 1714, the restoration of peace with Spain was the occasion of such a parade at Leeds, when, at the head of the procession, came 'Lieut. Southous on horseback, with drums beating at the head of the troop of H.M.'s Own Regiment of Dragoons commanded by the Earl of Stafford who marched by threes on horseback, with their swords drawn'.

A somewhat mixed comment on the *Household Cavalry* was passed by a visiting foreigner in 1710. Zacharias Conrad von Uffenbach, a student at Strassburg University, noted that 'Opposite the Chapel at the entrance to St James Park is the Corps de Gardes of the Cavalry, which is certainly magnificent. For they are all well mounted and have red uniforms laced with gold; two of them are always on guard on horseback with drawn swords.' As a result, possibly, of listening to malicious conversation, this initial enthusiasm was soon revised; for the following month he 'drove to Hyde Park to see the review of the royal horse guards, commanded by the Duke of Ormond. They are said not to be as gallant as they look; for when troubles lately broke out in Scotland, almost half of them wished to resign. They have, as all Englishmen have, a bad seat, looking like tailors on horseback.'

A new series of carbines and pistols was issued to the cavalry in the reign of Queen Anne. There was, however, little change from the previous patterns, except that the metal mountings were now brass instead of iron.

CHAPTER VII

HANOVER & STUART

From the accession of George I until the end of the first half of the eighteenth century the rival Houses of Hanover and Stuart contended for the British throne. The former was, of course, in possession; but the unpleasant personalities and habits of the first two Georges, coupled with the fact that they were foreigners, made them extremely unpopular. The Hanoverian tenure of the throne was, consequently, somewhat precarious.

The threat of Jacobite attempts on the throne led, amongst other preparations, to the raising of a number of new regiments of Dragoons. Typical of the Warrants to form these regiments was one issued to Brigadier-General Humphrey Gore for a regiment of Dragoons, which, much later, was to become the *10th Hussars*. The Warrant read as follows:

'George R.

'Whereas we have thought fit that a Regiment of Dragoons be forthwith raised under your command for Our Service, which is to consist of six troops of one Sergeant, two Corporals, one Drummer, one Hautbois and Thirty private Dragoons, including the Widdowsmen in each troop. These are to authorize you by beat of Drumm or otherwise to raise so many Volunteers as shall be wanting to compleat the said Regiment to the above numbers. And when you shall have Listed fifteen men fitt for service in any of the said Troops, You are to give notice to Two of Our Justices of the Peace of the town or Country wherein the same are, who are hereby Authorised and Required to view the said Men and Certify the Day of their so doing, from which Day the said fifteen Men and the Commission and Non-Commission Officers of Such Troops are to enter into our pay, and you are to cause the said Volunteers to be Raised and Levy'd as aforesaid to march under the Command of such Commission Officers as you shall direct to Hertford, appointed for the Rendezvous of the Said Regiment, and all Magistrates, Justices of the Peace, Constables and other Our Officers who it may concern are Hereby required to be Assisting unto You in providing Quarters, Impressing Carriages and otherewise, as there shall be Occasion.

'Given at Our Court at St. James' this 23rd day of July, 1715. In the first Year of Our Reign.

'By His Majesty's Command

'(*Sd*) Wm. Pulteney.'

The 'Widdowsmen' mentioned in the above Warrant were a peculiar institution. They only existed on paper, but pay was drawn for them as a means of providing a pension for the widows of officers who were killed or who died in the service. In reference to them a Warrant of 26th April, 1717, said: 'Our Commissary-General of the Musters to pass and allow upon the Muster, one man out of each respective Troop or Company of Our forces, both at home and abroad, to be and to remain as a fund for the payment thereof, of which Royal Bounty we do hereby establish, Direct and Appoint you to be the receiver and paymaster'.

In this same year another Dragoon regiment was raised by Colonel Charles Churchill which was given the title of *The Prince of Wales's Own*. It was disbanded three years later, and the sum of £600 was authorized to be paid 'to Colonel Charles Churchill, as Colonel of Our most dear son, George Augustus, Prince of Wales's Own Regiment of Dragoons, in consideration of their losses by horses killed and disabled, and other extraordinary expenses in their long and continued marches in a very rigorous season, in pursuit of the rebels who were taken prisoners at Preston'.

In Dragoon regiments at this period Sergeants were paid 14s. a week, Corporals 10s. 6d. and Dragoons 8s. 2d. In each case, however, there were weekly stoppages of 5s. 3d. for billeting, 1s. 5½d. for corn and 3½d. for the farrier, a total of 7s.

Lord Charles Cathcart was engaged in the military operations occasioned by the Jacobite rising of 1715. He was then Lieutenant-Colonel in *The Royal Scots Greys*, and was serving under the command of the Duke of Argyll. At the start of the campaign the Jacobites had occupied the town of Dunfermline in some force. Argyll promptly despatched a detachment of cavalry under Cathcart's command to reconnoitre and, if possible, destroy the Jacobites.

Cathcart has left an account of his successful little operation. He says, in a letter to the Earl of Loudoun: 'I have had the good fortune to draw the first blood of the rebels on this side. Sunday last the Duke of Argyll upon the intelligence he had of a detachment of 120 of their horse and 250 foot's being on their march to raise contributions in ffyfe sent me at five o'clock that evening with 150 dragoons in quest of them. At three o'clock of the munday's morning I arrived by byeways at the east end of the toun of Dunfermling the side from which they were to expect their friends. After taking my measures from knowing what was in toun, I found they were there, the foot people in the Abbey and the horse lodg'd in the toun. I consider'd if I should leave them till break of day the whole body wou'd get into the Abbey wher I could not attack them, and considering they had no guard of my side I resolv'd to beat up their quarters in the night. At five o'clock I sent in 30 dragoons on foot to take such a post near the Abbey as might keep up theirs, and give me time to deal with the horse. My 30 men beat their advanc'd post of foot and the fireing alarm'd the Cavalrie so that when I entered the town with a detachment of dragoons on horseback I found Major Gordon their Commandant in the streets mounted with a partie at his back. He advanced to challeng me, wee wounded him and tooke the most of those who were with him. I stay'd long enough in toun to pick up seventeen prisoners, ten of which are gentle men, one is Mr. Murray, brother to Abircany, a man that is us'd to travail between this and St. Germains, he was to have been Clerk to the Council. I retir'd out of the place before six without any loss, I had only one man and one horse wounded. I have had an account from Dunfermling since that they had 4 men killed and 2 mortally wounded. . . . At break of day I marched about to the west end of the town. Before the Abby I drew ther and show'd them ther freinds, my prisoners, to encourage them to attempt ther releife since I could not meddle with them within ther walls, but they would not take ther revenge so I return'd back to his Grace that evening who made me very welcome.'

The Jacobite version of the encounter is given in a scathing account by the Master of Sinclair:

'Everie one run a different way: some left their horses sticking in dunghills in the streets, and others, when their horses fell in anie narrow lane with justling or making too great haste to get away, left them on the spot and came to Perth on country horses and said they had horses shot under them; others run to Burntisland, some to different places of the countrie, some got under beds, others up to garrets, and most of this when the enemy was gone, who, knowing of the highlandman's being in the Abbey, did not stay to dally in the town and beat their retreat very quicklie after their coming in, for they seised nobodie in houses.'

In that same year of 1715 there was a review of the *4th Dragoons*, of which a very interesting account is given in *News Letters of 1715–16*, edited by Mr. A. Francis Steuart.

'I scarce think there is a more showy regiment in Europe. They drew up in two squadrons, three lines in each squadron, which made six companies in all; each company had a farrier, or hatchet man, with a very high black furred cap on, and a pock [bag] hanging behind tipped with fur. Instead of a sword, they had a saw at their side, and a shovel in place of a slinged carbine. They carried axes in their hands, and a hatchet under their belt instead of pistols. There were fixed two large things likest to muff cases where their horseshoes and nails were, they have clean white aprons and white gloves, and rode upon good grey horses.

'The 6 Drummers were Moors, with brass drums, and the Hautboys and they rode upon grey horses.

'The 6 Troops rode by the Duke [of Argyll] troop by troop, with a hatchet man and other proper officers. Before every Company there stood an officer where they were to wheel when they came up five in a rank, and to every file he said "Look the Duke full in the face".

'The 2 squadrons when they had passed thus, took up again their several grounds. The next they did was dismounting and fixing all their horses so that every tenth man held the nine horses, and then they drew out to that empty space betwixt the two squadrons and there performed their exercise on foot. Then they marched on foot by the Duke, who had dismounted with them. They took up their ground again when they were past, retired in order to their horses and remounted, and rode again in troops by his Grace, but as they passed him this time every horse singly from the right to the left filed off and rode by. You might see the vanity of some to make handsome caracole touch their horses to the quick with the spur. I never in my life saw so many fine black horses. The officers' led horses were extraordinary fine, with fine decks of different skins to cover them. There was something very shog and neat in the appearance of the regiment. . . .'

In 1728 the King reviewed *The Royal Horse Guards* on Datchet Common. The review is described in a letter written by the Adjutant to the Duke of Richmond, who commanded a troop in the regiment. The unit paraded at nine, and the King arrived at eleven and inspected it 'standing'. It was then ordered to dismount and carry out exercises on foot, 'which they did very well, then clos'd their Files to the Right and Whield in Nine Divisions and March by Fours before the King. The officers were Ordered not to pull off their Hats, but to salute on foot with their Swords, in the same manner as on horse back.' The regiment then mounted and 'went through the Evolutions on horse back in the Same manner as Ordered by the New Exercise'. He concludes, 'The Officers had Red feathers, we had new Trophies and Trumpet Cloaths, Most of the Men had new furniture and Boots, we had a glorious fine day and the Ground we reviewed upon was like a Bowling Green'.

In 1728 General Hawley (who wrote the accounts of the battle of Almanza) wrote a paper in which he proposed that a regiment of Dragoons should be formed to carry out the original functions of Dragoons. Hawley's paper was, in fact, the first scheme for what were later to be called Light Dragoons. The paper is of interest, not only for the proposed organization, equipment and training, but also for the light that it throws on existing practice.

The full title of the paper is 'A scheme for reviving a regiment of original Dragoons for the use they were first intended, since the modern Dragoons are become better Horse than ever was in England before'.

The following are extracts from the paper:

''Tis proposed that this regiment shall consist of 12 Troops of 50 effective men each, besides the pay of 3 men for remounting to the Captain, as other regiments have. That when on foot, it may be a tolerable battalion of nearly 500 rank and file.

'Each Troop to have a Farrier, a Gunsmith, a Saddler, besides the 50 effective men, to act as Pioneers. 3 Corporals to each Troop, 3 Sergeants, a Captain, a Lieutenant, and 2nd Lieutenant, a Quartermaster and 2 Drums.

'Besides this it is proposed to have 2 Standards or Ensign-bearers, upon Cornet's pay, called Guidons, exclusive of the 12 2nd Lieutenants.

''Tis proposed to cloathe this regiment every year, as the Foot are clothed, but their cloaks, boots, saddles and other accoutrements to be furnished as the Dragoons are.

'The accoutrements to be a cap, small boots, a cartridge box cross the left shoulder, and close under the right arm, with a good short sword or hanger, a small saddle with one pistol on the near side, a bill or hatchet on the other, a small hunting bit, a good firelock, bayonet and sling, in a bucket.

'The regiment to be raised of all the truss short men in the nation who have been discharged and are now refused for being too short.

98

''Tis proposed to raise this regiment in Yorkshire, to have it called the Yorkshire Horse, to give but £15 for each horse, and they to be really Yorkshire half-bred nags called bastards there.

'This regiment will march 30 miles a day, when a regiment of modern Dragoons can march but 10. This can be of use in the West, or any fast country where the modern Dragoons are of none. For westward they can go no farther than the open country, unless they are thrown away, as is evident to those who know that country.

'This regiment would kill all the others with fatigue, will go farther in 3 days than any other corps in 9. This regiment may loose their horses upon occasion by quitting them quite to be thrown into any place which the others can't afford to do. These are the only proper troops against smugglers. 'Tis the only proper corps upon an invasion, to harass and molest any body of troops that may have got a footing. 'Tis a very useful body to be interlined by troops on foot, between squadrons, in any day of business. 'Tis the only proper corps to go over 40 miles into Scotland, in case of any disturbance in the Highlands, where another corps can neither live nor march.

'By raising such a corps there is so many of the best men and horses of the nation made serviceable which are now lost, because they are not the size, nor the horses the shape nor sort now used.'

In fact, no light horse were raised until 1745. Captain R. Hinde says in his *Discipline of the Light-Horse* of 1778: 'The first institution of this useful corps that we know of in England was during the rebellion in the year 1745, when his Grace the late Duke of Kingston raised a regiment of Light Horse for H.M.'s service at his own expense upon an entire new plan, to imitate the Hussars in foreign service'.

In 1756 Hawley produced a revision of his former scheme and suggested that one troop of Light Dragoons should be added to each cavalry regiment. He paid some attention to camouflage in both men and horses:

'It is proposed that the colour of their clothing should be

99

green, or any colour but red, for the same reason that Franche Companies wear green, not to be discovered in ambuscades.

'Horses of all colours except grey, size from 14 hands to $14\frac{1}{2}$ of a moderate age, no very young ones, but to have some speed, and to have strength enough to carry forage.'

In 1729 Clothing Regulations were issued for the Army. The portions applicable to the cavalry were as follows:

'For a Trooper.

A new Cloth Coat, well lined with Serge.

A New Waistcoat.

A New Laced Hat.

A Pair of New Large Buff Gloves, with Stiff Tops, once in Two Years.

A Pair of New Boots, as they shall be wanting.

As it is difficult to fix a Period of Time for providing Saddles, It is to be left to the Judgement of the General-Officer, who may be appointed to Review them.

Housings, Caps, new Horse-Furniture, Bitts, and Stirrup-Irons; Cloaks faced with the Livery of the Regiment, entirely New and New Buff or Buff-coloured Cross-Belts, to be provided as they shall be wanting.

The Second Mounting is to consist of New Laced-Hats and Horse-Collars.

'For a Dragoon.

A New Cloth Coat, well lined with Serge.

A New Waistcoat.

A pair of New Breeches. [It is strange that breeches are not mentioned as part of the clothing for Troopers.]

A New Laced Hat.

A pair of New large Buff-coloured Gloves, with Stiff Tops.

A pair of New Boots, as they shall be wanting.

Saddles to be left to the Judgement of the General Officer, who may be appointed to Review them.

Housings, Caps, New Horse-Furniture, Bitts and Stirrup-Irons; and Cloaks faced with the Livery of the Regiment, entirely New, as they shall be wanting.

New Buff or Buff-coloured Accoutrements, viz. a Shoulder-Belt with a Pouch, a Waist-Belt sufficient to carry the Sword, with a Place to receive the Bayonet and Sling for the Arms, such as the General-Officers appointed to inspect the Cloathing shall approve of as they shall be wanting.

The Second Mounting is to consist of New Laced-Hats, Gloves, and Horse-Collars.

'The Size of Horse for a Trooper.

A strong well-bodyed Horse, from Fifteen Hands and an Inch, to Two Inches, and not exceeding.

'For a Dragoon.

A strong well-bodyed Horse at Fifteen Hands, and not exceeding.'

'Men not under Five Foot Ten Inches, in Stockings, is a sufficient size for the Horse and Dragoons; and that they be chosen Men with good Countenances, good Limbs, and broad Shoulders. And that the Size of Men for the Foot Guards be Five Foot Nine Inches; and Marching-Regiments Five Foot Eight Inches with Shoes, such as are given in the Cloathing.'

The horses for the Dragoons must have dropped below the standard required during the campaigns of the 'forties, for in 1746–7 the Duke of Cumberland issued the following order:

'It is H.R.H. the Duke's Orders that for the future no Horse shall be bought to mount the Dragoons above the size of Fifteen hands, at most, and that the Officer or Officers, who are appointed to Buy, choose, or receive such Horses have very strong Instructions given them to buy or take very Nimble kind of Horses that can Gallop, with short backs, broad Fillets for carrying of Forage, Small clean Legs, and as clear of Hair as possible. And to prevent the Excuse of Horses growing after they are Bought, it is His positive orders that no Horse be bought for any Regiment that is not rising five years old at least ye next Grass, and as they are for immediate Duty, if they are rising Six Years old, it would be better for the Service, and

His Royal Highness gives this further notice that if notwithstanding these orders, any Horses are bought above the size or under the age here directed and found so, when Received, by whom His Highness shall appoint it shall be to the Loss of the Buyer, receiver or chooser.

'It is H.R.H.'s opinion that the Sergeants of Dragoons should be mounted upon a much Lighter Nimbler kind of horse than the Dragoon.'

About 1727 the famous musket 'Brown Bess' made its appearance. This was an infantry weapon, but arms of the same general pattern were issued to the cavalry—carbines, musketoons and pistols. The Dragoon musketoon was something between a carbine and a musket. The respective barrel lengths of the three weapons were probably: musket 46 inches, musketoon 36 or 39 inches, carbine 35 to 36 inches. The 'Brown Bess' pistol had a 12-inch barrel and a 20/24 bore, and the weight of ball was 34 to the pound.

According to Bland's *Military Discipline* (1746 edition) the carbine was carried as follows: 'The carbine is to be placed in a bucket (which is fixed by straps to the right side of the saddle, so as to hang below the holster-pipe) and to be fastened about 12 inches above the lock by a strap that comes from the bur, or forepart of the saddle, the barrel upwards, and running between the man's right arm and side'.

Horse and Dragoons carried a similar type of sword. This was somewhat like the pattern at present carried in Scottish infantry regiments with a straight blade and a steel full basket hilt.

In 1726 there appears to have been some shortage of sword blades, for a Warrant of that year says that 'As the Colonels have represented that there are no sword blades to be had in England, His Majesty has been pleased to send orders to the Lord Commissioner of the Treasury to permit sword blades to be imported from Germany'.

On 17th July, 1737, *The King's Own Regiment of Horse* was joined by a new Cornet named Philip Browne. Browne remained with the regiment until he purchased a commission as Captain in the *3rd Troop of the Horse Guards* in 1745. In 1746 he was placed on half pay. During the period of his service in the Army Browne wrote a series of letters, part of which deal with his experiences during the operations on the Continent. The following are extracts from these letters:

'MARKET HARBOROUGH. Wednesday, 28 Septr 1737

'Monday morning I march the troop to Lutterworth about seven miles from hence, there being a Horse fair to be kept here, which begins a Tuesday, & holds a fortnight, & we go hence for the conveniency of the Inhabitants.'

'From the Camp near Newberry. 14th Sept. 1740

'We have had very high winds, & hard rains for some time past. The tents are never dry, the men are continually wet, & the horses stand footlock deep in water frequently.'

'HEREFORD. 18 October 1740

'We march for Worcester, a Monday morning, where shall be, till come for London in January. We leaving this place on account of the scarcity of forage, & hope to find it more plenty there. Hay here is four pounds a load, & oats twenty four shillings a quarter. In the march at Ross, twelve miles of hence, we paid three pence a quarter, a price never known before. . . . Ordinary low priced horses, are now to be bought or rather given away, oats & hay being so very dear.'

'GHENT. 1 O.S. (12 N.S.) September, 1742

'I writ from Ostend 19th Augst. O.S., where we landed, after a very disagreeable & fatiguing passage of twelve days. That morning we disembarked the horses upon the sands, the tide being half way up their legs.'

'From the Camp at Hanau. 18 June, O.S. 1743

'You will have heard of the battle that was fought between the French and us, on the 16th inst. between Aschaffenburg and this place. The public news will give you an account of the battle; shall therefore only inform you of what befell our regiment. For several hours we stood the cannonading of the enemy, from several batteries they had erected. . . . Our men &

horses stood it without the ranks being in the least disordered, & so soon as men or horses was killed they closed again, & at the same time we could see that as our cannon played upon them, they sett up a gallop in great disorder. . . . Before the left of the Brigade of Horse was formed, the Gens-Arms, the best troops of France, advanced to attack us, & a battery of their cannon flanked us; upon their advancing to attack Genl. Honeywoods & General Ligoniers regiments we marched forward & meet them sword in hand; at the same time their cannon ceased, & they flanked us on the left with their foot; then we engaged & not only received but returned their fire; the balls flew about like hail, & then we cut into their ranks & they into ours. . . . Had not the English foot come to our relieve we had been all cut to pieces, the Gens. Arms being nine deep and we but three, after which we rallied again & marched up to attack them again, but before we was ordered the French had retired & the English, Hanoverians & Austrians remained masters of the field. We then proceeded on our march & came to our ground at eight a clock, it pouring then with rain & continuing so all night, & not an officer had a tent the baggage not being come up, & we had nothing to eat nor drink, & we quenched our thirst by the rain that fell upon our hats, & we had nothing at all for our horses.'

The above account relates to the battle of Dettingen. The battle was also described in a letter from Private Sam Davies of the *3rd Dragoons* to his friend Abraham Debart, drawer at the 'White Hart' Inn in Colchester. Sam Davies was footboy to Major Philip Honeywood of the same regiment.

'Hanau. 26 June, 1743

'Friend Abraham,

I hope these few lines will find you very well and Mrs. Ann and my old Mrs. and Mrs. Wallis my young mistress and my young Mr. Joseph and all my old fellow-servants, as I am and have been ever since I came into this country. This is a very pleasant country we are now in. We have had a battel with French on Thursday, June 16, 1743. One battel lasted 5 ours, the first they played upon our baggage for about 2 ours with there cannon, and then we play upon there army and they upon us. There balls was from 3 lbs. to 6 lbs. and 12 lbs. each; our rigement was upon the left wing next the river, and they playing upon us all the time. The sarvants of the rigement went into the rear of the rigement with their led horses, I had a led horse so I was there. We stayed there till the balls came flying all round us. We see first a horse with baggage fall close to us. Then seven horses fall apeace, then I began to star about me, the balls came whisling about my ears. Then I saw the Oysterenns [Austrians] dip and look about them for they doge the balls as a cock does a stick, they are so used to them. Then we sarvants began to get of into a wood for safete, which was about 400 yards from ware we stood. When we got into the wood we placed ourselves against the largest trees gest as I had placed myself, a 12 pounder came, puts a large bow of the tree upon my head, the Ball came within tew yards of me. Then I began to stear, indeed it was about the size of your light puddings, but a great deal hevyer. Then we took fresh quarters, to the baggage of the whole army. We had not been there but a littel while, but the hussers were coming to take it, whilst the tow armies was swurd in hand, then the baggage made all haste they could away. I having good luck had a horse that would not follow, so I let him goe. Jist as I had let him goe the word came to halt. Then I had my horse to kich again and when I had my horse Cornet Car came to me. Sam, says he, your master is dead, so of all my troubels that was the worst; I takes my horse that I led and tyes him to a cart, then I went to see for my master. So when I came a littel higher in the ffield I saw Laftanent Lee, he told me that my master was taken by the French. I liked that better than the other. When I came a littel higher I saw some of our men lay on the ground, some dead, some wounded, some without Arms, some without Legs. I saw one Fryer of our Rigement that came from the oyspeatal [hospital] but that morning, he was afoot, the other men asked him to fech them some water from a well that was by them. He had been several times and as he was going agin a Cannon ball came, and went into his Back, takes his left Breast away and his Hart gumpt on the ground. Then I rides further up and at last I saw Sam and he tells me that his tow Horses was shot at once with a Canon Ball. He was upon the old gray Horse. At last they finds my Master on the ground naked for tow Freanch men had striped him of his Cloes, Watch and Money and left him for dead under a Tree. Sam was riding by him, as he had done before and did not know him. My Master happened to open his Eyes, saw Sam going close by him, calls him as well as he could considering he lay 4 ours naked upon the Cold ground. Thay got him to a village ware the King was, got him into a Bed, and now he is bravely, thank God for it. He has 6 Wounds, 2 cuts on the Head, a stab under his right Arm with a bagnet. One Ball went in at his Body, out at his Back, another Ball in at his Back, the other is but a little Cut—our Rigment is above half killed and wounded, for never any Men in the Field behaved as well as they did, so carry all the Honour. The King is meghtely pleased with them. But our English Army drive the Freanch so that some could not get fast eenuf over the Brige, but took to the Water and were drounded.

'And all the newes now is that the Emperor is going to come into our Army, and it is talked for Truth that the King has sent to the King of ffrance to desire Him to take the field farely, and not to doo as he did afore. If that he dont his Majesty says he will goo through France home with his Army, and the newes is hear that Prince Charles is coming with his army, and it is after a freanch Generll that as a small army coming to joyn the other. We have got 3000 of the Queen's Hussers a coming to help the freanch Hussars from our baggage. Those fellows have nothing but what they ketch, they ride upon small light cattel that goes light, they plunder and take all they come any, kill all they can of our Army. Ill tell you there Dres—First there Cap, which is made of hareskin, they ware no Cote but a Westcote, which is very tite upon them. There Briches and there Stockins are all of a peace, the Stockins lace down behind, the Boots are like your haf Boots.

They have a skin which they hang on one side, which side the wether comes. They carry a small Carbine slung over there Shoulder, so when they fire them they put it under there Arm, so look over there Shoulder. They have 2 pr of Pistolles and a Simmeter but when the Queen's hussers come, thay will soon put an end to thoase Gentlemen. The Queen's are the finest in all the Wourld. But there is one thing I forgot that I lost all the Baggage and was out of sight of any Body in the Wood. Up comes a man a horseback to me, he had no Saddell nor no Pistolls so I did not mind him. He asked me for to give him my led Horse in fraench, I told him no. At that he draws out a Sword, and runs it at me. Oh, thinks I, what sort of usige is this. So I takes a Pistoll out and shot him through the Shoulder. At that he makes off and I maks to the baggage. Thank God he did not hurt me, it went through my Grete Cote soo no more at present.

'Pray send me all the news you can out of the Town. . . . Your most sincere ffriend S. Davies.'

Writing from Brussels in December, 1744, Philip Browne announced his military ambitions. The letter is amusingly typical of a young officer of any period, both in its challenge to the 'powers that be' and in its flavour of military snobbishness:

'With regard to myself I shall write you very plain & don't care who may know or read it. I want the rank of Capt. of Horse in the Horse Grenadier Guards or Horse Guards, or a Troop in any one of the regiments of Horse, either abroad or at home, that is upon the English establishment, and in full pay. As for Dragoons I wont buy it, but if offered will accept of it. That rank in the Foot was offered me this campaign if I would accept it, which I refused. By being a soldier, I have learnt to be free, easy & bold, and if they won't let me have what I like, I defy them to make me dislike what I have.'

Quite another aspect on promotion is given in an official letter from Sir Robert Rich, the Colonel of the *4th Dragoons*. Writing on 12th April, 1745, he says:

'Captain Adamson of my regiment died lately at Ghent.

Captain-Lieutenant Pashlar is a brave honest old man, but from age and other infirmities of body and mind is, I am afraid, unfit for any further service. Lieutenant Bickerton, who is the eldest Lieutenant, is as good and as diligent an officer as any of his rank in the Army. . . . If H.R.H. do not think proper to promote Captain Pashlar, I hope he will give the troop to Lieutenant Bickerton who is the life of the regiment.'

Philip Browne's regiment was present at the battle of Fontenoy, and had a very trying, if inactive, ordeal. He described it as follows:

'From the Camp at Lessines, near Ath. 8th May. O.S., 1745

'The loss of the English and Hanoverians both in officers and men is very considerable; the killed and wounded is said to be upwards of six thousand, the Dutch nothing near the proportion; it is reported five hundred. Old officers that served the late war say they never saw so continual and so long a fire as the French played upon us from their batteries, during which time life was uncertain to each one for a moment as we was during the whole time, upwards of nine hours, within the command of them; four men was killed and an officer wounded by the same ball in the Major's squadron to whom I am Lieut. and three horses of his troop was killed just behind me by one ball likewise and they continually grounded and deadnd before us, dropped amongst us and flew over our heads— which never put any one squadron in the field into disorder, for so soon as the dead men and horses could be taken out of the ranks the whole was formed immediately again as at a review. There was no cavalry charged at all, but the troops expressed great inclination to engage sword in hand; but as the enemy continued in their lines, that could not be unless they had been first carried, but they showed a spirit of what they would do if they had an opportunity by the undauntiness and resolution they behaved with during the long cannonading.'

In the year of Fontenoy the centre of British military interest moved from the plains of Flanders to the Highlands of Scotland, where Prince Charles Stuart was gathering an army.

The Mounted Troops of the British Army

The Jacobite forces did not include many mounted troops. The cavalry which marched with the army into England consisted of the following units:

1st Troop, Life Guards, commanded by Lord Elcho; strength about 125.

2nd Troop, Life Guards, commanded by Lord Balmerino; strength about 40.

Horse Guards (and *Kenmure's Horse*), commanded by Lord Kilmarnock; strength about 100.

Pitsligo's Horse, commanded by Lord Pitsligo; strength about 120.

Hussars, commanded by Major Baggot; strength about 70.

The troops of *Life Guards* were composed of gentlemen and their servants. *Pitsligo's Horse*, similarly, consisted of gentlemen and their servants from Banff and Aberdeen. The *Hussars* were a troop of light cavalry, and their commander, Baggot, was an Irishman who had been in the French service.

There are a few references to mounted troops in the Orderly book of *Lord Ogilvy's Regiment of Foot* in the Jacobite army:

'An Officer and twelve Gentlemen of Pitsligo's Horse will come to Edinburgh about five o'clock this afternoon, where they will receive further orders.' (Edinburgh, 26th–27th October, 1745.)

'An Officer and twelve of the Life Guards are to patroll westward of Newhaven until break of day.' (Edinburgh, 28th–29th October, 1745.)

'Orders against all women but soldiers wives; and horses only allowed to Field Officers and Staff Officers, or such whom their Colonel can declare upon honour cannot march on foot.' (Kendal, 23rd–24th November, 1745.)

'The Baggage marches between Pitsligo's Horse and the Hussars which are to have the rear of all with an Officer of each Regiment.' (Kendal, 24th–28th November, 1745.)

'Lord Pitsligo's Horse are to patrol till the break of day with an Officer and 30 men on the road that leads to Lancaster. The Body of the Detachment are to be betwixt the Bridge and the Inn called the Cock and Dolphin, where half of them may unbridle and refresh the horses, whilst ten of them will patrol behind the bridge on that same road, unto the second great barn or house on the left hand.' (Kendal, 15th–18th December, 1745.)

During its retirement the Jacobite army was reinforced by a detachment of *Fitz James's Regiment of Irish Horse*. *Fitz James's Horse* (named after James, Duke of Berwick) was formed in France in 1698 by the amalgamation of two regiments of Horse in the Irish Brigade. Fitz James's fought at Fontenoy, and the following year part of the regiment was despatched to Scotland to join the army of Prince Charles Stuart. Some of the transports were captured at sea by the British fleet, but a detachment of three troops, consisting of 13 officers and 120 men, landed at Aberdeen from the *Sapphire* in February, 1746, the day before the Jacobite army evacuated the town. Some account of this detachment is given by Voltaire. No horses were brought from France, but the troopers carried their 'horse-furniture, arms, breastplates and baggage'. People who saw them arrive said that they were 'clothed with red turned up with blue'. Their arrival was received with 'great enthusiasm and by the country-people with joyful acclamations . . . the very women running out to welcome the strangers and leading the officers horses by their bridles'.

The squadron was present at Culloden, and Captain Shee's Troop of *Fitz James's Horse*, together with Balmerino's Troop of *Life Guards*, provided the escort for Prince Charles. After the battle, and having escorted the Prince from the field, the officers and men of Captain Shee's Troop were dismissed with orders to surrender to the Duke of Cumberland. Three officers and sixteen troopers did so the following day.

The ''Forty-Five' showed that there was a need for light cavalry in the Army. It was this need which led the Duke of Kingston to raise his regiment. Captain Hinde describes *Kingston's Light Horse* as 'mounted upon light horses of various colours, with swish or nick'd tails; their whole accoutrements were as light as possible, of every sort and species; their arms were short bullet guns or carbines, shorter than those of

Plate III

DUKE OF CUMBERLAND'S DRAGOONS.

(By gracious permission of H.M. The Queen,
from the painting by David Morier at Windsor Castle.)

Re-formed from Kingston's Light Horse in 1747. Disbanded in 1748.

the regiments of horse, and slung to their sides by a moveable swivel to run up their shoulder belt; their pistols upon the same plan, as they used both carbines and pistols on horseback indiscriminately; their swords very sharp, and rather inclined to a curve'. The regiment proved its usefulness at Culloden. After the battle it pursued the broken Jacobites for three miles, doing great execution.

Kingston's regiment was disbanded the following year, but it was re-established immediately as the *Duke of Cumberland's Light Dragoons*.

That the regiment must have distinguished itself in the field beyond the ordinary is shown by the circumstances of its disbandment. Each soldier received three guineas, together with his bridle and saddle, and every officer and man was presented with a copy of the following letter from the Secretary at War to the Duke of Kingston:

'My Lord,

'His Majesty has thought fit to order the regiment of horse under your Grace's command to be disbanded; but as the King considers the zeal and affection expressed for his person and government, in your Grace's offer to raise this regiment in the late important time of national danger, and the cheerfulness and alacrity with which it was raised, he cannot part with it without expressing his particular satisfaction therein; I am therefore, by his Majesty's command, and in his name to thank your Grace, and your Officers, for the seasonable and distinguishing marks you have given of your fidelity and attachment to his Majesty on this occasion.

'I am likewise commanded by his Majesty to desire your Grace, and the rest of your Officers, to thank the private men, in his name, for their services, before they are dismissed, in order that there may be no one person in your regiment unacquainted with the sense his Majesty has of their loyalty, activity, and gallant behaviour in his service: Qualities which have been so conspicuous in your Grace's regiment, that his Majesty, willing to retain as many as possible of such soldiers in his service, has been pleased to order a regiment of dragoons to be raised at the same time and place, when and where your Grace's regiment shall be disbanded, and to direct that as many of the Officers and private men belonging to your Grace's regiment, as shall be willing, may serve in the said regiment of dragoons, of which as a signal mark of honour and distinction, his Royal Highness the Duke of Cumberland will himself be Colonel.

'As this is a great and most honourable proof of his Majesty's royal approbation of your past services, so I doubt no but that your Grace, and the othere Officers of your regiment, will engage as many as may be of your men to enlist themselves, and thereby show, that the same zeal continues for their King and Country, which they have already so meritoriously exerted in defence of both.

'I am, with the greatest respect, My Lord, your Grace's Most obedient Most humble servant

H. Fox.

War Office, Sept. 1746'

The result of this appeal was that all except eight men of the old regiment re-enlisted in the new one.

Cumberland's Light Dragoons fought in Flanders in 1747, but at the peace of 1748 it was finally disbanded. In view of its record and the extraordinary efforts made to retain its personnel, it is difficult to find a reason for the disappearance of the Army's only regiment of Light Horse. Cumberland's Dragoons had a similar type of uniform and equipment to that of the heavy Dragoons. The horses were all chestnuts.

In 1747 some of the more senior regiments of Horse were reorganized into the more generally useful Dragoons. In order that they should not lose their place in the order of seniority they were designated 'Dragoon Guards'. Apart from certain items of uniform and equipment, the chief remaining distinction between Horse and Dragoons seems to have been on the emphasis placed on musketry. In 1726 it was noted that more powder was required by Dragoon regiments for musketry

Plate IV   [*Copyright H.M. The Queen*

1st TROOP, HORSE GRENADIER GUARDS.
(By gracious permission of H.M. The Queen,
from the painting by David Morier at Windsor Castle.)
Note the Grenadier cap, which is identical with that worn by
the Grenadiers of the Infantry, *circa* 1760.

practice, 'as their firing in the exercise is the same as the Foot's'.

A recruiting advertisement for the *2nd Dragoon Guards* appeared in *The Sussex Weekly Advertiser, or Lewes Journal* of Christmas Day, 1749, in the following terms:

'*All Gentlemen Volunteers* Who are willing to serve his Majesty King GEORGE, in his second Regiment of Dragoon Guards, commanded by the Right Hon. General Sir *John Ligonier*, on Application to Capt. *Frederick Frankland*, of the said Regt., at the *Star* Inn, in *Lewes*, shall receive a Good Horse, new Cloaths, Arms and Accoutrements, and all further encouragement they shall be found deserving.'

In the eighteenth century, and for much of the nineteenth, cavalry were frequently called upon for police duties. Some extracts from orders dealing with patrols and traffic control are given below. The occasion was the night of the Royal Fireworks on 27th April, 1749, when the *Horse Guards* and *Horse Grenadier Guards* were required to provide police detachments in the West End of London.

'Lord Delawair Orders. Gold Stick. April 25th, 1749.

'Relating to the Severall Detachments of Horse and Granadier Guards, disposed off the Night of the Royall Fireworks Thursday ye 27th Instant.

'A Party of the first Troop of Horse Guards, in Grosvenor Square to Patrole in Brook Street, Grosvenors Street, Mount Street, Bartlet Square, Dover Street, and the Small Streets joyning to the Square. . . .

'A Subaltern Officer and twenty men of the Second Troop of Horse Guards the upper end of St. Jameses Street to remain there unless sent for by the Guard or Party in St. Jameses Square, and not to suffer any stop of Coaches near his Guard. . . .

'An Officer and twenty men of the first Troop of Horse Granadiers to be in St. Jameses Park at three oclock, Disposed from the Scaffold where the Company gets out to Buckingham Gate, in order that there may be no stop with the Coaches, and when the Coaches is all gon thorow to march with his

Party to Hyde Park Corner, and Patrole along Pacadely, to Bolton Street end. . . .

'That the Severall Partys of Horse and Granadier Guards do Parrade at their own Stables on Thursday Evening the 27th Instant time anuff to be on their Ground by Six O'clock. . . .

'That the Commanding Officer of Each Party do take care that the Patrols do not stop or drink in the Streets but to keep moving slowly on their Ground till they are properly Releived.

'A Subaltern Officer to visit the Severall Patrols to see that the men do their duty Punctually, Each Party to march to their Quarters at three oclock in the Morning in case their is no Orders to the Contrary.

'If any Persons are taking up Committing Dissorders they are to be delivered to Constables of the Night at the Watch House.

'The Commanding Officer of each Party to make a Report in Writing Sealed up to Lord Delawair in the Morning.'

'Spit and Polish' received as much attention as in the most exacting regiment to-day. In the orders for a review to be held by Lord Stair, of 23rd October, 1742, it was laid down that:

'The Horse and Dragoons to take all their small accoutrements to pieces and see that they be very well cleaned and blacked, and then put them together again. The bosses, bits and curbs to be as bright as hands can make them. The boots to be as black as possible, and their knee-pieces not to appear above three inches above the boot-top. All their arms to be as bright as silver. The whole buff accoutrements to be of one light buff colour, the swords to be all brightened. The hats new cocked. 3 straps to each cloak. Care to be taken that the men do not ride too long. Officers to wear sashes over their shoulders.'

CHAPTER VIII

BEFORE THE FRENCH REVOLUTION

In the latter half of the eighteenth century equitation in the British Army was considerably influenced by an Italian named Domenick Angelo. Of him George II remarked that 'Mr. Angelo is the most elegant rider in Europe'. In 1754 Angelo became very friendly with Henry Herbert, tenth Earl of Pembroke, who was then about twenty years of age. Lord Pembroke, a keen officer and a court favourite, was an enthusiastic horseman. He started a private riding school at his house in Whitehall and another at his Salisbury seat of Wilton. Angelo was installed as his manager and riding master. When in due course Pembroke was appointed to the command of the *15th Light Dragoons* he sent a number of the riding instructors of the regiment to Wilton to be trained by Angelo. The influence of the Italian horsemaster soon became so widespread that his methods of breaking, training and riding horses were adopted in all mounted units of the Army. Lord Pembroke himself became an authority on equitation, and in 1761 he wrote his *A Method of Breaking Horses and Teaching Soldiers to Ride*, etc., which was based on Angelo's teaching.

Pembroke held strong views on the prevalent custom of docking horses; and his book contained the following passage:

'As I am very far from having any respect for a coachman's slapt hat, any more than for a groom's empty black cap, like many of my countrymen; I must own also that I am not possessed with the English rage of cutting off all extremities from horses: I venture to declare, I should be well pleased, if the tails of our horses, at least a switch, or nag tail, (but better, if the whole,) were left on. 'Tis hardly credible, what a difference, especially at certain times of the year, this single alteration would make in our cavalry: which though naturally superior in everything to all other cavalry I have ever seen, are however long before the end of the campaign, for what of that natural defence against flies, inferior to all; constantly fretting and sweating at picket, tormented and stung off their meat and stomachs, miserable and helpless; whilst the foreign cavalry brush off their vermin, are cool and at ease, and mend daily instead of perishing, as ours do, almost visibly to the eye of the beholder. The horses indeed of the foreign cavalry are always in better order than ours are, because their men at all times are more careful, and give more attention to them.'

Pembroke's strong representations bore fruit, and an Army Order was published in 1764 which laid down that:

'His Majesty having been pleased to order that all his regiments of Horse and Dragoons, except the Light Dragoons, shall be mounted only on such horses as shall have their full tails, without the least part taken from them; all breeders and dealers in horses for the service of the army, are desired to take notice, that, for the future, no horses but such as shall have their full tails, without the least part taken from them, will be bought for any of the Regiments of Horse and Dragoons, except the Light Dragoons.'

The Angelo influence spread to India, for Domenick's nephew, Anthony Angelo Tremamondo, was appointed Riding Master to the Bengal Army. (Tremamondo was the real surname of the Angelos.)

Anthony Angelo appears as a Lieutenant in the Bengal Army List of 1778. He was an officer of the Governor-General's Body Guard, and two years later he received the additional appointment of Riding Master: a position which he owed to his friend Warren Hastings, the Governor-General.

In a letter applying for the post of Riding Master, Anthony Angelo said:

'HONBLE SIR AND SIRS,—I beg leave humbly to submit the following outline of a Proposal for the better Training of all the Cavalry on the Bengal Establishment.

'I will be ready to receive two Troopers out of each separate

Troop of the three Regiments of Cavalry, and to instruct them correctly in the Art of Riding, agreeable to the Principles (recommended by Lord Pembroke) the most approved in Europe, and universally adopted in every Regiment of Cavalry, as well Horse as Light Dragoons. I will undertake to qualify the said Troopers of the different Corps to train their Cavalry Horses exactly conformable to the above method of the Armies in Europe, enabling them on their return to join their respective Corps, to instruct the rest of the Troopers belonging thereto, to ride, break, and train their own horses in the same manner, and in short to make them perfect Masters of the Art of Riding.'

For three years Anthony's riding school flourished. In 1784, however, as a measure of economy, the appointment of Riding Master was abolished, and the following year Anthony resigned his commission and returned to England.

After the Duke of Cumberland's Dragoons had been disbanded in 1748 there was no light cavalry in the Army for nearly eight years. In 1756, however, a troop of light cavalry was added to the establishment of regiments of Dragoon Guards and Dragoons. The Warrant introducing these troops directed a 'Troop of Light Dragoons to be added to each Regiment of Dragoon Guards and Dragoons on the British Establishment: 1 Captain, 1 Lieutenant, 1 Cornet, 1 Quarter-master, 2 Serjeants, 3 Corporals, 2 Drummers, 60 Privates including 1 Farrier. Height: 5 ft. 6½ to 5 ft. 8. To be light, active, young men. Horses 14 hands 3 in. and not under. They are to be well-turned nimble road horses as nigh to the colour of the horses of the Regiment as can be got. Arms: a carbine with ring and bar, 4 ft. 3 in. long with a bayonet 17 in. 1 pistol, 10 in. in the barrel, and of carbine bore, a straight cutting sword, 34 in. in the blade, with a light hilt without a basket. Accoutrements: a tanned leather shoulder belt, 3¼ in. broad, with spring and swivel, a tanned leather belt for sword and bayonet, a tanned leather cartouch-box with a double row of holes to contain 24 cartridges, with a tanned leather strap 1½ in. broad. The saddle to be with small cantles behind, as the jockey saddles are, and to be 22 in. long in the seat; on the right side

FIG. 9. LIGHT TROOP.
From 'The Discipline of the Light-Horse' by Captain R. Hinde, 1778.

of the saddle is to be the holster for the pistol, and on the left a churn, in which a spade and felling axe or a spade and a woodman's bill is to be carried. There is to be a bucket for receiving the butt of the carbine, and a pipe to receive the end of the horse-picket. The bridle to be a plain light bit with single reins; there is likewise to be a tanned leather headstall with a hempen collar. The Clothing and cloaks of these Light Dragoons to be the same as that of the rest of the regiment, only instead of hats the men are to have jockey caps ornamented in the front with our cypher and crown in brass, and the number or rank of the regiment. The crest is likewise to be covered with brass, out of which is to be a tuft of stiff horse-hair, coloured half red, and the other half of the facing of the regiment. Light jockey boots with small stiff tops. Horse-furniture: of the same colour and form as the rest of the regiment, and ornamented in the same manner, but to be less in proportion to the size of the horses.' (Frontispiece & Fig. 9.)

There is an interesting supplement to the description in the Warrant by Captain Hinde. He says of these light troops that they had 'a sort of carbine, with the bar and sliding ring, with a bayonet, but no sling; the carbine carried in a bucket, as the heavy horse; the belts tanned leather, the bridles and bitts small and light, as were the saddles, though made like the heavy, with bars and a cantle; they carried no side pouches, like the dragoons, but in lieu of it a swivel, which played up and down their shoulder belt, to which the carbine was sprung or fastened, and hung with the muzzle downwards during exercise, as they fired on horseback as well as on foot, contrary to the method of the horse in general, except the Hussars in foreign service. They also used their pistols, but at first they only had one each man, as they carried in their right holster either an ax, hedging bill or spades.'

Hinde describes the head-dress as 'a cap, or helmet, made of strong black jackt leather, with bars down the sides, and a brass bar at top; the front red, ornamented with brass work, with the cypher and crown, and number of the regiment; just before they were disbanded, they had a new sort of helmet, with a turban behind rolled round the whole, with two tossels at the back, tied in a knot to fall down over their neck in bad weather, as the former cap had a rolled-up leather flap round it for the same purpose'.

The horse of these light troops was, Hinde says, 'the nag or

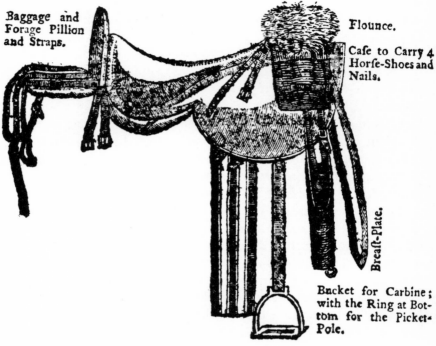

Baggage and Forage Pillion and Straps.

Flounce.

Cafe to Carry 4 Horfe-Shoes and Nails.

Breaft-Plate.

Bucket for Carbine; with the Ring at Bottom for the Picket-Pole.

FIG. 10. FORM OF THE NEW SADDLE.
From 'The Discipline of the Light-Horse' by Captain R. Hinde, 1778.

hunting kind, and from 14 hands three inches to 15 hands one inch high'.

The straight-legged seat, which was later to become an unfortunate riding fashion in the British Army, was not practised by the Light Horse, who were taught to have their stirrups sufficiently short for the rider to be clear of the saddle when standing in them.

Something of the methods and spirit adopted in training the Light Dragoons is shown in the following quotations from instructions written by Lieutenant-Colonel Campbell Dalrymple of the *King's Own Regiment of Dragoons*:

'Love to the horses should be strongly inculcated from the beginning. . . . The instructor must speak mildly to the recruits. . . . Things impressed with good humour will be eagerly listened and attended to; for though we meet with great awkwardness, yet we find a desire to learn in almost every recruit.'

In that one last sentence Colonel Campbell Dalrymple not only paints an affectionate picture of the type of recruit which every regular officer yearns for, but he dispels the popular notion of the type of horse soldier which the Army recruited in the eighteenth century.

On the tactical employment of the light troops, Hinde says: 'Light troops should never form squadrons; the levity of the men, from the nature of their employment, and the want of weight on their horses absolutely incapacitate them from forming a corps which requires so much solidity. They should therefore march, act, and always form by troops in two ranks, without standards, and having only one trumpet.'

Hinde had strong views on the quality of the officers required for the light troops: 'Care should be taken to post officers to the light troops, who are distinguished for activity and address, and above all by a spirit of enterprise; a man who raises scruples and difficulties, has mistaken his talents, and should dispose of himself better immediately'.

In 1759 it was decided that complete regiments of Light Dragoons should be raised, since the light troops had proved extremely useful. Five regiments, the 15th to 19th, were accordingly formed in the same year; and two more, the 20th and 21st, followed early in 1760. The last of these was raised by the Marquis of Granby and given the title of the *Royal Foresters*.

These Light Dragoon regiments were considered as *corps d'élite*, and recruiting orders were issued impressing on officers that the men enlisted 'must be light and straight, and by no means gummy', and that they were not to be under

A Troop of Light-Dragoons, Drawn up.

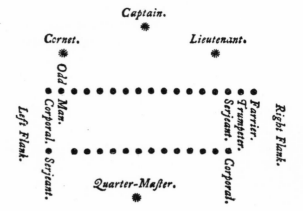

The Troop marching by Twos or Files.

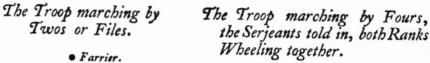

The Troop marching by Fours, the Serjeants told in, both Ranks Wheeling together.

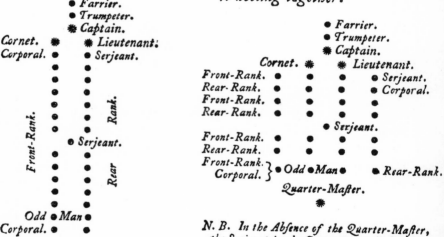

N. B. In the Abfence of the Quarter-Mafter, the Serjeant in the Center may take his Poft.

FIG. 11.

From 'The Discipline of the Light-Horse' by Captain R. Hinde, 1778.

Plate V

THE 4TH QUEEN'S OWN DRAGOONS, 1802
by John Scott

(By kind permission of The Executors of the late Lieutenant-Colonel F. E. Hugonin, O.B.E.)

5 ft. 5½ in. or above 5 ft. 9 in. The arms of the Light Dragoons were, according to Captain Hinde, 'carbines about 2 Feet 5 inches Long in the Barrels, (with or without a Bayonet about 1 Foot Long in the Blade,) and a Pair of Pistols 9 Inches Long in the Barrels, and a Sword about 37 Inches Long in the Blade, either crooked or straight according to the Regulations of the Regiment, in a belt worn over the Right shoulder. . . . A Shoulder-Belt over the Left Shoulder, with a Swivel, Chain and T at the end to spring the Carbine to, to carry it by the Men's Sides, hanging with the Muzzle downwards.'

In 1763 the light troops in the regiments of Dragoon Guards and Dragoons were disbanded.

The Light Dragoons certainly appealed to popular imagination. The *Weekly Journal* of 23rd May, 1758, for instance, announced that 'The nine Troops of Hussars [*i.e.* Light Dragoons] belonging to the nine regiments of Cavalry are now preparing to go on this expedition [*i.e.* the descent upon the coast of France]. The flower of these Hussars is the Troop commanded by Captain Lindsay [*i.e.* the Light Troop of the *11th, Ancram's, Dragoons,* commanded by Captain William Lindsay], quartered at Maidenhead, where they have been practising the Prussian exercise, and for some days have been digging large trenches and leaping over them, also leaping high hedges with broad ditches on the other side. Their Captain on Saturday last swam with his horse over the Thames and back again; and the whole Troop were yesterday to swim the river.' It all sounds like the commando training of some 200 years later.

The *21st Light Dragoons*, or *Royal Foresters*, was the regiment of Captain Hinde, whose well-known work, *The Discipline of the Light-Horse*, has already been frequently quoted. The book was published in 1778, and in presenting his 'Compliments to the Officers of Light Dragoons', the author announces that he 'has Retired on Half-Pay, having a Wife and twelve Children at this Time alive, the Eldest of whom is now in the Army'. If Captain Hinde is a typical example, the Light Horse deserved well of their country!

Fig. 12. Light Dragoon.
From 'The Discipline of the Light-Horse' by Captain R. Hinde, 1778.

In an account of the action near Hombourgh, on 24th June, 1762, Captain Hinde gives an interesting illustration of co-operation between light and heavy cavalry.

After a dashing attack, the *15th Light Dragoons* had become somewhat isolated, and 'the enemies cavalry facing about immediately, and falling sword in hand upon Elliot's Light Dragoons, that regiment would have suffered greatly, had not Colonel Harvey, at the head of the Blues, seeing the danger, passed the village on full gallop, and notwithstanding he could oppose only eight or ten men in front, to formed squadrons, he overthrew all that came in his way, and saved Elliot's regiment.

'The situation of the two regiments was at this time very critical, but the mutual support which they gave each other, Elliot's Light Dragoons by continual skirmishing with the enemy, and the Blues by their manœuvres in squadrons, and their steady countenance, kept the enemy at bay till the infantry could come up.'

Captain Hinde's notes on horse management probably applied to all cavalry. The following are extracts:

'Feeding—The horses feed is always to be measured to the men, in the standard measure of the regiment.

'The feed is never to be left in the stables, but taken care of in the Men's rooms.

'The Quarter-Master to be answerable under penalty of severest censure, that troop-horses never eat more than *twenty pounds of hay* in the *twenty-four hours*, and when the regulation of other provendor is at or above a *peck*, they are then not to eat more than *sixteen pounds of hay* in that time.

'Riding-Regulations—Every officer newly come into the regiment is to attend the Riding-School, as long as the commanding officer thinks necessary.

'Instructions for the Care and Preservation of Horses in time of War—An officer must always go with the horses to water, and never more than one troop, or half-squadron be suffered to water at a time.

'The Officers to take particular care that the men fodder

their horses regularly; that they rub down, and curry them well; and further, that they imbibe a regard for them, and learn to be sensible of the many advantages accruing to themselves, in consequence of the pains they bestow upon them; for which reason it is necessary to be inculcated as much as possible by all Officers, that for the Horses to be in good condition, whether in an engagement, or on the march, is of the highest utility.

'If a regiment or party is posted near the enemy, the horses will receive no damage, though kept saddled for the space of *twenty-four hours*, provided that the Commanding-Officer only takes care that the men loosen their girths a few times in the day, and wipe their backs.

'The Method of Embarking Horses—When the Horses arrive at the Water-Side, their Saddles and Bridles are to be taken off, but the Collars are left on, then they are led into the Flat-Bottomed Boats, over a stage erected for that purpose from the Beach to the Boats; which are railed on that account, the Dragoons holding their Horses by the Collar-Rein; about ten or twelve Horses are put into each Boat; when they come along side the Transport Vessel, a Sling is placed round their bodies, made of sacking, which reaches from their withers to their flanks, and incloses the body very securely, having a Breast-Plate and Breeching of sacking also to prevent them from slipping out; on the top of the Sling are fastened two strong pieces of wood to stretch it out, in the centre of which a hole or loop is made, to put the Tackle-Hook through for hoisting them on board; then a Rope is tied to the end of their Collar-Rein, which is given to a Man on board the Transport, which prevents the Horse being unruly, and likewise keeps his head down; on a signal being given, they hoist him up, and lower him down into the Hold. Some of the Cavalry sling their Horses the whole time they are on board, and others only occasionally: it is best to have a standing or two vacant on each side the ship, in case a Horse should be taken ill or prove unruly, as many Horses may be preserved by that means, as it often happens for want of such a convenience, many Horses are obliged to be killed when there is no room left to shift them: there is also a Rail placed between each Horse, and the Horses stand with their heads fronting one another. The King's own Troop of Lord Albemarle's Regiment, only slung their Horses (on the Expeditions to the coast of France) in the evening, if the sea was calm, on which account their Horses were in the best condition when landed, by not keeping them slung in a rough sea: from *thirty-eight* to *fifty Horses* are put into each Transport. The Disembarkation is performed in the same manner. If the Horses are Embarked from the Warfs, then they are immediately slung off from thence into the Transports in the same manner as before described.'

At the time when Captain Hinde wrote, the American War of Independence was in progress, and he includes a few anecdotes to illustrate the initiative and resourcefulness of the Light Dragoons. In one of these: 'Colonel Abercrombie, with a Light-Dragoon, first discovered the Famous Partizans, *Randall* and *Coomes* behind a Farm-House. The Former shot the Colonel's Horse, and wounded the Dragoon in the neck; he then jumped over a Rail Fence, the Light-Dragoon pursued and shot him through the Shoulder, then offered him Quarter, which he refused; he then engaged him with his Sword, and obliged him to submit; which *Coomes* perceiving, cried out, "*Damn you, Randall, will you take Quarters from such a Bloody-Backed Scoundrel?*" but he soon found himself reduced to the same Dilemma, and they are now safely lodged in Brunswick Guard-House.'

The Duke of Cumberland was considerably exercised with regard to the heavy Dragoons. He was anxious to ensure on the one hand, that they did not become assimilated to the Horse, and on the other, that they should be of a very high standard as Dragoons. About 1755 'Standing Orders to be Observed by the whole Corps of Dragoons by His Royal Highness' Order' was published. The following extracts present a good picture of the Dragoons of the period.

'The Dragoon Officers are to remember that they are still Dragoons, and not Horse, that they are to march and attack on Foot, if there is occasion when dismounted therefore the Men's Boots are not to be encumbered with great Spur Leathers and Chains, to hinder them from getting over a Hedge, Ditch or Works when they are ordered to attack. . . .

'All Serjeants of Dragoons are not to be fixed to the Ranks like Corporals of Horse. . . . They are to be mounted upon Horses like the Officers as near as possible, Horses that can Gallop, and have speed enough to stop the men upon occasion, and not Dock't Close like the Men's Horses, but such as make a good Figure. . . .

'Whereas a Dragoon has a multiplicity of things to do more than a Foot Soldier, and ten times more Arms, Accoutrements &c. to keep clean, and take care of and carry. Particular care must be taken not to overcharge him with unnecessary trifles, nor load him or his horses with useless things. NB: a Soldier can't have too few things to be taken care of, it disgusts him, and makes him so much longer getting ready, besides Galling his Horse, which renders him unserviceable.

'Neither does his Royal Highness approve of a whole Basket hilt to the Officer's and Men's Swords, which deprives them of the use of their right hand in case their Bridles are Cut, or broke, and no Officer can possibly salute well with them, besides no Officer is supposed ever to Fight himself, any more than to defend his Head, his Business is to see the Men fight and do well; that's sufficient. . . .

'All Dragoons shall have Links, and not silly Snaffles, and to link their Horses the same way alike, when they are ordered to Dismount, leaving three Men mounted in each Rank, of each Squadron, the Quarter Master and Farriers to remain with the Horses. . . .

'His Royal Highness cannot approve of the large footed, hairy leg'd Cart Horse that are too commonly bought for the Dragoons, by being ill chose; a Dragoon Horse should be from fifteen, to fifteen two inches, with light feet, and clean Sinewy legs, well coupled and good fillets, no flat ribs, but even made with an oval Croupe, and good thin Shoulders and nimble and active movers.

'And if all Recruit Horses could be bought at rising six years, or even coming seven, it would be much better for the Service, they being fit for immediate use, besides there having got over all Distempers incident to Young Horses, such as the Strangles &c., they are also cheaper than Five year old Horses coming, for they are a year past Market, they are also quite formed, and don't grow nor alter their Shape, as Colts of four or five Years do. . . .

'As a Serjeant Major is a new thing in the Dragoons (being introduced by lazy Adjutants) it is forbid for the future. . . .

'No Dragoon shall be made a Corporal merely because he can write a good hand, as has been hitherto the Custom, in Consequence of which restriction; the Non-Commissioned Officers will be compleat Soldiers and not simple Scribblers. . . .

'All the Farriers' and Drummers' Baggage to be examined every time the Men's Wallets are, which should be once a week at least especially in Camp, or else their Baggage will daily increase, and whenever they March their Wallets should be inspected narrowly to hinder them from carrying their wives' things and spoiling their Horses.'

There are a number of other administrative records of the period.

An order book of the *King's Dragoon Guards* of the Seven Years War shows that in the Minden campaign a regiment was allowed two waggons for the baggage of the Captains and one for that of all the Subalterns, whilst two more were allotted to the regimental headquarters and two to each squadron. On the march from Emden these latter had carried the tents and at other times they were loaded with the men's blankets. In addition every squadron had a forage cart, and there are also references to farriers' carts. A General had a 'coach' or 'chaise' in which to travel.

Manes and tails caused some concern in *The Royal Scots Greys*, as the following comments show:

At an inspection on 10th May, 1777, it was said as an excuse for the badness of the horses' tails that, on account of the colour, the tails were frequently plucked and the hairs

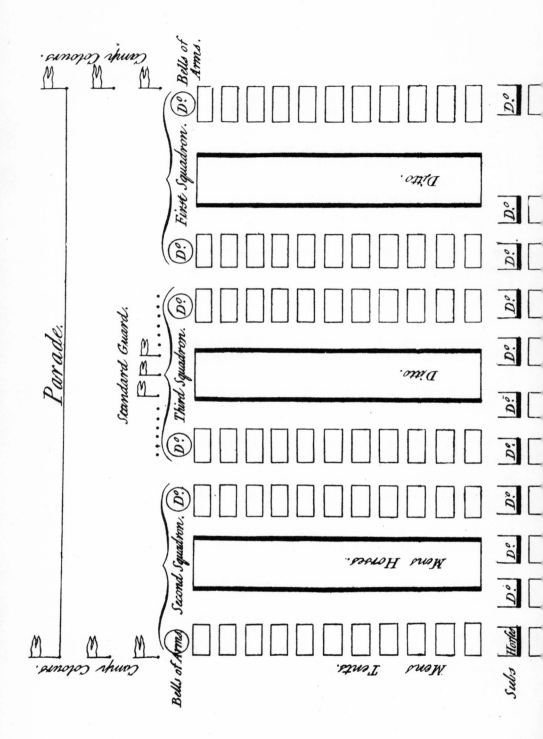

Parade.

Camp Colours. Camp Colours.

Camp Colours. Camp Colours.

Bells of Arms.

Standard Guard.

First Squadron. D.º Dº Bells of Arms.

Ditto.

Third Squadron. D.º Dº

Ditto.

Second Squadron. D.º Bells of Arms.

Mens Horses.

Mens Tents.

Subs Horses. Dº Dº Dº Dº Dº Dº Dº Dº Dº Dº

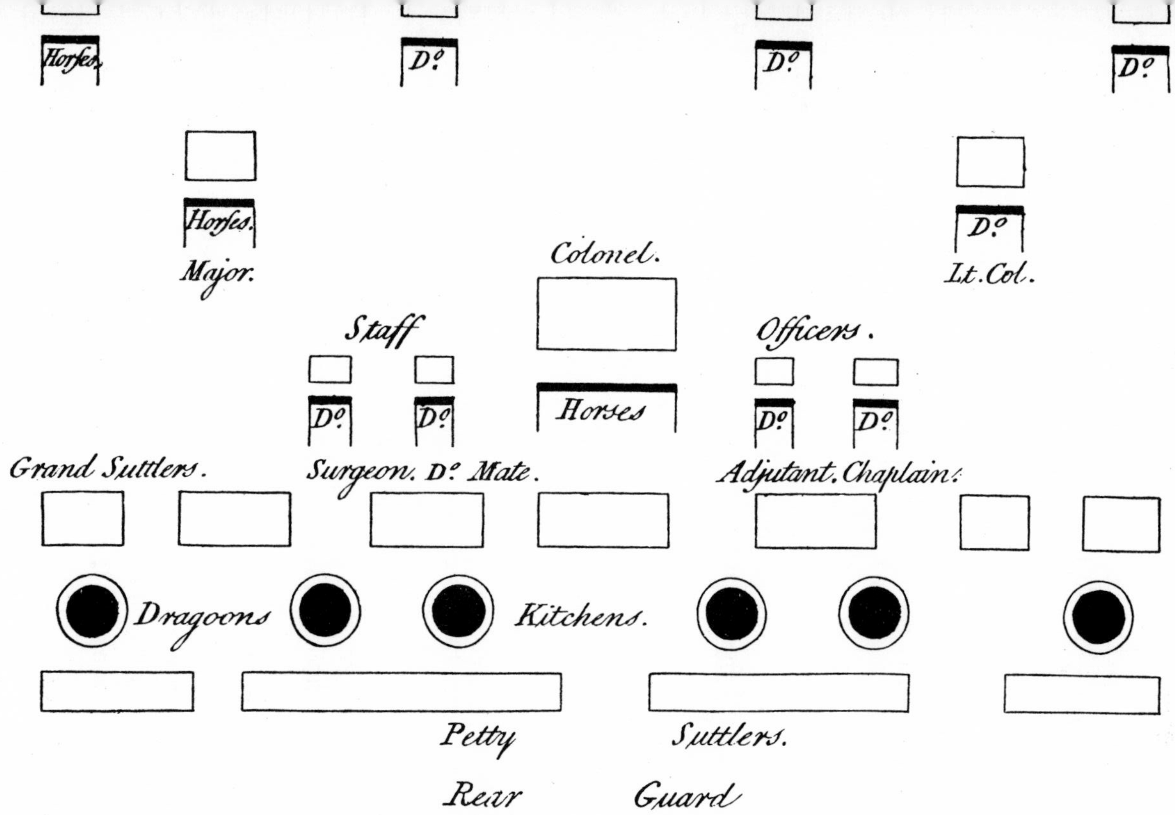

Dº

Dº   Lt.Col.

Officers.

Dº
Dº   Adjutant, Chaplain:

Colonel.

Horses

Suttlers.

Guard

Dº

Dº
Staff   Dº   Surgeon, Dº Mate.   Kitchens.   Petty   Rear

Hoyer.
Major.

Hoyer.   Grand Suttlers.   Dragoons

FIG. 13.   THE ENCAMPMENT OF A REGIMENT OF LIGHT DRAGOONS.

From 'The Discipline of the Light-Horse' by Captain R. Hinde, 1778.

stolen. The late Mr. S. M. Milne commented, 'I expect the hairs were stolen for fishing purposes, silk-worm gut not yet having come into use'.

On 15th November, 1780, it was ordered that the horses' tails were to be firmly tied with a piece of tape; and on 8th December that two inches were to be cut off each of the horses' tails in order that they might grow full and square.

On 9th May, 1782, the men were ordered to plait their horses' tails and tie them up close to the end of the rump, and to use all means to prevent them from being pulled by the inhabitants.

In preparation for a review it was ordered on 8th September, 1782, that the horses' manes and tails were to be clean washed, and the manes plaited, which, if opened out, were to be again plaited up till the morning of the review.

On 7th May, 1783, the men's hair, for a change, was the subject of a peculiar order; to the effect that, 'All men who have their hair too thin for plaiting to be furnished with additional hair before the Review, and the men are warned to put it up under their caps in a neater manner than some of them have done of late on Field days'.

A manuscript book, now in the officers' mess of the *15th/19th Hussars*, gives the colours of the horses of the *15th Light Dragoons* in 1779. These are:
'The Rt. Hon. Gen. Eliott's Troop—horses mostly chestnut, with one grey.
Lieut.-Col. Ainslie's Troop—horses mostly bay, with one grey.
Major Eliott's Troop—horses all black, except one brown.
Captain Bain's Troop—horses mostly bay.
Captain Churchill's Troop—horses mostly brown.
Captain Murray's Troop—(page missing).
The sizes of the horses are all small, some only 14¾ hands.'

An order book of the *10th Light Dragoons*, of the period 1784–8, contains a reference to 'marching to grass'. It was the custom in the eighteenth century to turn the horses of the cavalry out to grass during the six summer months. This resulted in a considerable saving in the expense of feeding.

There was little loss in efficiency, for the quarters of the various troops of a regiment were too scattered to permit any combined drills or training, and for slow troop training, such as patrolling, a grass-fed horse was quite adequate.

In this same order book there is mention of trumpet and bugle calls. These include, 'Trumpet for Stables 6.30 a.m. Boot and Saddle, 7.30, and Bugle 8.30 to turn out'.

Light Dragoons had originally carried drums, in common with all Dragoon regiments. The issue of trumpets to Dragoons in place of the drums may have owed something to an essay written by Lieut.-Colonel Dalrymple of the *King's Own Dragoons*. In this he said, 'It will be observed that trumpets are proposed preferable to drums: it is because they are infinitely more animating than the hoarse unaccompanied sound of the latter; they pour an acid into the blood, which rouses the spirits and elevates the soul above the fear of danger'.

Of the change from drums to trumpets in the Light Dragoons Hinde says:

'In the year 1764, his Majesty thought proper to forbid the use of brass side drums in the Light Cavalry, and in their room to introduce brass trumpets, so that each troop has one trumpet, who when they are dismounted form a band of music, consisting of two French horns, two clarinettes and two bassoons and also one fife to a regiment; but when mounted, the trumpet only carried.

'They use also a bugle horn, which is slung over the shoulders of one of the trumpeters, and is a signal to assemble the troops, in the same manner as beating to arms was formerly. It is of an antique form, and is also used during the exercise as occasion requires.'

The bugle, which is illustrated in Hinde's book, is of the same pattern as that shown in the badges of Light Infantry regiments. It was suspended over the shoulder by the cord.

The most famous cavalry soldier of the latter eighteenth century was undoubtedly Lieutenant-General Sir Thomas Dallas of the East India Company's Army. (Plate VI.) A vivid description of this colourful character is contained in

Cavalry; its History and Tactics, by Captain Nolan (the same Captain Nolan who took the fatal order to the Light Brigade, and who was the first to be killed in the charge). Nolan says:

'The Mysorean cavalry of Hyder Ali and Tippoo abounded in clever horsemen and first-rate swordsmen, who used their sharp weapons even with more effect than that with which the Sikhs have since been found to wield their tulwars. They frequently challenged our dragoons to single combat, and they generally had the advantage over them in the duels. But there was an officer riding with our troopers who had trained himself and his steed, and who could always give a good account of the best of them. This was Major Dallas—afterwards Lieut.-General Sir Thomas Dallas—a cavalry hero and a *model*—a sort of English Murat. Like that dashing Frenchman he was remarkable for his horsemanship and swordsmanship, for the strength, symmetry, and beauty of his person, for his daring courage, and for his love of hand-to-hand combats. He was sometimes seen to cut down three or four Mysorean champions the one after the other, on the same day. He signalized himself, in the view of admiring armies, by many daring feats, throughout the wars of Coote, Medows, Cornwallis and Harris; and left a name that will be long remembered in India. Dallas's single combats, famous throughout the Army, were usually fought on the line of march: Mysorean officers would ride up and challenge him by name. His great height (6 ft. 1 in.) and physical strength helped by his famous black stallion, which entered into the fray with equal enthusiasm, brought all his encounters to a successful end—the only exceptions being those when the combatants, after several rounds, feeling respect for skill, saluted and retired. In one encounter Dallas cut off his adversary's sword hand at the wrist, the weapon flying through the air to descend between Dallas's shirt and back. On another occasion, being too close to his foe to be able to draw his sword, he seized him by his cummerband and, lifting him off his horse, threw him to the ground, breaking his neck.

'Dallas was posted to the 6th Madras Native Cavalry as

134

Plate VI

LIEUTENANT-GENERAL SIR THOMAS DALLAS, G.C.B. (1758 to 1839).
(By kind permission of Her Grace the Duchess of Portland, from the original oil painting by Alexander Nasmyth.)
Note the heavily curved sabre of the Indian type, which is no doubt typical of the weapon preferred by this noted swordsman.

Cornet in 1775. In 1781 he was Lieutenant commanding the two companies of the Bodyguard in Eyre Coote's army in all the battles of the Carnatic between 1781–3, and was with General Stuart at Cuddalore. In 1790 he was Brigade Major of the cavalry of General Medows' army and principal staff officer to Colonel Floyd in all the battles fought near Sattimungalum in 1790 against Tippoo's army. It was mainly due to his exertions that both the detachments and Medows' supporting force were saved from disaster. After three days of heavy fighting without food, Dallas having led every charge in person, the last onset finally routed the enemy. It was then found, however, that Medows' force was in grave danger of capture. Dallas volunteered to ride alone by night and inform Medows of the situation, there being no one else capable of riding the distance.'

There were some interesting developments in cavalry firearms during the period.

A new pattern of carbine was produced about 1770, which was used by some regiments until after the end of the Napoleonic wars. It was very similar to the previous model, but had a barrel which was only 28 inches in length. This appears to have been the first carbine to be carried by Light Dragoons muzzle down in a bucket.

In 1772 the Adjutant General sent a letter to General Conway, giving comments made by Lieut.-General Elliot and Major-General Burgoyne on this carbine. After listing some minor suggested modifications, he concluded, 'They much wish for a rifled barrel carbine to be made, as a pattern, as they apprehend it may be well worth considering if rifled barrels for the Light Dragoons will not be essentially useful for H.M.'s service'.

In 1786 six carbines, three with rifled barrels and three with plain barrels (*i.e.* smoothbore), and of three different lengths, were sent for trial by Light Dragoon regiments. The following report from the Commanding Officer of the *11th Light Dragoons* is typical:

'The rifle 3 ft. 2 in. and plain, of the same length too long and too unwieldy for a Light Dragoon to manage on horseback.

'The rifle 2 ft. 9 in. and plain, of the same length, found by much too heavy for a Light Dragoon to carry.

'The rifle 2 ft. 4 in. Nothing can be better adapted for a Light Dragoon than this carbine, provided the spear which is a weight of 1 lb. 1 oz. was taken from it. It carries and will with exactness do execution at the distance of 500 yds. and is to be preferred to any of the plain barrels, as 'tis impossible to lose the ball.

'The plain 2 ft. 4 in. is objectionable as the ball from the motion of the horse is frequently lost, and renders the fire useless, which is the case with the present carbine which is loaded with a ramrod. (Signed) Col. R. Dundas, Lt. Col.'

As a result of the reports furnished by commanding officers, the Board of General Officers on Swords, Carbines, etc., of cavalry made the following recommendation in 1788: 'The Board give a preference to the shortest rifled barrel (viz. of the length of 2 ft. 4 in.) as the best adapted for service'.

In spite of this strong recommendation, however, the short rifled carbine was never issued.

In 1762 the British Army lost an honourable opponent in the disappearance of *Fitz James's Regiment of Horse* from the French Army. Together with the rest of the French Army, the regiment was overwhelmed at the battle of Wilhelmsthal, on the Hesse–Cassel border, by the Allied Army under the command of Ferdinand of Brunswick. FitzJames's was posted near the village of Grobenstein in an apparently invulnerable position. They were attacked, however, on all sides; the British cavalry charging in from the left under the command of the famous Marquis of Granby. The Irish regiment was almost annihilated. Two standards and 300 horses were captured and seventy men were made prisoners. An English cavalryman remarked on the gallant behaviour of FitzJames's in its last fight, and added, 'We cannot help, in this place, lamenting the fate of FitzJames's Horse, tho' in the service of our enemies; they proved themselves our brethren, though misled'. The regiment was disbanded on 21st December, 1762.

4TH ROYAL IRISH DRAGOON GUARDS, 1849

(*By kind permission of the Commanding Officer of the 4th/7th Royal Dragoon Guards.*)

The Mounted Troops of the British Army

The latter part of the eighteenth century saw the start of the formation of voluntary mounted corps, which were to become such prominent feature of the armed forces during the Napoleonic wars, and which were the forerunners of the Yeomanry cavalry. *The London and Westminster Light Horse Volunteers*, a very famous unit, was formed in 1779 by a number of gentlemen who belonged, for the most part, to mercantile firms in the City of London. In the Jorrocks' tradition, they were in the habit of hunting together on the borders of Kent and Surrey. The regiment was raised to meet a threat of invasion; but the following year it was called upon to do duty in the London area during the Gordon riots. It was disbanded at the peace of 1783, but was destined to be re-formed eleven years later.

Very few mounted troops served in America during the War of Independence. Of regular cavalry there were only two Light Dragoon regiments; the 16th and 17th. The 17th Dragoons left Ireland in 1775 and landed at Boston just before the battle of Bunker Hill, and a detachment of the regiment took part in the battle. After the retreat from Philadelphia in 1778 the headquarters of the *16th Light Dragoons* was returned to England, and the men and horses were transferred to the 17th. The amalgamated regiment was known as the *Queen's Dragoons*, and acquired a great reputation. A detachment served with Tarleton's Legion in the southern theatre of operations. Tarleton's were dressed in a green uniform with black facings, and this was offered to the *Queen's Dragoons* in replacement of their own threadbare clothing. The *Queen's*, however, insisted on retaining their old red uniforms, and patched them up as well as they could.

Some of the recruiting posters of the period make entertaining reading. One for the *Royal Dragoons* in 1764 stipulated that:

'Young men wishing to be entertained as Royal Dragoons must be well made, and well looking, perfectly sound and healthy, having no bodily Infirmity whatever, from the Age of Sixteen to Twenty One Years, and from five Feet eight inches and a Half, to five Feet eleven inches high.

137

'No Tramps or Vagabonds need apply, nor any Seafaring Men; likewise Militia Men not having served their Time, or any Apprentice whose Indentures are not given up; nor will any Man be entertained that is not known something of, as it is the intention of the Regiment to inlist none but honest Fellows, that wish to serve their King and Country with Honesty and Fidelity.

'God Save The King.'

Another for *The Prince of Wales's Dragoon Guards*, which appeared in the *Ipswich Journal* of 8th December, 1770, announced that:

'Any young Men of good Character and Figure, ambitious of serving his Majesty, in the Third (or Prince of Wales's Dragoon Guards) may have an opportunity of entering that Corps, there being at this Time a few Vacancies, by applying to the Commanding-Officers, either at COLCHESTER, IPSWICH, WOODBRIDGE or BECCLES. They will receive his Majesty's Bounty, and every other Encouragement they can wish; likewise Horse, Arms, Accoutrements, and every other Appointment becoming a Dragoon-Guard.

'To save unnecessary Trouble, none need apply whose Character and Figure are not unexceptionable; or who are more than 23 years of Age, or less than five Feet 8 and a half inches high.

'N.B. Any young Man, troubled with Inquietude of Mind, from Connections with the Fair Sex, or any uneasy Circumstance whatever, may, by enlisting in this Corps, find a Release from his Cares, and enter on a Life of Ease and Jollity.'

It would seem that the unexceptionable character was interpreted in a fairly broad-minded way!

At this period standards and guidons still played a large part in all regiments of cavalry, and every squadron carried one. Standards, however, had almost reached the end of their tactical use on the battlefield. They were rarely, if ever, carried in the Peninsular campaign, and they were ultimately withdrawn from the Light Cavalry altogether. Hussars seem to have discarded them from their formation as such, though they

A SERGEANT, 10TH LIGHT DRAGOONS, 1793.

(By kind permission of the Society for Army Historical Research, from the drawing by the late Rev. P. Sumner.)

The carbine will be seen to be carried in a muzzle bucket.

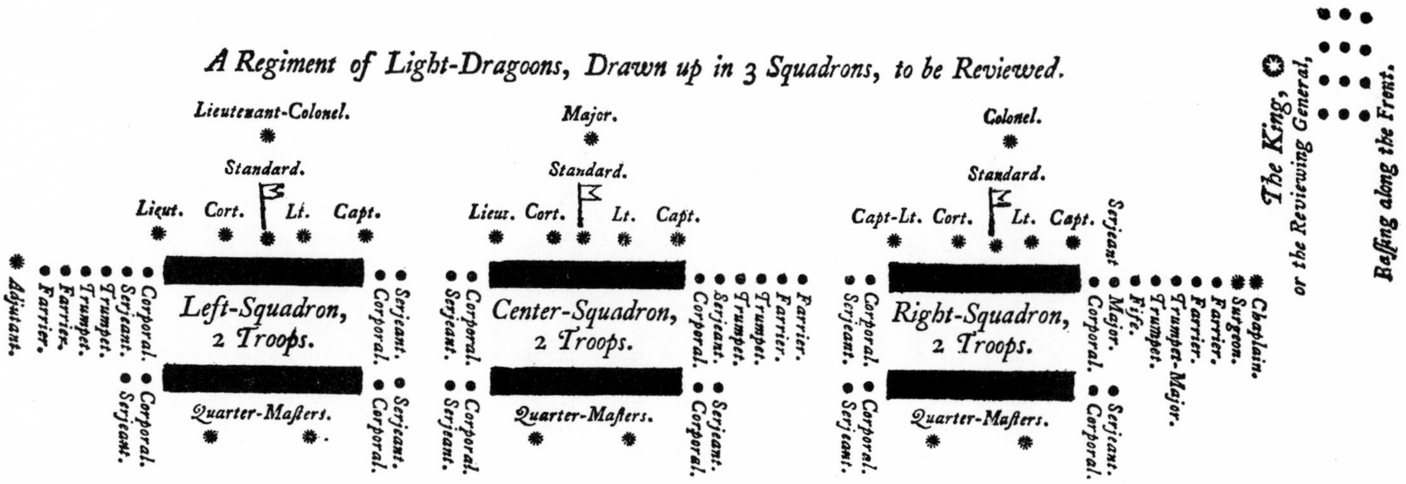

A Regiment of Light-Dragoons, Drawn up in 3 Squadrons, to be Reviewed.

Bassing along the Front.

The King, or the Reviewing General.

Chaplain.
Surgeon.
Farrier.
Farrier.
Trumpet-Major.
Trumpet.
Fife.
Serjeant • Major. • Serjeant.
Corporal. Corporal.

Colonel.
Standard.
Serjeant Capt-Lt. Cort. Lt. Capt.

Right-Squadron, 2 Troops.
Quarter-Masters.

Corporal. Corporal.
Serjeant. Serjeant.

Farrier.
Farrier.
Trumpet.
Trumpet.
Serjeant. Serjeant.
Corporal. Corporal.

Major.
Standard.
Lieut. Cort. Lt. Capt.

Center-Squadron, 2 Troops.
Quarter-Masters.

Corporal. Corporal.
Serjeant. Serjeant.

Lieutenant-Colonel.

Serjeant. Serjeant.
Corporal. Corporal.

Standard.
Lieut. Cort. Lt. Capt.

Left-Squadron, 2 Troops.
Quarter-Masters.

Corporal. Corporal.
Serjeant. Serjeant.
Trumpet.
Trumpet.
Farrier.
Farrier.
Adjutant.

FIG. 14.

From 'The Discipline of the Light-Horse' by Captain R. Hinde, 1778.

were retained for some time for purely ceremonial purposes by the remaining regiments of Light Dragoons.

Captain Hinde has given an account of the ceremony which accompanied the 'fetching' and 'lodging' of the guidons of a regiment of Light Dragoons. The Light Dragoon guidon of this period was of silk, slit at the fly, and the two tails tapered at top and bottom. The King's, Colonel's, or 'first' guidon was carried with the right squadron; the Lieutenant-Colonel's, or 'second', with the left squadron; and the Major's, or 'third', with the centre squadron. Of these, the first guidon was crimson with in the centre the badge of the crowned rose and thistle, in the first and fourth corners the white horse, and in the second and third corners the number of the regiment within a wreath of roses and thistles. The other two guidons were of the regiment's facing colour with the regimental badge (or number if it had none) in the centre; in the corners the same badges as on the first guidon, except when there was no regimental badge, when the rose and thistle appeared in the second and third corners. The third guidon was further distinguished by the figure 3. It is apparent from Hinde's opening words that the guidons were carried by the regiment on tactical training:

'When the regiment is formed in the field for exercise, the Major orders the trumpets (except one to remain with each squadron) to the centre squadron, where they are to be formed into ranks according to their number, all facing outwards. This being done, he orders the eldest Cornet to march for the standards, with a quarter-master and four or five files, or a quarter rank from the centre of that squadron, the Cornet marching at the head of the detachment, the trumpets in his front, and the quarter-master in the rear of the whole. When the Cornet comes to the place where the standards are lodged, he is to form his detachment into a rank intire, facing the house; then the Cornet orders his men to draw their swords, except those men who are to carry the standards, as it is usual for the party to march for the standards without sound of trumpet or swords drawn; on receiving the standards the trumpets are to sound a flourish, then he is to march back to the regiment, the trumpets sounding a march; but instead of marching along the front of the regiment, he is to march in the rear of it, untill he comes to the interval, which was made by their marching out, and then he is to wheel and march his men into their former places; as soon as the standards are come near the regiment, the Major orders the whole to draw their swords, on which the trumpets remaining with the squadrons sound a march; this is a ceremony always to be paid the standards, both in bringing them to, and carrying them from the regiment. When the standards are come, the eldest Cornets of the right and left squadrons are to march with three men from the centre of the front rank, along the front, and when they come opposite to the standards to return their swords, and take their several standards. The Cornets are then to march back with their standards, taking with them their respective trumpets, who are to sound a march, and as soon as they have got to the centre of the intervals between the squadrons, they are to wheel to the rear, and march until they come opposite to the intervals of the front and centre or rear ranks, and then to wheel to their squadrons, and march between those ranks until they come to their places and then wheel up. The trumpets are then to go to their posts, and the regiment to return their swords.

'When the standards are to be lodged, the major orders the Cornets of the right and left squadrons to carry the standards to the centre squadron, which they are to do in the same manner as they brought them from thence, the trumpets sounding a march; and when they have delivered them to that squadron, the Cornets are to return with the men to their squadrons, marching between the first and centre or rear ranks, if two deep only, until they come to their own places, and then wheel up; the trumpets are to remain with the standards, except one to each squadron; when the Cornets of the other squadrons are returned, the Cornet that brought the standards is to march back with the same number of files (the trumpets sounding a march) and lodge the standards, drawing up his men in a rank intire as he did when he received them, on which

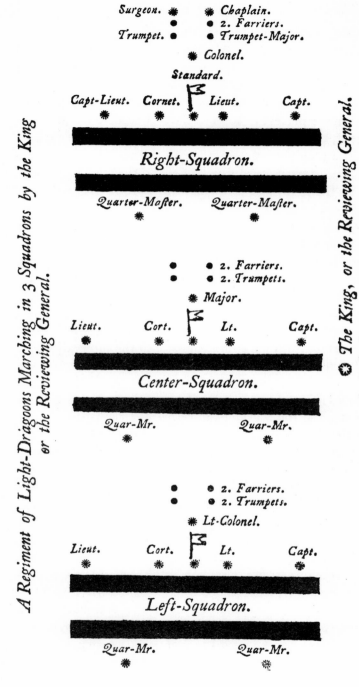

A Regiment of Light-Dragoons Marching in 3 Squadrons by the King or the Reviewing General.

Surgeon. ✳   ✳ Chaplain.
● ● 2. Farriers.
Trumpet. ● ● Trumpet-Major.
✳ Colonel.
Standard.

Capt-Lieut.   Cornet.   Lieut.   Capt.
✳   ✳   🚩✳   ✳

Right-Squadron.

Quarter-Master.   Quarter-Master.
✳   ✳

● ● 2. Farriers.
● ● 2. Trumpets.
✳ Major.

Lieut.   Cort.   Lt.   Capt.
✳   ✳   🚩✳   ✳   ✳

Center-Squadron.

Quar-Mr.   Quar-Mr.
✳   ✳

● ● 2. Farriers.
● ● 2. Trumpets.
✳ Lt-Colonel.

Lieut.   Cort.   Lt.   Capt.
✳   ✳   🚩✳   ✳   ✳

Left-Squadron.

Quar-Mr.   Quar-Mr.
✳   ✳

✳ Adjutant.

⊛ The King, or the Reviewing General.

● ● ●
● ● ●
● ● ●
● ● ●

Fig. 15.

From 'The Discipline of the Light-Horse' by Captain R. Hinde, 1778.

the trumpets sound a flourish; then he orders the swords to be returned, and marches back to the regiment without sound of trumpet.

'Before the standards are carried to the centre squadron, the Major is to order the regiment to draw their swords, and as soon as the standards are gone, to return them.'

At the beginning of the reign of George III the Light Dragoons were given the curious duty of relieving the Household Troops in the provision of travelling escorts for the King. The following order shows the method of providing escorts for such a royal journey:

'His Majesty will leave Kew on Monday morning at 6 o'clock precisely, and will travel at the rate of 10 miles an hour. This information will enable you to calculate the exact time of the King's arrival at the several posts of the Detachments under your command, so you will accordingly have the escorts in perfect readiness to fall in, and proceed to their respective points of relief.'

The King must presumably have been travelling on horseback, for, as will be seen in a later chapter, it is most unlikely that there were any roads which would have permitted a carriage to be drawn at ten miles per hour.

CHAPTER IX

THE NAPOLEONIC WARS—
THE FIRST PHASE

During the long period of the Napoleonic wars there was a considerable expansion in the auxiliary cavalry force of the Army. The genesis of the Yeomanry was a letter of 14th March, 1794, which the Government sent to Lords Lieutenant asking them to raise Corps of Yeomanry Cavalry for the internal protection of the country and its defence against invasion. As a result, 27 Yeomanry Cavalry regiments were formed the same year.

Training of this force must have presented a considerable problem, and it is not known how it was tackled. No permanent staff was appointed from the Regular Army, as happened at a later date. The following extract from the *Salisbury and Winchester Journal* of 14th July, 1794, shows the desperate need for instructors:

'Wiltshire. Wanted immediately. Several Men who have been used to or understand the Dragoon Services, to act as Serjeants and Rough-Riders in the several Troops of Gentlemen and Yeomen Cavalry, now raised in the County. Apply to Mr. William Cox, Devizes.'

A typical advertisement to raise the men for the new regiments was that issued for the Yeomanry of Rutland, as follows:

'19 April, 1794. Rutland Light Dragoons. Not to be employed out of Great Britain nor to be drafted, Such gentlemen as like a pleasant ride this summer and are hearty tight fellows, for no bad hands need apply, will do well to offer themselves to serve in the Corps now being raised. . . .'

All the yeomen were, of course, volunteers; and as such they regarded it as a point of honour to attend drills, obey the orders of their officers and N.C.O.'s, and parade at a moment's notice when required. There was no code of discipline to which they were subject except their own rules; and these could only be enforced by public opinion. The only punishments were fines or dismissal from the regiment. The following account of a regimental court martial provides an amusing example of the working of such discipline:

'27 Sept., 1794. A Court Martial was held on Thursday last on the Race Ground on a Private in our new raised Corps of Cavalry for damning the Colonel, the Captain, and the Troop for a set of awkward Squads. It appearing that the words were uttered when the person was inebriated the charge was voted frivolous.'

The *Western Flying Post* of 6th July, 1795, published a notice of the expulsion of a yeoman:

'John Dyke, of Weston, Yeoman, voluntarily enrolled in the First Troop of Somerset Yeomanry Cavalry, having positively refused to embody himself, although repeatedly summoned, in consequence of directions from the Sheriff, that the said troop should be held in readiness to aid the Civil Power, AND having denied also in the most direct manner the payment of Twenty Pounds, a penalty he had incurred, and which he had promised voluntarily under his hand to pay, if he ever refused to embody when called upon, either by order from His Majesty, the Lord Lieutenant, or Sheriff of the County, A General Meeting of the Troop was this day held, when it was unanimously resolved, That as no obligation will bind that man, who can violate the strong and solemn tie of honour, the named JOHN DYKE BE EXPELLED, with every possible ignominy as a disgrace to the Corps, and to the Yeomanry. I do, therefore, in this public manner, as the greatest punishment a person with any degree of feeling can suffer, Expel the said JOHN DYKE. He is about 27 years of age, near 5 feet 10 inches high, stoops in his shoulders, black complexion, full face, large eyes, lank hair, and a down-cast look. (Signed) ROBERT STEVENS. Captain.'

A scathing commentary on the clothing of some of the

Yeomanry is contained in the *Gentleman's Magazine* of November, 1795, of which the following is an extract:

'It has been always judged wise . . . to cloathe the guardians of their country in a way that may strike with respect and awe. In the cloathing of the volunteer cavalry in the midland counties some of the committees have brought forth a kind of non-descript body, a kind of go-between thing in dress, neither soldier nor yeoman; somewhat like a recruit from the plough, just enlisted, seen at the head of a recruiting-party, with a sword, belt, and a serjeant's hat or helmet on, and in his rustic dress; at once a figure of ridicule and the sport of the boys. An absurdity of this nature, but in a far less degree, occurred on the day of the presenting of the standards to the Leicestershire regiment; a regiment excepting in that particular, truly military and respectable, both in cloathing and arms. They were accoutred in a dingy-coloured brown farmerly cloak, or great coat, in the place of one the colour of the uniform of the regiment. No one could wonder, if this regiment should ever be called into actual service on the sea-coast, if detachments of the men be taken for smugglers, on a rainy day, and fired upon by their brothers more regular in arms.'

The London and Westminster Light Horse Volunteers, when they were re-formed in 1794, had a strength of six troops. In the *General Regulations* of the regiment, issued in 1797, it is stated that: 'As the Light Horse Volunteers have neither Sergeant or Corporal by name, eight gentlemen from each troop have obligingly agreed to take on themselves the duty of N.C.O.'s'. The regiment also had 'a detachment of Horse Artillery with two six-pounders, appointed by the Government'. The *General Regulations* say too that the 'corps being composed of noblemen and gentlemen of almost every profession, is generally considered a corps of Officers serving as Private Soldiers, in support of our King and constitution'. The regiment, indeed, had the privilege of submitting the names of all applicants for enrolment to the King for his personal approval.

Probably the first occasion in which the services of the

Yeomanry were required was in aid of the Civil Power. This was during the Nottingham Bread Riots of April, 1797, when a troop of the *South Notts Yeomanry* assisted a troop of the *Inniskilling Dragoons* to disperse unruly mobs. On this duty a junior officer of the Yeomanry performed a remarkable feat. Some of the rioters had retreated behind the protection of some iron railings in the market-place of Nottingham, from which apparently secure position they hurled stones at the yeomen. Cornet Alexander Madden of the *South Notts Yeomanry*, however, rode his horse straight at the railings, leaped over them into the midst of the mob, and dispersed them with the flat of his sword.

The Earl of Pembroke, who had fought so hard for the comfort of the horses of the Army, died in 1794. The cavalry regulations of 1795, in the compilation of which he had been consulted, fixed the length of a horse's tail as to reach 'half way between the hoof and the fetterlock'. In the following year the Adjutant General wrote to the Board of General Officers on cavalry matters requesting information as to 'The long Tail'd Chargers, on which the Officers of Heavy Cavalry are now requir'd to be mounted; and whether on account of their present scarcity, as well as of the exorbitant Price demanded for them, the Board might be induc'd to recommend the use of Nag Tail'd Chargers in their stead'.

The trouble was that civilian fashion had not followed the Army need; and it was the normal practice to dock horses' tails.

As a result of the Adjutant General's enquiry the Board submitted a report on 18th May, 1796, which dealt with the matter as follows:

'Considering the great difficulty found by Officers in providing themselves with long-tailed Horses, we are most humbly of opinion, that it would be attended with material convenience to them, and that they would be supplied with better Horses, were they mounted in future with Nag-tailed Horses, of Strength, Figure, & Activity, & not under the size of Fifteen Hands one Inch.' This proposal was approved until (as in so many and other later cases) 'the end of the war'.

Docking was officially reintroduced into the Army by an Army General Order of 10th August, 1799, in the following terms:

'His Royal Highness the Commander-in-Chief has directed His Majesty's Pleasure relative to the Horses of the Heavy Cavalry, to be immediately circulated to the Colonels or Officers Commanding those Regiments.

'The Heavy Cavalry, with the exception of the two Regiments of Life Guards and the Royal Regiment of Horse Guards, are to be mounted on nag-tailed Horses.

'The 1st (or King's) Regiment of Dragoon Guards; The 1st (or Royal) Regiment of Dragoons; The 3rd (or King's Own) Regiment of Dragoons, are to be mounted on Black nag-tailed Horses.

'The 2nd (or Queen's) Regiment of Dragoon Guards are to be mounted on nag-tail'd Horses, of the Colours of Bay and Brown.

'The 2nd (or Royal North British) Regiment of Dragoons are to be mounted on nag-tail'd Grey Horses.

'All the other Regiments of Heavy Cavalry on the British Establishment are to be mounted on nag-tail'd Horses of the Colours of Bay, Brown and Chestnut.

'The custom of mounting Trumpeters, on Grey Horses, is to be discontinued, and they are in future to be mounted on Horses of the Colour, or Colours, hereby prescribed to the Regiment to which they belong . . .'

Rather strangely, it was by no means the universal practice, at the end of the eighteenth century, to teach the horses of heavy cavalry to jump. Light cavalry, on the other hand, were generally expected to be able to cross any normal country. In a book written by an anonymous author ('A Field Officer') in 1809, entitled *Strictures on the Army*, etc., the author emphasizes the importance of teaching cavalry horses to jump:

'War is never carried on, on a lawn, and seldom on a plain. When the horse is bitted, the next essential thing is to teach him to leap, . . .

'The Light Dragoons that left Ireland, for the West Indies

in 1795, were most efficient cavalry. They could individually hunt their horses; for leaping was made a part of their regular exercise. A heavy regiment, the 4th Dragoon Guards, commanded by the late Lieut.-General Warde, who possessed the

FIG. 16. CUT TWO AGAINST INFANTRY.
From 'Rules & Regulations for the Sword Exercise of the Cavalry', 1796.

soundest ideas of what cavalry ought to be, and who for some years commanded the troops in Ireland, and was so partial to Cavalry, that he exercised his own Regiment regularly five times in the week; although he was then upwards of seventy, he had an utter aversion to any but quick movements.

'Notwithstanding it was a heavy regiment, he, at the head, often took it across a country.

'To such a high perfection did he bring this corps, as to be able to trot in line, with the reins thrown loose on the horses' necks: this gave the men an excellent seat, & taught them to direct the horse by the calf of the leg, which at length was effected with the greatest precision.'

New swords were introduced into the cavalry by a Royal Warrant of 1796. Rather oddly, the sword for the Light

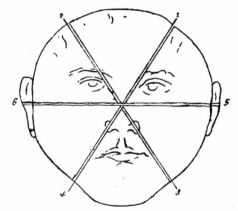

FIG. 17. THE SIX CUTS.
From 'Rules & Regulations for the Sword Exercise of the Cavalry', 1796.

Dragoons was outstandingly good; whilst that for the heavy cavalry was thoroughly bad.

The Light Dragoon weapon was a short sabre of 32½ or 33 inches; the blade being measured in a straight line, though it was, in point of fact, curved. This heavily curved and broad-bladed sabre, fitted with a steel stirrup hilt, remained the light cavalry weapon throughout the Napoleonic wars. As an offensive weapon, it was probably the finest cutting sword which was ever produced as a general military issue. Its weight and balance gave it tremendous cutting power, and it is said that during the Peninsular campaign a French commander made official complaint as to the fearful wounds inflicted by this sabre.

The sword for the heavy cavalry had a straight 35-inch

blade. It was no use for thrusting, however, as the blade had a
hatchet point; and its poor balance made it a bad cutting

Fig. 18. Guard.
From 'Rules & Regulations for the Sword Exercise of the Cavalry', 1796.

weapon. In addition, the design of hilt gave very little protection to the hand.

An official book, *Rules and Regulations for the Sword Exercise of the Cavalry*, was issued from the Adjutant General's Office on 1st December, 1796. In spite of its title the contents are concerned solely with the Light Cavalry sword, and all the illustrations are of Light Dragoons.

There is an interesting discussion on the use of this weapon in cutting and thrusting. The book lays down that:

'The *thrust* has only one mode of execution, whether applied to cavalry, or infantry: but a greater degree of caution is required in its application against cavalry than against infantry; for if the *point* is parried, the adversary's blade gets within your guard, which is not to be recovered again in time, as with a small sword; the weapon being too heavy to be managed with the requisite degree of quickness; for which reason the point should seldom or never be given in the attack, but principally confined to the pursuit, when it can be applied with effect and without risk.

'The case is different in acting against infantry, as the persons against whom you then direct your *point* are so much below your own level, that the weight of your sword is not so felt; consequently it is managed with greater facility than with an extended arm carried above the level of the shoulder. Therefore in many instances against infantry, the point may be used with as much effect as the edge and with the same degree of security.'

As regards the difference in cutting against cavalry and infantry, the regulations say that in the case of cavalry it must be an affair of wrist and shoulder, without bending the elbow; for to do so would expose the forearm. Against infantry, on the other hand, because the horseman is so elevated above the man on foot, it is necessary to bend the elbow to obtain sufficient sweep for the cut to take effect.

The book emphasizes the importance of horsemanship:

'To become a perfect cavalry swordsman, horsemanship is indispensably necessary, and without it, very little benefit can be derived from the science. Good riding does not consist in urging a horse forward with precipitation and checking him

IT is His MAJESTY's pleasure, that the use and exercise of the Sword shall in future be regularly taught at the drills of the Cavalry, as an essential part of the instruction of a horseman; and, in order to establish uniformity of execution on a proper system, the following regulations must be strictly observed.

The first principles are to be acquired and shewn on foot, under the direction of the adjutant, until such time as the squads are in a sufficient degree of forwardness to execute their lessons on horseback, when it will become the particular duty of the riding master to instruct them in the mode by which horsemanship and the use of the sword are combined.

His MAJESTY's Regulations for the Formations, Movements, and Field Exercise, of the Cavalry, do not suffer the smallest alteration in the practice of this system, which is calculated to give the horseman, when acting singly, that decided advantage over an enemy, which horsemanship, and a conscious superiority in the use of his sword must always produce.

FIG. 19. THE INTRODUCTION TO 'RULES & REGULATIONS FOR THE SWORD EXERCISE OF THE CAVALRY', 1796.

with violence, but a dragoon and his horse should be so formed to each other to act as one body; for which purpose the rider should make himself acquainted with the temper and powers of his animal, so that by judicious management, the horse may be rendered docile, and execute readily whatever may be expected of him. . . . It is alone 'by temper and perseverance, not by severity, that vice is to be conquered, and those tricks surmounted which in horses generally originate in timidity.'

Captain Hinde has some words to say on how to set about this desirable aim:

'In the riding school it is usual to hold a swish in the right hand, to shew how the sword is to be carried, and to employ the hand which otherwise might on a violent motion of the horse, or apprehension of falling, be apt to catch hold of the mane or saddle; as the horseman is to depend upon his seat, and not offer to hold himself on by any other disgraceful means.'

During this first part of the Napoleonic wars active operations by mounted troops were practically confined to the long and unsatisfactory campaign in the Low Countries. An orderly book of the *Scots Greys* of 1793 gives an insight into some unit administration of the period. The following is an extract:

'Directions for Carrying Camp Equipment.—Mallets, tents, pins and hatchets carried in water buckets fixed to the near ring of the saddle behind. The powder bag to be carried by the Orderly Corporal. Kettles to be fixed with strings upon the baggage, till straps can be provided. Canteens to be slung on the right side, haversacks on the left side. Picket posts strapped to firelocks. Corn sacks with corn divided between the ends, across the saddle. Hay twisted in ropes and fixed upon the necessary bags. Water-decks neatly folded and placed upon the hay. Nosebags fixed to the off-ring of the saddle behind. Forage cords upon the baggage. Scythes wrapped with haybands and strapped with the handles to the firelock. Sneads, stores, etc., to be carried by the same men. Old clothing, hats and spare things not wanted at present to be properly packed

Fig. 20.

FRONT GIVE POINT. HORSE NEAR-SIDE PROTECT.
LEFT GIVE POINT.   THE ST. GEORGE.

From 'Rules & Regulations for the Sword Exercise of the Cavalry', 1796.

and lodged at the regimental store at Robert Cantrell's, grocer, St. George Street, Newton, Ostend, this evening.'

Although the campaign in the Netherlands was, in the long run, an unsuccessful one, it was noteworthy for some brilliant actions by the British cavalry. Mr. J. H. McGuffie gives a vivid description of them in his book *Peninsular Cavalry General* (General R. B. Long). Long served in this campaign as a subaltern. Mr. McGuffie says:

'At Villers-en-Cauchies, on April 1794, three hundred men of the 15th Light Dragoons attacked and dispersed five thousand Frenchmen. At Beaumont the 1st Dragoon Guards also came into action, when they, with the 3rd and 5th Dragoon Guards, the Blues, Royals and 16th Light Dragoons, together with six squadrons of Austrian Cuirassiers, burst upon the flank of over 20,000 Frenchmen and in a few minutes whirled them away in a torrent of destruction.

'On this glorious day Long, with most of the first squadron, began by falling in a deep ditch, where he was overrun by our supporting troops, but escaped unhurt. His horse, Conqueror, was not so fortunate. In Long's own words, used when writing home, Conqueror "received a wound in his off foot near the hoof, by a musket shot which a scoundrel, whom I had pardoned the instant before on condition of his laying down his arms, fired at me. My sword soon gave him the reward which such Criminal Ingratitude justly merited." '

Captain Gronow, in his *Reminiscences and Recollections*, mentions an unusual addition to the officers of the *10th Hussars*, as follows:

'Amongst the curious freaks of fortune there is none more remarkable in my memory than the sudden appearance in the highest and best society in London of a young man whose antecedents warranted a much less conspicuous career. I refer to Beau Brummel. He was endowed with a handsome person and distinguished himself at Eton as the best scholar, the best boatman and the best cricketer. . . . He made many friends amongst the scions of good families . . . and his reputation reached a circle over which reigned the celebrated Duchess of

Devonshire. . . . At last the Prince of Wales sent for Brummel, and was so much pleased with his manner and appearance that he gave him a commission in his own regiment, the 10th Hussars. Unluckily, Brummel, soon after joining the regiment was thrown from his horse at a grand review at Brighton, when he broke his classical Roman nose.'

It was said that Brummel could never master the names of the men in his troop, and, further, that his only means of recognizing the troop at all was by one old soldier with a bottle nose who was always placed in the front rank. On one ceremonial parade, however, in order to make the other troops up to strength, Brummel's, the most junior, was divided amongst them. Brummel arrived late on parade, after the Colonel had already taken up position, and rode to the place where he expected to find his troop. Not finding it and somewhat disturbed he galloped down the line. Eventually, to his relief, he spotted the bottle-nosed trooper and took post in front of him. The Colonel, who had been watching this performance, shouted out, 'How now, Mr. Brummel; you are with the wrong troop!' 'No, no,' Brummel protested, turning round in his saddle for a confirmatory look at his landmark. 'I know better than that. A pretty thing, indeed, if I did not know my own men!'

Brummel did not remain long in the regiment. After he had been in it three years it was ordered to Manchester; and Brummel resigned his commission on the plea that he could not go on foreign service.

A new horsed element was introduced into the Army at the end of the century. Its appearance was signalized by appeals for recruits, of which the following advertisement in *The Nottingham Journal* of 15th February, 1800, is a typical example:

'His Majesty's Royal Waggon Train

'Wanted to engage for the term of Three Years, or during the war, some young men of good character, to take care of Horses and drive the Waggons of the Army. Farmers' Servants or such Young Men who have been accustomed to

Horses are the description of people wanted. They will be well used and receive 1s. 3d. per day with comfortable good cloathing and many other advantages. Such young men as are desirous to engage in the above employ are required to apply to Lieutenant Bigsby.

'Each person he engages will be allowed Two Pounds to purchase such articles as he may have occasion for.

'*Likewise wanted*

'In the said Regiment one Smith, one Farrier, and one Wheelwright. *No* man will be accepted but those who can bring testimonials of their abilities and good character; those willing to engage have the pay of one guinea per week.

'The men wanted for the *Royal Waggon Train* are not to do duty as Soldiers but to be solely employed with Waggons and Horses of the Army.

'God save the King.'

Before the institution of army barracks it was the custom to billet troops at inns. With the considerable growth of the Army during the Napoleonic wars this presented a difficult problem. An account of the billeting of soldiers at Springfield (a parish which formed part of Chelmsford) shows that on 19th July, 1795, the six inns in the village (the 'White Hart', the 'Plough', the 'Red Lion', the '3 Cups', the 'Two Brewers' and the 'Duke's Head') had to accommodate between them seventy-six men and horses of the *1st Royal Dragoons*. From the 19th to the 22nd August they got off more lightly with a troop of twenty men and sixteen horses of the *32nd Light Dragoons*.

In the days of sail it was no easy matter to arrange for the provision of horses for any distant expedition. A force was almost certain to embark without its proper complement of horses for mounted troops, artillery and transport. An example of the difficulties which were encountered is provided by Sir James Craig's expedition to Naples in 1805. Craig was informed that he would have to undertake defensive operations in the mountainous areas of Sicily. He embarked with 300

159

dismounted men of the *20th Light Dragoons*, and without any horses for his artillery or transport. He considered, of course, that for the static operations envisaged he would have plenty of time to make up his limited requirements from local re-sources. However, during his passage his instructions were altered and he was put under the Russian commander in a rôle which would require a lot of cavalry, and for his guns and vehicles to be immediately mobile. Craig was forced to rely on the efforts of the Neapolitan government to procure horses. The British Minister managed to purchase 200 horses for the Dragoons; but though the government, in their efforts to supply draught horses, even requisitioned the carriage horses of the nobility, their efforts met with little success.

As always in the British Army, war seemed to have little effect on the observance of regimental customs. *The History and Topography of Ipswich*, written by G. R. Clarke in 1830, contains an account of the celebration of St. Andrew's Day in the *Scots Greys* in 1805. In May of that year the regiment arrived in the district from Canterbury; six troops being stationed in Ipswich and four in Colchester.

On 29th November, according to the account, 'The cere-mony of introducing St. Andrew into this town, was observed by the Scots Greys, in garrison here. A soldier of the regiment represented the venerable saint: he was mounted on a fine grey horse, and wore a bear's-skin cloak and a long white beard; he had a roll of paper in his right hand, and a cross affixed to his breast; two men led his horse, and a guard of twelve soldiers, in the Highland dress, with their broad swords drawn, kept off the crowd; the procession was proceeded by the band of the regiment, who played several national airs, this being St. Andrew's day.'

The affair was also mentioned in the *Ipswich Journal* of 7th December, 1805, which added the information that the pro-cession drew up at the house of Major Heron (a former officer of the regiment), where the Highlanders danced Scottish reels and the band played. Finally the Major's health was drunk and the cavalcade returned to barracks.

The Mounted Troops of the British Army

In 1805 the *15th Light Dragoons* were converted into a regiment of Hussars, and they were dressed in the exotic uniform, including busby and slung pelisse, which was worn by this type of cavalry on the Continent. Colonel Liddell, in his *Memoirs of the Tenth Hussars*, says that the word 'Hussar' was derived from two Hungarian words, 'husz' signifying twenty, and 'ar' meaning pay. This, he relates, derived from the time that Matthias Corunus succeeded to the throne of Hungary, and decreed that one man out of every twenty should be enrolled as a cavalry soldier; and that the families which supplied these men should also provide for them.

Although the *15th* appear to have been the first British regiment to be designated Hussars, the *10th Light Dragoons* were the first to be issued with Hussar pattern uniform. The relevant order is as follows:

'Clothing Regulations, 22nd April 1803, for 10th Light Dragoons.

'Once every four years—1 pelisse, 1 dress jacket, 1 hussar cap. Once every 8 years—1 sash. (Sd) Jas. Pulteney.'

However, it was not till the inspection of the *10th* on 20th October, 1820, that the general reported that 'the standards were deposited in the Pavilion at Brighton when the regiment became hussars'.

The busby had a curious history. It appears to have been introduced into Europe by the Turks, and in its original form it was probably similar to the headgear now worn by the Uzbeks of Bokhara. This is a conical cap of silk or cloth bordered with fur; the top falling over to make a hanging bag. The hanging bag was probably intended to protect the neck against a sabre cut. There was a corps of cavalry in the old Ottoman army called the Gunalis who wore a similar cap, with fur and hanging top, which was called a kalpak. They also had the slung pelisse. The Turks continued to wear the kalpak, generally with a turban twisted round it, until Sultan Mahmoud the Reformer changed the national head-dress to the fez in the nineteenth century. From Turkey the kalpak and pelisse spread to Hungary, where it was gradually modified into the well-known Hussar dress. The fashion was taken up in France and Germany, where the busby was known as the 'Colback'. The hanging bag is still retained as a kind of flap on the modern busby, worn as the full-dress cap of the regiments of *Hussars*, the *Royal Artillery*, the *Royal Engineers* and the *Royal Signals*.

The busby was not at first viewed with unmixed favour. The early pattern was very high in the crown, clumsy-looking and unwieldy. An inspection report on the *15th Hussars* of May, 1808, says, 'Officers and men disfigured by a large cap'; and Dr. Adam Neale in his *Letters from Portugal and Spain*, referring to the charge of the *10th* and *15th Hussars* at Sahagun, on 21st December, 1808, says: 'Our dragoons complain much of their new-fashioned fur caps, which from being top-heavy, either tumbled off during the charge, or were cut down by the heavy French swords like so much cartridge-paper'. Fortescue states that, 'The fur caps were very tall, so much so that an M.P. called them "monstrous muffs" '. In 1812 the busbies were withdrawn from the *15th Hussars* and were replaced by shakos of red cloth.

Whatever they may have thought of the busbies, however, the men appear to have liked the smart pelisses. On 3rd November, 1806, it is recorded in the Adjutant's Journals of the *15th Hussars* that, 'The senior Privates in each Troop assembled by order and consulted on their choice of the clothing to be received in 4 years. They unanimously agreed to receive 1 pelisse and 2 dress jackets, instead of 1 pelisse, 1 dress jacket, 1 stable jacket and flannel waistcoat.' And on 8th March of the following year it is stated that, 'The men remarkably pleased with the pelisses'. The serjeants of the regiment, on 5th November, 1806, 'sent in a statement of the clothing for 4 years, requesting to be permitted to furnish their own pelisses'. This last is a nice touch. No doubt serjeants could, by the expenditure of a little extra money, obtain a rather smarter pelisse than that worn by the rank and file.

A subaltern in the new Hussar regiments had considerable expenses to meet. On 9th September, 1806, a Board of

Officers was held by the *15th Hussars* to enquire into the expenses which were incurred by an officer on first joining the regiment. Apart from uniform, the following are some of the charges which had to be met:

'First charger, £63; second charger, £42; one regimental saddle and bridle complete, £9 17s.; one plain ditto, £6 4s. 6d.; two suits of horse clothing, collars etc., £8 8s.; small stable articles, corn chest, etc., £2 12s. 6d.; a dress shabracque, £16 16s.; a velisse, £1 1s.; a field collar, 10s. 6d. . . . Present to the men on joining the troop to which he is appointed, £2 2s.; riding master £5 5s.; sergeant-major, rough rider, etc., £2 2s. . . .'

The presents which a subaltern had to make on joining his regiment are interesting, and the custom was probably fairly general. No doubt the arrival of a new officer was awaited with pleasant anticipation by a great many people.

The firearms of the heavy cavalry received long overdue attention in 1796. In that year the Board of General Officers, expressing the opinion that the firelock then in use had long been useless, inconvenient and cumbersome, recommended a carbine of 26 inches in the barrel and of a musket bore. They further recommended that until such a weapon could be provided, the barrel of the existing firelock should be cut down in size, and a swivel bar added to enable it to be carried butt downwards. The bayonet should, they said, be reduced to 15 inches and each man should carry only one pistol, with a 9-inch barrel and an iron ramrod fixed to the holster pipe.

These recommendations were put into effect in the same year.

In 1800 the light cavalry 'Paget' carbine and its companion pistol were adopted. This carbine was the first of its class to have a barrel less in length than 26 or 28 inches, and the reduction was considerable, for the length was only 16 inches. 'Paget' carbines and pistols had a long life, for they were carried by the light cavalry until the appearance of percussion arms in the 1840's. They were named after General Paget, who was credited with the invention of the ramrod attached by a link to the barrel, so that it was never detached from the weapon—a great convenience to horsemen, who were liable to drop their ramrods.

In 1803 there was an issue of rifled carbines. The War Office order said, '9th August 1803, Rifle carbines to be supplied, one hundred to a regiment, to the several regiments of Light Dragoons'.

CHAPTER X

THE PENINSULA & WATERLOO

The difficulty of supplying an adequate number of horses for an expeditionary force made itself felt at the outset of the campaign in the Iberian Peninsula, and resulted in a great shortage of artillery in the Vimiero operations. The only animals provided by the Portuguese were nineteen mares and eighty-six mules, of which many of the latter were used to carry entrenching tools. Six guns were landed at Mondego bay: four light 6-pounders and two howitzers. Three of these had to be sent back. The remaining three were drawn by mules to Leyria and then left. The nineteen mares were distributed amongst the eighteen guns which had been landed with the first part of the force. These consisted of five 9-pounders, ten 6-pounders, one $5\frac{1}{2}$-inch heavy howitzer and one light howitzer of the same bore. The 9-pounders and 6-pounders were organized in three five-gun brigades, and, with the Portuguese mares, there were just enough horses to draw these guns and their carriages. They were the only artillery to go into action, however, for the howitzers had to be left behind.

Later on the normal light 6-pounder brigade consisted of six guns, and required some 104 horses or mules to draw it. A light 6-pounder was hauled by a six-horse team, but the heavier pieces had eight-horse teams.

The horses sent out to the Peninsula from England were not always satisfactory. A note in the diary of Captain Henry Neville of the *14th Light Dragoons* on 1st July, 1809, says: 'We received today a Remount of 61 (I may almost say Cart) Horses from the *Irish Commissariat Corps*! What makes this more ridiculous is that they are chiefly Horses that have been *cast* in *England* as being unserviceable for the *Heavy Dragoons*!'

The Heavy Dragoons were the most archaic-looking part of the early Peninsular army. They were still wearing the large cocked hats, which had been largely discarded in the rest of the Army, and heavy jack-boots. The Light Dragoons, the most numerous of Wellington's cavalry, had the blue laced jacket and black leather helmet, with bearskin crest and plume at the side, which had been introduced during the American war. A similar uniform was worn by the Horse Artillery.

The British cavalry early acquired a feeling of superiority over that of the French. This is well illustrated by the action which took place at Sahagun in December, 1808.

Lord Paget, commanding the Hussar Brigade, planned to launch a surprise attack on Sahagun, with the object of seizing the town and destroying its garrison, the French *16th Dragoons of the Guard*. Paget wrote his own account of the affair a few days later:

'You will be pleased to hear that I have had an affair with the French Cavalry, and have given them a good licking. It was those lucky rogues the 15th,—who always happen to be under my hand, when there is anything to be done.

'The following is the history:—Hearing that a French General with 700 or 800 cavalry was at this place, I determined upon trying to catch them, and for this purpose ordered Gl. Slade to march with the 10th and 7 Guns on our side the River, to make a Show and if possible push into the town, whilst I marched at 1 o'clock A.M. to get round the town with about 400 of the 15th and about 12 men of the 7th. In the night my advanced Guard fell in with a Patrole of the Enemy, from whom 5 Prisoners were taken, but as the others escaped, I was obliged to push very fast, lest they should take the alarm and escape. I judged right, for having come to my point before daylight, I found the Enemy formed without the town. I judged them to be between 6 and 700 Men, but from the reports of Prisoners they must have amounted to 750. As soon as they could distinguish us they made off in good order. I marched in column Parallel, but a good deal behind them,

PRIVATES, SCOTS GREYS, 1807.

(By kind permission of the Society for Army Historical Research, from an unpublished coloured plate by
J. A. Atkinson.)

Note the archaic head-gear of the heavy cavalry of this period.

gaining however upon them. At length seeing they must be caught, they halted and formed; I pursued a little further to secure them, halted, wheeled into Line and charged, just as you have often seen us do at Ipswich. The French fired at us, and stood firm to receive us. We broke them and the result was several killed, 19 wounded, 2 Lt. Cols., 1 Capt, 10 Lieuts. between 150 and 160 Men and 125 Horses and some Mules made prisoners.—Col. Grant, Ajt. Jones and 22 Men of the 15th wounded. The March and the attack were beautiful, nothing could exceed it, but the pursuit was sadly disorderly. I gave the Regiment a good scolding for it after the affair was over, and the answer they gave me was three cheers, and a request that I would accept as a token of their regard the two best Officers' Horses that were taken. You would be pleased, if you were to hear all they say about me. I cannot write it. I am quite well and was not touched. I rode Harlequin,—he carried me admirably over the roughest and most difficult ground that can be imagined. The 18th have had two or three little affairs with the enemy and acquitted themselves admirably. In the last, a Captn, Subn, and about 30 Men attacked 100, killed 20, and made 5 Prisoners. All this is very well, but Spain is gone, nor are the People worth saving. Aff. yours PAGET.'

The orders given to Brigadier-General Slade, commanding the *10th Hussars*, were as follows:

'The 10th Hussars with 4 guns will march from the Monasteries so as to arrive at the Bridge of Sahagun at half-past six in the morning. . . . The object of the movement is to surprise Sahagun. The picquet at the Bridge will be driven in briskly. If serious resistance is shown, a squadron or more may be dismounted, who, followed by a mounted squadron, will enter the town, make for the General's and principal officers' quarters to make them prisoners. The grand object is to drive the enemy through the town, on the other side of which Lt-General Lord Paget will be posted with the 15th Hussars. The moment this object is in way of being accomplished two squadrons of the Tenth must be detached to the left, where the

167

enemy has a piquet of from 60 to 100 men. These must be briskly attacked and made prisoners. This done they will return to Sahagun. (Sd) Paget.

'Morgel de Alaxo; 20th Dec., 1808, ½ 9 p.m.'

Slade records subsequent events in his diary: 'A more dreadful night troops could not be exposed to, as it was particularly dark, a severe frost with sleet falling, and the snow drifted in many places to the depth of four feet. Many horses fell, and one man had his leg broken. We arrived at the bridge at the hour fixed, but the French were gone. We followed through the town and found that the 15th had not ten minutes charged and put them to rout. We joined in the pursuit, when 140 prisoners were made. One of the lieutenant-colonels taken is said to be a relation of the Empress Josephine. The French were prepared for the attack, and were drawn up ready to receive the 15th. I must here observe that the French load their baggage every night, and keep their horses bridled and saddled, the men sleeping in the stables. Had we surprised them, the regiment under my command would in all probability have had hot work, as they were all in a convent, where they could very easily have defended themselves. This convent the Hussar Brigade occupied on the night of the 21st.'

It was said that Napoleon himself had witnessed the action, and had been so annoyed at the poor showing of the French regiment that he degraded it from the Guard to the Line.

An interesting sequel to this engagement took place some four and a half years later, which will be recounted in due course.

Lack of control in the pursuit was a constant failing of the British cavalry in the Napoleonic wars, which cost them the fruits of many a success and heavy casualties in men and horses. They received many strictures from Wellington in consequence and the Duke's comments on his cavalry and its commanders were more often uncomplimentary than not. This was not always so, however; for, at Salamanca, after witnessing the brilliant charge of the Dragoons, Wellington turned to Sir Stapleton Cotton (later Lord Combermere), who commanded the first Cavalry Division, and exclaimed: 'By God, Cotton, I never saw anything so beautiful in my life; the day is *yours*'.

Mr. J. H. McGuffie's book, *Peninsular Cavalry General*, which has already been quoted, gives a vivid picture of the day-to-day life of a cavalry Brigadier during the campaign.

Writing from Villafranca on 29th May, 1811, Major General Long describes a successful cavalry action at Usagre, shortly after the battle of Albuera. He says:

'If the Enemy leave us in peace and quietness for three days more I shall try to fulfill the promise made in my last letter of sending you a bumper, viz.: a Journal of our proceedings since my last. The period is so long and has been so interesting that it is a formidable task to undertake and one I could not accomplish until I am a little recovered from the fatigue of fourteen as hard days and nights work as ever I experienced in my life.

'My present object is merely to tell you that having followed the Enemy's retrograde movements from Albuera, and keeping quite close to them, we advanced on the 24th inst. to Usagre (in the direction of Llerena) where we found one Regiment of Cavalry which was very soon dislodged from the village, and they at the same time evacuated Benvenida. The next day, however, they returned with all their force of Cavalry, and six pieces of artillery, to recover the ground. At first M. General Lumley had determined to meet them on the other side of the Village. I strongly advised him against it as from the nature of the ground if beaten, the greater part of our force could scarcely escape destruction; and I can never put reliance on any other than the British Troops, which in point of numbers are scarcely one third of the Enemy.

'Accordingly, having ordered back our only 3 Regiments, the whole retired across the defile as the Enemy advanced. They established themselves on the heights on the opposite side of a deep ravine, and likewise took possession of the village. They then formed their guns into a battery and opened a cannonade which we answered. Soon after they pushed 3 Regiments of Dragoons thro' the village to attack our right.

Two of them formed in Columns of attack, the other deployed. This took place in front of the 4th Dragoons and 3rd Dragoon Guards. General Lumley was with the latter Regiment, and not observing the enemy, was actually making a change of position during the time they were advancing. From the badness of the ground which the 3rd Dragoon Guards had to move their column over, I observed them broken and apparently in confusion, the Enemy within 200 yards. To rescue them from this critical state, I immediately directed the 4th Dragoons, supported by the 13th Dragoons to attack, and proceeded to the charge. Scarcely had I advanced 50 yards, when I observed the 3rd Dragoon Guards wheel into line and also move forward to the attack, which in consequence was made simultaneously by both Regiments, and as well as if the whole had been preconcerted and arranged. The Enemy received us, were overset, and having a wall and defile to their rear, were completely broken and beaten with the loss of about 30 to 40 killed (we counted 30 on the ground, the rest were killed in the village) and 78 taken prisoners. Among the latter one Colonel, one Major and 2 Lieutenants; one officer besides killed. The number of horses about 60, exclusive of those seized and carried off by the Spaniards, when delivered over to them in the rear. Our loss not above 3 killed and four wounded.'

Some six weeks after this affair Long had doubts about his military future, and a letter of his expresses a mood which nearly every professional soldier feels at times:

'I also hear of great expected changes at the Horse Guards. I never was enamoured of that pile, even when it contained the friends I value most. How it will appear when big with frowns and haughtiness instead of smiles and condescension, I leave you to judge. There is room enough, thank God! both in front and rear of it, to *turn a horse about*, and I must practice mine to expertness in this manœuvre. Neither beggary nor wooden shoes shall ever make me a Courtier, therefore prepare your cabbage seeds and when these squabbles are over I will bury all ambition (should a remnant remain) in the Bay of Biscay, and prepare to cultivate them for you. The thanks of Parliament, recently bestowed, shall be folded up with the Parchment Roll of Family Pedigree, and indexed

Thanks of the Country

to

Robert Long

Major General and Cabbage Planter

Who had luck enough to do his public duty

Sense enough to know when he had done it,

and

Wisdom enough to prefer Cabbage-planting

to

Dependence upon Princes or Power

for

More substantial happiness

Bello finito

Requiescat in pace!

'I have just received an invitation to dine at Head Quarters to meet the Prince of Orange, who has just arrived to take a lesson in the art of human butchery.'

Another letter of Long's shows the sort of equipment which was required for the mess of a cavalry brigade commander on active service:

'I must now send you some commissions which you will have executed for me as well as you can. First of all I am much distressed for plates and dishes, my canteen holding only half a dozen of rusty tin ones. Now I think you might procure me a small set of the cheapest Wedgewood, sufficient let us say for 12 persons; viz:

'1½ dozen soup plates; 4 dozen meat plates; a Soup tureen; 4 *Medium* sized dishes for joints of meat; 10 or 12 small side dishes for made dishes, vegetables, etc.; 2 Butter boats; 1 dozen good sized tea cups; 1 dozen saucers; A good Wedgewood teapot and milk jug and slop dish.

'The whole of the above to be neatly, equally and securely packed in two baskets covered with oil cloth or horse skin, so as to be quickly and easily put up and taken out, to be as nearly as possible of the same weight, and a small space to be left in each basket for table clothes. In general plates travel

171

best when arranged edges upwards. I wish the whole to go in the smallest possible space consistent with security and celerity in packing. Now the sooner the above could be procured and sent the better. Let them be plain but neat, but strapped round with canteen straps and brass padlocks. When ready they may be sent to Portsmouth to the care of Lt. General Whetham, the Lt. Governor, to whom I will write, addressed to me as follows;

'M. General Long, Portugal, To the care of Captain Brayman (King's German Legion), Town Major's Office, Lisbon.

'Pay for them by a draft on Greenwood and Cox. Likewise wish Windeler to send me a new plain undress Major General's coat, for I am in rags. I believe I begged a hat in a former letter. I think you will find in the drawer in my room bureau, some very good table-cloths. Send a few with the baskets, and let Windeler enclose in the box he forwards (adressed as above) a pair of calico sheets, which I think are also to be found in the same bureau.'

Long gives a melancholy picture of the state of the cavalry after the retreat of 1812. He says:

'The remounts for my Brigade, with James, etc., were within two days march of us, but were ordered back on our retiring from the Tagus, and I have heard no more of them. I hope they will not wander into the Enemy's clutches.

'My Brigade is nearly unfit for the field. The 9th and 13th Dragoons scarcely muster 400 swords, the men are naked and starving with cold, the horses upon their last legs. Nevertheless we appear to be preferred for harassing services, and in a short time more we shall cease to exist as a Brigade. Slade's Brigade destroyed nearly 50 horses in one day from inability to proceed. The Northern Cavalry has I am told suffered equally, and if so our force in this arm will not be very formidable.'

A curious incident of the Peninsular campaign is related in his recollections by Private James Smithies of the *1st Royal Dragoons*. His regiment moved to Santarem in January, 1810, and returned there again after the battle of Busaco in September of that year. The incident occurred during the advance, and he writes:

Plate X

OFFICER, THE 6TH (INNISKILLING) DRAGOONS, 1811.

*(By kind permission from the original water-colour by Dighton now in
the possession of Captain Russell Steele.)*

Note the Service-dress overalls with the leather bottoms and
the shako which had practically replaced the uniform cocked-
hat for active service.

'It was now coming on for winter, and it would have to be decided whether the French should be allowed to encamp in Portugal, or, if possible, we were to drive them out of the country. Various rumours were afloat in the army to the effect that the French were meditating a retreat, and to discover the truth of this rumour, several of the commanding officers went out upon a reconnoitring tour—our chief officer went, and took me as his orderly. We could see by the telescope the place where the French had been encamped, but could perceive no sign of life whatever, though the sentries seemed to be posted in their usual places. We approached these sentries as cautiously as possible, not wishing to attract any attention, and when we got nearer to them we noticed that they continued to face us in the same manner as when we first saw them. My officer ordered me to challenge the one nearest to us, which I did, but received no reply. I thought I'd make the fellow either speak or run, so I charged him at full gallop, and cut him in two, but great was our surprise to find, instead of a living sentry, it was a dummy on horseback stuffed with straw. We discovered other dumb sentries placed along the line. It was found that under cover of darkness, and during a very heavy mist which hung over the mountain sides, they had broken up their position and beat a retreat.'

A complete brigade of Hussars was sent out to the Peninsula from England in 1813. A colourful character, Colquhoun Grant, was appointed to the command of this new formation; being preferred before Long, who was recalled to England. Grant's brigade adjutant was a Lieutenant Charles Jones of the *10th Hussars*. In his *On the Road with Wellington* Augustus Schaumann says: 'The latter [*i.e.* Jones] was a small man with fox-red hair, a red moustache and red whiskers, and he also wore a red shako. It was very funny to see him galloping behind the tall, black-whiskered general, who wore an enormous three-cornered hat with a long fluttering feather; and from that day those two were never spoken of in the brigade except as the black giant and his red dwarf.'

On 2nd June, 1813, the Hussar Brigade encountered again

the *16th French Dragoons*, whom it had defeated at Sahagun in 1808. Wellington mentioned the ensuing engagement in a letter to Sir Thomas Graham. He wrote:

'The Tenth had a very handsome affair this morning with the enemy's cavalry between this and Morales. Their loss is small, but they must have destroyed the enemy's 16th Dragoons, of whom they took 200 prisoners. The enemy showed in great strength in cavalry about Pedrosa del Rey.'

Wellington gave the following fuller account in his official despatch:

'The troops have continued to advance since the 31st of last month, and were on the 1st at Zamora, and on the 2nd they arrived at Toro. The English Hussars being in the advanced guard, fell in between Toro and Morales with a considerable body of the enemy's cavalry, which were immediately attacked by the Tenth supported by the 18th and 15th. The enemy were overthrown and pursued for many miles, and 210 prisoners, with many horses fell into our hands. I enclose Colonel Grant's report of this gallant affair, which reflects great credit upon Major Roberts and the 10th Hussars and upon Colonel Grant, under whose directions they acted.'

The young Marquess of Worcester was an officer in the leading squadron in this attack, and he relates how his regiment overthrew the French in one fierce charge, and continues: 'It then became a chase across country over the prickly pear hedges, the pace being so good that the rest of the Hussar Brigade in support could not get up; and nearly the whole of the enemy's dragoons were destroyed or taken prisoners'.

The long pause on the French frontier gave opportunities for more peaceful recreation. Colonel R. S. Liddell records in his *Memoirs of the Tenth Royal Hussars* that two packs of hounds were kept at St.-Jean-de-Luz. One of these belonged to Lord Wellington, and the other to a Commissariat Officer named Marsden. The meets drew a large number of enthusiastic officers, some of them well mounted, but others on any mount they could find; mostly the local ponies, but often, even, mules.

On one occasion the fox crossed the River Bidassoa and ran right into the enemy's lines, the hounds following. The field halted on the British side of the river, whilst the French, in some bewilderment, stood to arms. Marsden, the Master, however, rode forward holding his white handkerchief above his head as a flag of truce, and explained what had happened. The French, with great courtesy, permitted him to enter their lines and recover his hounds!

A very interesting addition was made to the Army during the Peninsular campaign. This was the Royal Staff Corps, which was formed to undertake a number of different duties under the direction of the Quartermaster General's Staff. (In the Napoleonic wars and for very many years afterwards the Q.M.G. Staff was responsible for those staff functions which are performed by the General Staff to-day.) From the Royal Staff Corps, in turn, was formed the Corps of Staff Guides, a mounted unit which was specifically charged with the collection of information. Part of the Corps of Staff Guides, however, was diverted to the running of the 'army despatch office' and the transmission of messages by semaphore. The unit was, therefore, the forerunner of *The Royal Corps of Signals*, the last horsed soldiers to be added to the Army List. These signal communications became so much an integral part of the Peninsular Army that in the Waterloo campaign reference is made to the 'department of Military Communications', despite the fact that by this time the Corps of Staff Guides had ceased to exist. To a certain extent, however, the Royal Staff Corps seems to have undertaken the communication duties of its offspring; for Colonel Basil Jackson, in his *Recollections of Waterloo*, says, 'On the portentous night in question, several (mounted staff officers) chiefly belonging to the Royal Staff Corps . . . were employed in conveying duplicates of the instructions previously forwarded by hussars, in order to guard against the possibility of mistake'. The Hussars employed on these intercommunication duties were probably under the direction of the Royal Staff Corps.

The concentration of the Army for the Waterloo campaign

entailed the movement of a considerable number of troops from the United Kingdom. The movement of a troop of Horse Artillery is described in the diary of Lieutenant Ingilby of G Troop, *R.H.A.* The following are extracts:

'Colchester. 24 March, 1815. Intelligence having arrived that Napoleon Buonaparte had relanded in France, it was certain war would recommence, and on the 24th it was intimated that the Troop would be sent to the Netherlands.

'26. Ordered to be in readiness to march at the shortest notice, but we did not receive a route 'till 8th April.

'9 April. Marched to Harwich and embarked a part of the Troop the same afternoon.

'10. Embarked the whole of the remainder of the Troop, carrying the horses off to the transports in boats. My division, in transport Letter "V", proceeded to Ostend.

'11. Wind failed. Dropped anchor on what is called the rolling ground.

'12. At anchor the greater part of the day.

'13. At 2 p.m. anchored in the harbour of Ostend and immediately commenced disembarking the horses, which was accomplished during the daylight, and the whole guns and material by 10 o'clock at night. Each horse had to be dropped into the water and then swum to shore. We were conducted by torch-light to some sheds at a village called Sars, leaving the guns and carriages where we had disembarked.

'May 1. Strythem (10 miles due W. from Brussels). The Officers quartered in an old unfurnished chateau surrounded by a moat. We understand the whole of the Cavalry and Horse Artillery are cantoned in this neighbourhood, from the great plenty of forage it produces of every kind—indeed every inch seems fertilised by the greatest industry.'

Captain Edward Kelly of the *1st Life Guards* distinguished himself at Genappe and Waterloo, and tales of his gallantry on the battlefield became widespread. The following extracts are taken from letters written to his wife during the campaign:

'Canterbury, 29th April, 1815. . . . Our men being all young soldiers makes our march rather laborious and the weather has not been very favourable, having two wet days. We march into Ramsgate tomorrow to embark and we hope to sail on Monday. My little long-tailed horse knocked up, he was too young and I gave £15 back between him and a very good one at Maidstone. . . .'

'Ostend, 3rd May, 1815. . . . I have the pleasure to inform you that we have just arrived here after a passage of three days from Ramsgate, and my horses have been disembarked safe, with the exception of a severe blow on the eye to one of my favourite mares, which I fear will end in her losing the sight of it. I was, as usual, ill the whole voyage and never took off my *cloaths*. I am now pretty well, and we march to Bruges this night—15 miles. . . .'

'Ninove, 18th May, 1815 . . . the whole British Cavalry are within seven miles round, in the finest possible condition and waiting for the ball to open. . . .'

'Ninove, Flanders, 14th June, 1815. . . . We are in hourly expectation of moving—The French are within 20 miles of us and very inferior to our Cavalry. . . . Our Brigade is the admiration of all here and they never looked better in Hyde Park—I command the left squadron as Lind is ill, and I hope to command it in the campaign. . . . My horses are in fine condition. . . .'

'Brussels, 19th June, 1815. . . . The very day after I had the pleasure in addressing my last letter to you we were ordered to March and on the same day after a march of nearly 50 miles arrived upon the field of battle near Nivelle where the French Army commanded by Bonaparte in Person attacked the British and Belgian army commanded by the Duke of Wellington at four o'clock the same day, and the enemy was repulsed with severe loss on our side and the night being so dark the Cavalry could take no part in the engagement of that day. . . . We being on the field of battle that night with our Bridles in our Hands and at Half past 2 o'clock in the Morning, the action recommenced by a Cannonade—We retired from our position— covered by the Cavalry and Horse Artillery and the moment we commenced our retreat one of the most dreadful storms of thunder and rain came on that ever I experienced—the Enemy taking advantage of it pushed forward his Lanciers and Cavalry and came up with Lord Uxbridge after we passed through the town of Genappe. Our Hussars the 7th gave way and left Lord Uxbridge alone on the road within 15 yds of the Lancers of the Imperial Guard.

'The 1st Life Guards were halted and Fronted to them Whale's squadron next the Enemy who came charging in close column up the road in most gallant stile with Spears and Flags in their front. Our men at first gave way and retreated a little when Whale was wounded by a Lancier in the back slightly. I left my squadron and went to the one next the Enemy and charged the Lanciers of the Guard twenty yards in front of my own men and altho there were two of them at me at one time I had the Good Fortune to Kill their Colonel and one of the Privates when our Corporal Major came up just in time to save my life. Our charge was successful and we drove them under their own guns back into the village of Genappe—on our return Lord Uxbridge thanked the Regiment in face of the Whole Cavalry of the army and said Capt Kelly I have marked your conduct and shall mention *you* particularly to the Duke of Wellington.

'The Blues suffered by the Cannonade a little and we lost only two or three men and horses in the charge, we bivouacked again that night near the enemy under a most heavy rain the whole night. I then commanded Whale's squadron the next day, when the enemy attacked at 11 o'c and one of the most bloody engagements that ever was fought took place and continued until dark,—then the enemy was obliged to give over the attack and I was unfortunately obliged to leave the field from a cannon shot having torn away part of the flesh of my right leg. . . .

'I had three horses wounded under me and at last mounted a trooper who is also much cut in the head by the French Cuirassiers of the Guard who were also repulsed and beat twice off the field to the rear of their own infantry. . . .

'P.S. My beautiful bay mare was wounded in the head by a

Plate XI

TROOPER, 6TH (INNISKILLING) DRAGOONS, *circa* 1815.

(From the water-colour drawing now in the possession of
Lieutenant-Colonel Peter Young.)

The same regiment as the previous plate, four years later.

Lancier and I fear she is lost she carried me beautifully in action and I would almost prefer being wounded myself to having lost her. . . .'

The charge of the Union Brigade at Waterloo is well described by Lieutenant A. J. Hamilton of *The Royal Scots Greys*:

'I was returned on full pay when the Emperor landed from Elba, and was appointed galloper to General Sir William Ponsonby, who commanded the Brigade, and as I was the only subaltern in it whom he knew, he asked me to be with him on the 17th and 18th June. When the General appeared on the ground I joined him, his A.D.C. being at Brussels whither the General had sent him, not expecting the action to begin so early, if at all that day. His Major of Brigade and an officer who acted as extra-A.D.C. were however with him. After he had looked at the Brigade we proceeded to the top of the hill, leaving the Brigade drawn up close at the bottom of it. The French cannonade began, and I was sent to desire the commanding officers of the different regiments to draw them up as close to the hill as possible as they began to suffer both from shot and shell.

'The cannonade now greatly increased and under cover of the smoke from their cannon and our own the French advanced. The General observing what was about to take place, immediately sent me down to bring up the Brigade with all speed. I did so. The General met us just before we reached the summit of the hill. Our three regiments of Dragoons were not quite in line, the [Royal] Dragoons on the right and some yards in advance, so the General placing himself in front of them they charged a little before the others did. The French gave us only a partial volley, being in some disorder, having no knowledge of our Brigade being so near at hand; we accordingly went right through them—not a horse as is usually the case went round from the fire—and the enemy threw down their arms. The other regiments coming up, we again charged, the General riding along the whole line to the left of the Brigade, so that we saw the whole three regiments charge—the result the same—the enemy throwing down their arms and begging their lives. In the conflict two eagles were taken. We ought to have stopped and reformed the Brigade, but our men still went on. The General however had collected about thirty of his men, when Colonel ―― came past us at full gallop with about twenty of his men, in a second all those we had collected set off in the same direction. In the hopes of stopping them we followed, and passed between the columns of French infantry when the Red Polish Lancers closed in behind us. After a hand-to-hand encounter with them, the first person I saw was Captain ――, the General's extra-A.D.C., who had lost sight of him some minutes before I had. We sought for assistance to rescue the General and others from the hands of the French. I went to Lord E. R. S., who commanded the Life Guards Brigade, to Sir J. V.'s Brigade and to another Regiment without avail. "No orders", was the reply to my request. I then joined my regiment.'

Major General Sir William Ponsonby was killed in this charge.

James Smithies of the *Royal Dragoons* has something to say about Waterloo. He comments that, 'for the first time ever known in our army, the cavalry were ordered to grind the backs of their swords, as so our Captain Clarke said, we should have to use both sides. It was thought by the men that this order had been given because we had to contend with a large number of French Cuirassiers, who had steel armour, and through this we should have to cut.'

In Smithies' account of the charge he describes how some of the opposing troopers caught hold of each other's bodies, wrestling fashion and fighting for life. He adds that he did the same as the rest and got through as well as he could. He tells how when they encountered the French Lancers they found that they had the lance fastened to a foot, 'and when we reared them, they sent it out with all their might; and if the man at which they aimed did not manage to parry the blow, it was all over with him'.

Some of the experiences of the Light Cavalry in the battle

Plate XII

OFFICER, 8TH THE KING'S ROYAL IRISH HUSSARS, *circa* **1823.**

(Reproduced from a contemporary water-colour.)

This picture shows well the lavish dress of both officer and horse at this period.

were narrated by Captain Charles Wood of the *10th Hussars* in a series of letters, of which the following are extracts:

'I got hit just as the Duke moved to the attack and bled like a pig. I took up my stirrups into the hunting seat and made the best of my way back to Waterloo. With the assistance of a Dragoon I afterwards got into Brussels, and found a lodging in the Rue Royale. Arnold [Lieutenant Robert Arnold] will come home with me. He was shot through the lungs. They tell me he must not eat meat for six months. He says, "Wait till I get to Northampton with five hunters next November. . . ." Quentin [Lieutenant-Colonel Quentin, the commanding officer] is going to Paris to-morrow in a carriage [He was wounded in the ankle]. . . . Bob Manners [Lieutenant-Colonel Lord Robert Manners, second-in-command] was struck in the shoulder by a lance, and did not find it out until the next day. . . . You should have seen us all the night before the fight. Every one wet through. We had a shower that came down like a wall. Our horses could not face it, and all went about. It made the ground up to the horses' fetlocks. We got into a small cottage close to our bivouac, about a mile in rear of the position, most of us naked, and getting our things dry at the fire. I managed to get "Paddy" [Wood's charger] a shop for the night. Old Quentin burnt his boots, and could not get them on. . . . We had to feed on what we found in the hut, beginning with the old hens for supper and the young chickens for breakfast. I see the English papers say, "The Light Dragoons could make no impression on the French Cuirassiers". Now our regiment actually rode over them. Give me the boys that will go at a swinging gallop for the last seventy yards, applying both spurs when you come within six yards. Then if you don't go right over them I am much mistaken. . . . I have found the ball which went right through my thigh into the pad of my saddle, very high up. I think it hit the bone, which drove it upwards.'

Of the cavalry at Waterloo, Wellington said in his official despatch:

'The enemy repeatedly charged our infantry with his cavalry, but these attacks were uniformly unsuccessful, and they afforded opportunities to our cavalry to charge, in one of which Lord E. Somerset's brigade consisting of the life guards, royal horse guards, and 1st dragoon guards, highly distinguished themselves, as did that of Major General Sir W. Ponsonby, having taken many prisoners and an eagle.'

CHAPTER XI

THE GOLDEN AGE OF HORSES

After the Napoleonic wars the Army returned to an England which was being transformed by the magnificent roads and bridges which, due primarily to two Scottish engineers— McAdam and Telford—were forming a network of good and rapid communications over the country. Until the end of the eighteenth century the roads had been appalling. In summer they frequently had great three-foot deep ruts which could break a horse's leg, and in winter they were often churned into impassable bogs. A waggon which stuck in rut or mud might require twenty or thirty horses to drag it out, and horses sometimes sank up to their girths where traffic and rain had formed deep pools of liquid mud in the unmetalled roads. As late as 1796 a Mr. Robert Bealson had suggested fixing a roller to the bottom of a carriage so that when the wheels dropped into ruts the broad surface of the roller would prevent the vehicle from sinking to the axle and getting stuck. In the winter of 1797–8 the main road from London to Oxford was over a foot deep in mud for most of its length.

Under these circumstances wheeled transport was slow and uncomfortable and most people, who could afford it, travelled on horseback. There was little change in the speed of wheeled traffic in the eighteenth century. The following stage-coach advertisement of 1706 is probably typical:

'YORK Four Days
Stage-Coach
Begins on Friday *the* 12*th of* April 1706
All that are desirous to pass from *London* to *York* or from *York* to *London* or *any* other Place on that Road; Let them Repair to the *Black Swan* in *Holbourn* in *London,* and to the *Black Swan* in *Coney street* in *York.*

At both Places they may be received in a Stage Coach every *Monday*, *Wednesday* and *Friday* which performs the whole Journey in Four Days, (*if God permits*) And sets forth at Five in the Morning.

And returns from *York* to *Stamford* in two days, and from *Stamford* by *Huntington* to *London* in two days more. And the like Stages on their return.

Allowing each Passenger 14 ls weight and all above 3d a Pound.

Performed by
$\begin{cases} Benjamin\ Kingman \\ Henry\ Harrison \\ Walter\ Baynes \end{cases}$

Also this gives Notice that Newcastle Stage Coach sets out from York every Monday, and Friday, and from Newcastle every Monday, and Friday.'

At the foot of the copy of this advertisement, in the writer's possession, is the following manuscript note:

'Recd. in pt 05.00.0 of Mr. Bodingfold for 5 places for Monday the 3 of June 1706.'

In 1742 the Oxford coach left London at 7 o'clock in the morning and took ten hours to cover the forty miles to High Wycombe. There it stayed the night and went on to Oxford the following day. Night travel seems to have been unusual; probably due both to the badness of the roads and to the danger of attack by highwaymen.

Half-way through the century the speed of coach travel must have actually decreased; for in 1754 an advertisement for the 'Flying Coach', which was to be started between London and Manchester, said that, 'incredible as it may appear, this coach will actually arrive in London in four days and a half after leaving Manchester'. The distance was 187 miles, so that the average speed was considerably less than that of the London–York coach of 1706. In 1779, according to the *Edinburgh Courant*, the London Coach 'will run every Tuesday, occupying ten days, resting all Sunday at Barrowbridge'.

The first great improvement came in 1784 when the first mail coach ran from London to Bristol, covering the journey of

Plate XIII

AN OFFICER, 15th HUSSARS, *circa* 1827.

(By kind permission of the Colonel of the 15th/19th Hussars.)

117 miles in seventeen hours, at an average speed of nearly seven miles an hour, which was about double the speed of the mounted post-boys, who had previously carried all the mails. Eight years later sixteen mail coaches left London every day, and by the end of the century the number had risen to about eighty.

In the early years of the nineteenth century the work of McAdam was beginning to bear fruit. Between 1798 and 1814 he travelled over 30,000 miles of road, and in 1818 his system was officially approved.

McAdam's method consisted of spreading small pieces of hard stone over the surface of the subsoil to a depth of about a foot, none of the pieces being more than 6 ounces in weight. The solid, closely knit mass of stone was covered with a carpet of finer-grained stone and then stamped or rolled into a smooth and compact crust, which was cemented by the setting of the powder. These 'macadamized' roads, combined with Telford's engineering of bridges and improved roadways, resulted in a revolution in road transport. As an old coachman said, in describing the bad roads of earlier days: 'Then came Mr. McAdam, with his hammers, sand, and resin, and the crooked places were made straight, and the rough places plain and hard'.

Some idea of what military movement of guns and transport must have entailed on the old roads is conveyed in a vivid description given by Daniel Bourn in his *Treatise of Wheeled Carriages* of 1763. He says: 'So late as thirty or forty years ago the roads of England were in a most deplorable condition. Those that were narrow were narrow indeed, often to that degree that the stocks of the wheels bore hard against the bank on each side, and in many places they were worn below the level of the neighbouring surface, many feet, nay, yards perpendicular; and a wide-spreading brushy hedge intermixed with old half-decayed trees and stubbs hanging over the traveller's head intercepting the benign influence of the heavens from his path, and the beauties of the circumjacent country from his view, made it look more like the retreat of wild beasts and reptiles than the footsteps of man. In other parts where the road was wide, it might be, and often was too much so, and exhibited a scene of a different aspect. Here the wheel-carriage had worn a diversity of tracks which were either deep, or rough and stony, or high or low as Mother Nature had placed the materials upon the face of the ground; the space between these were frequently furzy hillocks of thorny brakes, through or among which the equestrian traveller picked out his entangled and uncouth steps.

'To these horrible, stony, deep, miry, uncomfortable, dreary roads the narrow-wheel waggon seems to be best adapted, and these were frequently drawn by seven, eight, or even ten horses, that with great difficulty and hazard dragged after them twenty-five or thirty hundredweight, seldom more.'

As the network of macadamized trunk roads spread across the country, so the great towns became linked by a really fast service of stage and mail coaches. There grew up, in fact, the fastest and most efficient land transport system that the world had ever seen; a system which has caught the imagination of men to such an extent that the great days of the stage-coach have become enveloped in an aura of romance out of all proportion to the length of time which they lasted. The best coaches ran to an overall average speed, including all stops for meals and changing horses, of ten miles an hour and upwards. The inns of England formed the framework of the system. The coaches started and finished at inns, and it was the stables of the inns along the routes which housed the horses for the stage and mail coaches, and also, together with post-boys, for the private carriages. It was the golden age of the horse, but before it had reached its prime it was suddenly extinguished by the rapid advance of the iron rail and steam. By 1840 the stage-coach, except as a feeder to the railway, had gone. It disappeared so rapidly that almost overnight the once-thriving inns were almost deserted; their stables empty and dining-rooms silent.

Nevertheless these marvellous coaches were the foundation on which our modern transport system was built; for they set an example of smartly timed and rigidly adhered to schedules

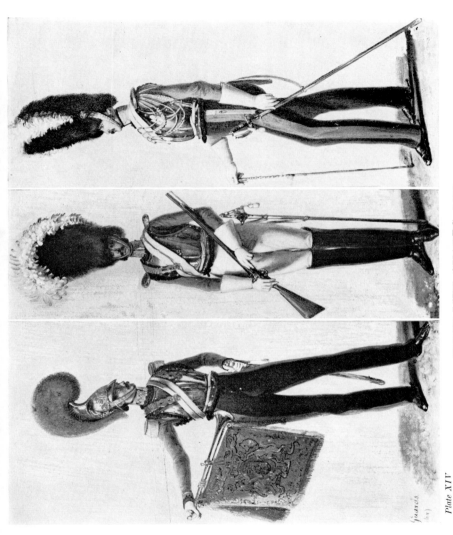

Plate XIV

FIRST LIFE GUARDS. 1833.

(By gracious permission of H.M. The Queen).

Note the new bearskin head-dress. The trumpeter is wearing the old helmet.

which the public came to expect, and the railways had therefore to follow.

There was some difference between the mail and the stage coaches. Most of the mail coaches started their journey from London at night. Those for the north and south assembled in Lombard Street between 8 and 8.20 every evening to receive their mails, and formed up in double file. Each coach was called forward in turn by the name of its destination, and, on being summoned, broke ranks and came up to the door of the post office to receive its mails. The bags were tossed into the boot, and the slamming shut of the lid was the signal to start. Most of the mails for the West started at 7 P.M. from the Gloucester Coffee House in Piccadilly. The bags for the coaches were brought in gigs from the General Post Office.

The mail coaches were painted black with red undercarriage and wheels, and had the Royal Arms emblazoned on the door panel. Above this was the route served; *e.g.* 'LIVERPOOL LONDON ROYAL MAIL'. On each upper quarter was one of the stars of the four chief Orders of Knighthood: the Garter, the Thistle, St. Patrick and the Bath. Four persons could be carried inside, and three or four outside, in addition to the coachman and the guard. The latter had a small seat behind all to himself, and carried a sword, a blunderbuss, and the long horn popularly known as a 'yard of tin'. No baggage could be carried on the roof of the mail coach.

The stage-coaches were considerably more heavily loaded. Under an Act of 1810 they could carry luggage up to a certain height on the roof, and nine outside passengers in addition to the coachman and guard.

These light, fast coaches created a demand for lighter and more active harness horses, and in the production of these England became celebrated. This development was, of course, of considerable benefit to the Army. The demand for coach horses was so enormous that the modest requirements of the Army could be met easily, and the improvement in the roads was accompanied by a much better type of horse for the haulage of guns and transport.

The number of horses required to work a coach was approximately the same as the distance in miles of the journey one way. That is to say, that if a coach had to run between two towns 200 miles apart, 200 horses would be necessary. Horses normally worked over a stage of about ten miles, and for this ten horses were required. Of these four provided a team for the up coach, four a team for the down coach, and two were resting. A coach horse, therefore, did one hour's work a day for three consecutive days and rested the fourth day. But the pace was hard, and four years was the average time that a horse could last in first-class service. He would then have to be transferred to lighter or slower work.

The fastest coach in the country was the 'Quicksilver', or Devonport Mail, which carried the foreign mails to the Falmouth Packet station. In 1837 it was timed as follows:

Miles	*Place*		*Time*	
0	London, St. Martins le Grand	dep.	8.0	P.M.
29	Bagshot	,,	10.47	,,
67	Andover	,,	2.20	A.M.
80	Amesbury	,,	3.39	,,
125	Ilchester	,,	7.50	,,
154	Honiton	,,	11.0	,,
170	Exeter	arr.	12.34	P.M.
		dep.	12.44	P.M.
190	Ashburton	,,	2.41	,,
214	Plymouth	,,	5.5	,,
216	Devonport	,,	5.14	,,
234	Liskeard	,,	7.55	,,
246	Lostwithiel	,,	9.12	,,
254	St. Austell	,,	10.20	,,
268	Truro	,,	11.55	,,
279	Falmouth	arr.	1.5	A.M.

The above timings do not show the meal stops, but there was usually one for breakfast and one for dinner (a midday meal), each of about twenty minutes. In addition there were a few other stops of five minutes each for the convenience of passengers. Including all these, however, it will be observed that

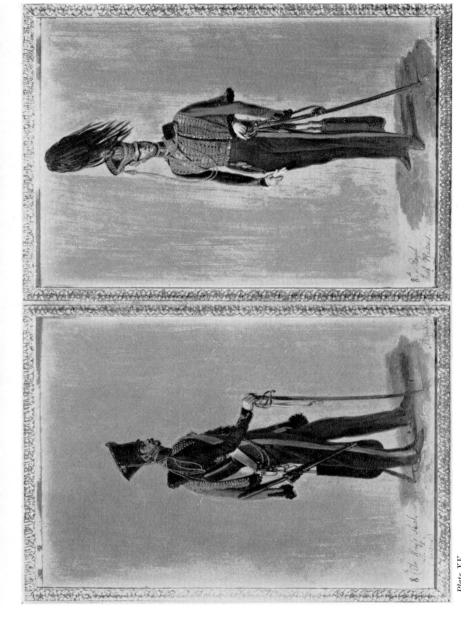

Plate XV

8TH HUSSARS, 1833.

(By gracious permission of H.M. The Queen, from the painting by Dubois Drahonet at Windsor Castle.)

The Hussars at this period were not wearing the busby.

this coach averaged just over ten miles per hour from London to Devonport. The speed from there on was slower, but it included the crossing of the Tamar to Saltash and very hilly roads through Cornwall.

Even when they were running there was a glamour about these coaches which no other form of land transport ever seems to have acquired; and in spite of the derogatory remarks which have been made in latter days about their discomfort, they fascinated contemporary society. It was never considered to be in any way derogatory to drive a stage-coach. The coachmen of the crack coaches were treated with respect, and often awe, by everybody; and many of Wellington's old soldiers, both officers and other ranks, were to be found on the box.

An old coachman, Jerry Drag, who drove the 'Highflyer', the 'Red Rover' and the 'Marquess of Huntley', said what many felt:

'Them as 'ave seen coaches, afore rails came into fashion, 'ave seen something worth remembering; them was happy days for Old England, afore reform and rails turned everything upside down, and men rode as natur' intended they should, on pikes [*i.e.* turnpike roads] with coaches and smart active cattle, and not by machinery, like bags of cotton and hardware; but coaches is done for ever, and a heavy blow it is. They was the pride of the country, there wasn't anything like them, as I have heard a gemmen say from forren parts, to be found nowhere, nor never will be again.'

A song called *The Tantivy Trot*, which became very popular about the time when the threat from the railways first became felt, expresses something of the spirit of these great days of the horse:

> Here's to the heroes of four-in-hand fame,
> Harrison, Peyton and Ward, sir;
> Here's to the dragsmen that after them came,
> Ford, and the Lancashire lad, sir.
> > Let the steam pot
> > Hiss till it's hot
> > Give me the speed
> > Of the Tantivy trot.

189

Here's to the arm that holds them when gone,
Still to a gallop inclined, sir.
Heads to the front with no bearing reins on,
Tails with no cruppers behind, sir.
    Let the steam pot
    Hiss till it's hot
    Give me the speed
    Of the Tantivy trot.

Here's to the dear little damsels within,
Here's to the swells on the top, sir;
Here's to the music in three feet of tin;
Here's to the tapering crop, sir.
    Let the steam pot
    Hiss till it's hot
    Give me the speed
    Of the Tantivy trot.

Before the advent of railways fifty miles a day was not considered too much for a pair of horses to do; and there was a recognized routine for such a journey which may well have been used in the Army as well as for civilian carriage horses. After the first ten miles there was a halt for fifteen minutes, during which each horse was given an opportunity to wash out his mouth and a wisp of hay. The next six miles was followed by a halt for half an hour. Harness was taken off and horses were rubbed down and given a peck of corn each. Another ten miles was then done, after which there was another fifteen minutes' halt, with mouth wash and wisp of hay. After the next six miles there was a halt of two hours, and the horses were given hay and a feed of corn. This was followed by another ten miles and the same procedure as after the previous ten-mile stretches. The rest of the journey, of eight miles, was done without a stop. Before their night meal the horses were given a bran mash and, if the weather was cold and wet, some beans thrown in as well.

The great coaching period coincided with the early part of the Industrial Revolution, and with the civil disturbances which went with it. In the absence of a police force, the Yeomanry

Plate XVI

14TH **LIGHT DRAGOONS**, 1833.

(*By gracious permission of H.M. The Queen.*)

The trooper on the right has removed his carbine from the swivel.
Officer, sergeant and trooper.

was largely responsible for keeping the peace, and was frequently called out for lengthy periods.

Even at this period there seems to have been some difficulty in obtaining regulars for the permanent staff of the Yeomanry regiments. After two months' active duty by the *Wiltshire Yeomanry*, it was discovered that Lieutenant Pettit, the Adjutant, was unable to perform his duties efficiently owing to his advanced age. He was seventy-six! The Colonel of the regiment applied for a younger officer, and recommended that Pettit should be retired on pension. The War Office replied that there was no regular officer available, and refused to sanction the appointment of an officer who had never served in the regular cavalry. They also refused to retire Pettit. Six years later Pettit died at his house in Salisbury aged eighty-two, and still Lieutenant and Adjutant!

Pettit's record appears to have been beaten, however, by at least one other cavalry officer. In the churchyard of St. Mary-at-the-Walls in Colchester there is an epitaph on a tombstone which reads:

SACRED
To the Memory of
JOHN ANDREWS
late a Lieut. of British Cavalry
who Died the 3ᵈ of Dec. 1817
Aged 97 Years
He served his Country 81 Years with Fidelity
and was present in the following
Campaigns & Battles
with Prince Eugene in the year 1736 and 1737
at the Battle of Dettingen in 1743 where he was
distinguished as Orderly Dragoon to
GEORGE the Second
at the Battle of Fontenoy in 1745
at the Battle of Culloden in 1746
and at the Storming of the Moro Castle
in the Island of Cuba in 1762

It does not appear, however, that all horse soldiers kept themselves as physically fit as is inferred by these records. In the Journals of Francis Smet, who was Surgeon to the *8th Hussars* from 1815 to 1824, there occurs the following letter written to a patient in India on 16th September, 1815:

'Dear Sir, I told you in my last note that your Fevers depended on your way of living, and that it was of no use to take medicines for their removal unless you altered your way of life, which I believe you either cannot or will not do. . . . I shall not mention to the Adjutant that I have repeatedly urged your being on horseback every morning at 5 o'clock, the restoration of your health and keeping healthy depending hereon. It will depend on yourself to follow my directions given in the way of my Profession, or to act for yourself whatever the consequences may be.'

From this deplorable officer one turns with pleasure to Cornet W. H. B. J. Wilson of the *3rd Dragoon Guards*. In later years he wrote *Green Peas at Christmas: Hunting Reminiscences of William Wilson*, which was published under that title, edited by Sir Guy Fleetwood Wilson. According to the Reminiscences, Cornet Wilson joined the *3rd Dragoon Guards* at the Royal Barracks in Dublin in 1825, where he was 'very kindly' received by Colonel George Holmes, whom he describes as 'a little round country fellow . . . not much of a soldier according to present ideas, but a rare judge of a horse'. Wilson says of his new regiment, 'We were one of the best mounted regiments in the service—fine, strong, upstanding, good shouldered, good-quartered horses, with action and showing breeding. The London carriage horse as he was—tails about eight inches long and squared, which at any rate set off the quarters, and on and off parade we were one of the cleanest regiments in the service.'

In the *11th Light Dragoons* in 1836 each troop had, apparently, horses of one colour; and this may have been the practice in other regiments. Sergeant-Major G. Loy Smith, who joined the regiment at Meerut in that year, says, in his reminiscences, that the two right troops had bays, the third from the right chestnuts, the fourth duns, the fifth piebalds, skewbalds and horses of all colours, the sixth blacks, and the

Plate XVII

TRUMPETERS AND DRUMMERS, 1st KING'S DRAGOON GUARDS, 1927.

(By kind permission of Messrs. Gale & Polden Ltd.)

seventh and eighth greys. He adds that all the horses had very long tails.

In 1819 the first official manual of instruction in riding was issued. It was called 'Instructions in Military Equitation and in the elements of Field Movements of Cavalry'. In this manual it was directed that stirrup leathers should be lengthened two holes. This was in imitation of the very long stirrups and almost straight leg which was in vogue on the Continent. It was an unfortunate habit to copy, for it led to too much dependence on balance and some loss of control over the horse. (Plate XVIII.) However, the British Army has often been cursed by the adoption of some showy stupidity from its military neighbours. This straight-legged seat lasted for about ten years, but for many years after that stirrups were longer than became the custom in later years.

Another retrograde cavalry innovation was the introduction in 1820 of a new sword for light cavalry. It was a much inferior weapon to the sword which had been used with such devastating effect in the Peninsular campaign. The stirrup hilt was retained, but it had a narrower and considerably less curved blade, with its length increased to 34 inches. The long, straight, narrow blade was suitable for thrusting, but the lack of weight and curve made it a very poor weapon for cutting. Two years later the bad heavy cavalry sword was somewhat improved by the substitution of a sharp point for the hatchet end.

In 1829 bayonets were, apparently, at last withdrawn from the cavalry. *The Royal Scots Greys* had them up till this year, though the *1st Royal Dragoons* appear to have got rid of theirs after the Waterloo campaign. It is unlikely that any cavalry regiment actually used bayonets after 1820 at the latest.

Following the official withdrawal of bayonets, a *Horse Guards* Memorandum of 20th July, 1829, directed that all cavalry sentries were in future to mount without carbines, and to salute with swords in the manner prescribed for the sentries of the Household Brigade.

There was certainly no lack of original experiment in cavalry weapons at this period, for the *Essex Standard* of 26th September, 1834, printed the following extract from the *Maidstone Gazette*:

'Experiments are now trying in the depot as to the practicability of arming both heavy and light dragoons with the lance, and lancers with the carbine . . . each will have pistol, carbine, sword and lance.'

Luckily for the unfortunate trooper this extraordinary proposal was never adopted!

CHAPTER XII

EARLY VICTORIAN

The attractive life enjoyed by the early Victorian horse soldier was portrayed in most inviting terms in a *Royal Artillery* recruiting poster of 1845. It read as follows:

'FINE YOUNG MEN

of respectable Parents and Good Character, have an opportunity (if not married or Apprentices) of joining the

ROYAL ARTILLERY

In which Superior Service they may be made gentlemen of and treated accordingly. They must measure 5 feet 8 inches in height and be between Eighteen and Twenty-two years of age. Growing lads not more than Seventeen may be admitted. They will all receive the same Liberal Bounty of £5 15s. 6d.

On their arrival at Head Quarters they will be taught the art of Riding, Driving, Fencing, Gunnery, and the Mechanics, The making and use of Gunpowder, Sky Rockets, and other Fireworks, and by the power of the lever to move a 42-pounder Battering Gun with the same facility as a Penny whistle.

The Cannon used in the Field are called

FLYING ARTILLERY

from the astonishing rapidity of their movements. The Gunners (for so Artillerymen are styled) wear a

SPLENDID UNIFORM

and are well mounted on taking the field.

They are lodged in the finest Barracks in the World. They have Light Work and Good Pay, the best Beef that Kent can afford, and a comfortable place in the Barracks called "The Canteen" set apart for them to see their Friends in and take a cheerful glass; also a splendid Library and Reading Room; a Park and Pleasure Grounds, with a select number of Horses for their Instruction and Amusement. After their "Education" is completed they will have an opportunity afforded them to Travel to Foreign Countries, where they may drink their Wine at Two-pence per Bottle by the new Tariff!! If well conducted they will be promoted to

Non-Commissioned Officers

from whom the Quartermasters are selected, who are the best paid in the Army, and return to see their Friends with money, manners and Experience!! . . .'

Few would disagree with the last word in this remarkable composition, but serving Gunners may well have regarded much of the rest as open to comment!

From Queen's Regulations of 1844 it appeared that for all practical purposes there was now little, if any, difference between heavy and light cavalry. It is there said that: 'The number of Cavalry in the British Army being small . . . it is of the utmost importance that this portion of the Army should be of the best description, that is that both Heavy and Light Cavalry should be equal to the Charge in Line as well as the Duties of Outposts. The Horses which are selected and trained for the Cavalry should therefore be of sufficient height and strength to be capable of performing the duties of that branch of the Service with the greatest efficiency.'

There are some interesting comments on the British cavalry horse of the period in a book called *Cavalry; its History and Tactics*, which was written by Captain L. E. Nolan, and published in 1853. Nolan was the gallant officer who carried the order for the charge of the Light Brigade at Balaclava, and was the first person to be killed in the charge. Nolan writes:

'The power of heavy cavalry lies in the strength and breeding of the horse, and the courage and activity of the rider. The size of the rider, his cuirass, defensive armour, and heavy equipments, detract from the speed and lasting qualities of the horse. . . . In the last war the French Cuirassiers were reduced

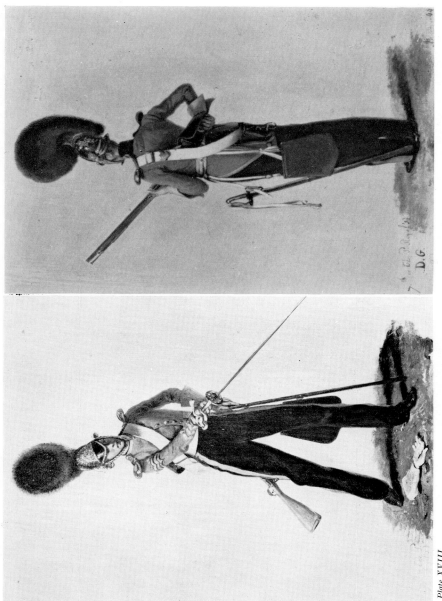

Plate XVIII

7TH DRAGOONS, 1833.

(*By gracious permission of H.M. The Queen.*)

The sergeant's carbine is on its swivel.   The trooper is removing a cartridge from his pouch.

to charge at a trot, their horses being unable to carry such a weight at a quicker pace. . . .

'No horse can compare with the English,—no horse is more easily broken in to anything and everything,—and there is no quality in which the English horse does not excel, no performance in which he cannot beat all competition. . . .

'The English cavalry in India is well mounted. On an emergency any one of these Indian regiments would gallop fifty miles in a pursuit, leave few horses behind, and suffer but little from the effects of such exertion. The horses on which they are mounted are small but powerful. The Arab, the Persian, the Turcoman, the horses from the banks of the Araxes, are all unrivalled as war horses. I have seen a Persian horse fourteen hands three inches carrying a man of our regiment of gigantic proportions, and weighing in marching order twenty-two and a half stone: I have seen this horse on the march alluded to, of eight hundred miles, carrying this enormous weight with ease, and keeping his condition well; at the crossing of the Kistna, a broad, rapid, and dangerous river, the owner of this horse (Private Herne of C Troop) refused to lead the animal into the ferry-boat to cross, but saying "An hussar and his horse should never part company", he took the water in complete marching order, and the gallant little horse nobly stemmed the tide, and landed his rider safely on the opposite bank.

'An officer in India made a bet that he would himself ride his charger (an Arab, little more than fourteen hands high) four hundred measured miles in five consecutive days, and he won the match; the horse performed his task with ease, and did not even throw out a wind-gall. The owner, an officer of the Madras Artillery, died shortly afterwards.

'General Daumas relates that the horses of the Sahara will travel during five or six days from seventy-five to ninety miles a day, and that in twenty-four hours they will go over from one hundred and fifty to one hundred and eighty miles, and this over a stony desert. Diseases of the feet and broken wind are almost unknown amongst them.

'The fine Irish troop-horses, formerly so sought for, are not now to be procured in the market. Instead of the long, low, deep-chested, short-backed, strong-loined horse of former days, you find nothing now but long-legged, straight-shouldered animals, prone to disease from the time they are foaled, and whose legs grease after a common field-day. These animals form the staple of our remount horses.'

At this period most officers in India of average weight rode Cape chargers, and there was a very large import of horses from South Africa. Australian horses, the well-known 'Walers' (from New South Wales), were, however, becoming popular, and in due course replaced the Cape horses. The local horses mentioned by Nolan, known as 'countrybreds', were nearly all entires. In spite of their qualities they were brutes to ride out of the ranks and they were a nuisance in the horse lines. In the tremendous marches which took place during the later campaigns of the Mutiny neither Cape horses nor Walers could stand up to the same amount of gruelling work as the countrybreds.

A *R.H.A.* gunner of the 'forties rode over 18 stone and a driver 16 stone. A gun horse of five years old would probably be 16 hands and weigh 11 hundredweight. Some of the horses in the Artillery lasted for an extraordinarily long time. On a Waterloo Day parade on 18th June, 1846, there was one horse and his rider, both of whom had taken part in the battle. Horses of the Heavy Cavalry carried the biggest weight. About 1860 this, with rations and forage for one day, was about 20 stone 9 pounds.

An interesting side-light on the horse soldier of the 'forties at the battle of Moodkee is contained in a letter written by William Hoff, camp clerk to the Governor General, on 18th December, 1845. He says:

'A pretty long march. On the way, a brush with the enemy was fully expected. Major Broadfoot, who was riding in advance with a few irregulars, had seen a body of Sikh horsemen, and had supposed that a large detachment of their army was at hand. The baggage camels were instantly stopped, and

Plate XIX

THE ROYAL HORSE GUARDS, 1833.

various orders were shouted out, which caused the Cavalry and Horse Artillery to thunder past towards the front. I was uncertain whether a pitched battle was about to take place, or whether we had come upon a hostile fort. After a few anxious moments, I was glad to hear the word passed, that the march should be resumed. Pushing on ahead, I came up with the guns, which were moving in a compact column. Ladies had been sternly prohibited from following the army; it was therefore with surprise that I saw one of that sex on horseback in the midst of the thronging multitude. . . . At 4 o'clock, to the great astonishment of every one, some of Major Broadfoot's men brought us intelligence that the Sikhs were almost upon us— that they were only a mile off! . . . Some of the Artillerymen had no time even to pull their boots on. What a strange wailing sound the trumpets had, or appeared to me to have! How many heard it for the last time! On all sides were the thundering of horses' hoofs and the heavy tramp of men. With incredible speed, they all hurried forward; and silence prevailed in our camp!'

With the coming of steam, trooping to India became a much simpler operation than it had been in the past. But, nevertheless, the movement of mounted units was not carried out without difficulty, and often considerable inconvenience. Troops going to India were normally moved in ships which went all the way, and necessarily travelled via the Cape; the voyage taking about two and a half months. Horses were not taken. If a cavalry regiment was relieving another one in India, which was returning home, it generally took over its horses; otherwise it had to be re-equipped on arrival, which might take some months.

Typical of this latter type of move was that of the *10th Hussars* in 1846. The regiment received orders to proceed to India in March. It was then dispersed in a number of small stations. The concentration of the regiment was the first step, followed by the disposal of the horses. These, with the exception of the few required for the depot troop, were handed over to other regiments to complete establishments or sold locally.

The regiment then had to be increased from six to eight troops in accordance with the Indian establishment. This entailed a real increase of three troops, since one of the original troops was to be left behind as the regimental depot troop.

The additional officers required were made up by those wishing to purchase a commission into light cavalry, by transfer from both cavalry and infantry units, and by the recall of officers on half-pay. Other ranks were required not only to complete the three new troops, but to take the place of men who were either unfit for service in India, or too near their date of discharge to warrant sending. The number necessary was obtained easily from volunteers in other cavalry regiments.

The *10th Hussars* were completed to their new establishment and ready for inspection by the end of April. The inspecting general commented on the remarkably high average height. From which it follows that the regiment was able to pick and choose, and that therefore there must have been a large number of men who found the idea of service in India attractive.

The *10th* embarked in the vessels *Larkins*, *Hindostan* and *Persia*, and sailed between 5th and 7th May, only two months after receiving its first orders. Disembarkation was completed at Bombay by 26th August. Three days later the regiment left by march route for its final destination, Kirkee, reaching there on 7th September.

However, the *10th Hussars* were in for long months of frustration. They were not relieving another regiment, and there were therefore no horses for them. The Commanding Officer had tried to anticipate this difficulty by despatching in advance by the 'overland' route (*i.e.* through the Mediterranean and across Egypt to the Red Sea) a party consisting of a captain in charge, the riding master, the veterinary surgeon and a number of rough riders. But on reaching Bombay they found that suitable horses were quite unprocurable at that time of year. The Arabs, which provided the bulk of the remounts, did not arrive much before the end of October, and the comparatively small supply of Cape horses was temporarily exhausted.

Plate XX

[By gracious permission of H.M. The Queen

THE ROYAL HORSE ARTILLERY, 1833

Note the similarity of the uniform to that of the Hussars in Plate XV.

It was not, in fact, till the middle of March that the first 200 horses were received. Of these some 150 were more or less pure-bred Arabs and Persians, and the remaining 50 were Cape horses. Initially, the regiment was disappointed at the small proportion of the bigger and stronger Cape horses, but they soon came to appreciate the endurance and qualities of the little Arabs. As has already been mentioned, nearly all of them were entires, but in spite of the trouble they gave in biting and kicking and occasionally fighting with one another, the troopers became devoted to them.

Eight years later the *10th Hussars* were ordered to move to the Crimea complete with their horses. They accordingly moved with 738 horses, which included a mount for every man and a percentage of replacements for casualties.

At Bombay men and animals were first embarked in open native boats and taken out to the waiting transports. These were a very mixed bag. They consisted of:

The *Punjab*, a steam vessel of the Indian Navy, which was only just off the stocks and had not yet been fitted with engines. She had, therefore, a lot of accommodation and was able to receive 220 horses. She was, in fact, a floating stable, and it was intended that she should be towed by a steamer on the voyage to Suez.

The *Sultana*, a sailing ship.

The *Auckland*, a steamer which was to tow the *Punjab*.

The *Victoria*, a steamer detailed to tow the *Sultana*.

The *Precursor*, a steamer.

The *Feroze*, a steamer.

The *Clare*, a sailing ship, to be towed by the *Precursor*.

The *Jessica*, a sailing ship which was to be towed by the *Feroze*.

The *Earl Grey*, a sailing ship travelling independently.

The voyage was not without its troubles. The right wing of the regiment sailed ahead of headquarters and the left wing, and ran into a bad storm. The *Jessica* had a particularly bad time. She was carrying over a hundred horses and had a deck load of hay of such proportions that it reached half-way up to the cross-trees. Moreover, the *Feroze*, which was towing her, was herself having such difficulties in the heavy seas that the captain signalled his intention of casting off the tow, as the strain was too great. On learning, however, that the deck load did not allow the *Jessica* to use her sails, and that, furthermore, she was undermanned, the captain of the *Feroze* agreed to carry on as long as the rope held out. Fortunately the storm soon abated. The *Punjab*, on the other hand, though only jury rigged, was found to sail so well that she was constantly getting ahead of her tug, and had to heave-to for the little *Auckland* to catch her up.

Under these conditions the Arab horses gave a lot of trouble, and some became so ferocious that they had to be destroyed. In addition there was an outbreak of glanders which resulted in the loss of some horses.

The two portions of the regiment disembarked in turn at Suez and marched overland to Cairo, the march taking four days. In preparation for this march very efficient arrangements had been made by officers of the Honourable East India Company's Commissariat and Quarter-Master General departments. At each of the planned halting places in the desert, water troughs had been constructed and supply depots established for provisions and forage. Transport for the carriage of supplies and baggage had been obtained from the Egyptian government, who had also undertaken to furnish a daily provision of water from the Nile.

In Cairo the regiment was quartered in the cavalry barracks at Abbassia.

The sailing ship *Earl Grey* sprang a leak during the voyage and had to put into Aden for repair, with the result that the troops on board her did not arrive at Cairo till about a fortnight after the remainder. Five days after their arrival the march was resumed to Alexandria. The going was far worse than the desert portion of the march, owing to the trackless and broken country, and it was twelve days before the *10th* reached Alexandria.

The transports *Etna* and *Himalaya*, which were waiting to

Plate XXI

[From the Coloured Print by William Heath

AN OFFICER OF THE 12TH ROYAL LANCERS, 1820.

(By kind permission of the Commanding Officer, 9th/12th Royal Lancers
(Prince of Wales's).)

take the regiment on to Balaclava, had insufficient accommodation, and 170 men and 168 horses had to be left behind.

One hundred and nine days after leaving Kirkee the *10th Hussars* disembarked at Balaclava, where some months previously had taken place the two most famous cavalry actions in the history of the British Army.

There is an excellent eye-witness account of the charge of the Heavy Brigade which was recorded by an officer of *The Royal Artillery*. The following is an extract:

'On the morning of the 25th October, 1854, "C" Troop, R.H.A. (Captain Brandling), was ordered down . . . in support of the Cavalry Division under Lord Lucan. As the troop came down into the valley a portion of General Scarlett's Heavy Brigade, which was moving away from the direction of the troop's advance, was seen to wheel its left into line and halt. At the same time, Lord Lucan was seen coming down fast from the ridge in their front and Russian cavalry appeared in sight up on the same ridge. The troop . . . passed within 150 yards of the rear of the Heavies and halted about 300 yards to their right rear. Lucan and Scarlett were then seen to be in front of five squadrons, of which three were helmeted and two were in bearskins. On the right was one squadron 6th Inniskilling Dragoons, in the centre were two squadrons 2nd Dragoons (Royal Scots Greys), one behind the other, and on the left were two squadrons 5th Dragoon Guards (Princess Charlotte of Wales's), also four deep. A second squadron Inniskillings was in sight some distance to the right rear. Farther back to the left rear, and not seen by the gunners, were two squadrons 4th Royal Irish Dragoon Guards and two squadrons 1st Royal Dragoons.

'The left wing of the Russian cavalry had shown first on the ridge trotting fast. Their commander, General Ryjoff, was on their left, and as they cleared the ridge they wheeled slightly until their centre was opposite Scarlett's, and then came slowly on. . . . At between 400 and 500 yards from Scarlett they halted, the flanks pulling up slightly after the centre . . . , and moved on, without correcting the dressing, at a hand's jog. As

Scarlett advanced with the first squadron of The Greys the Russians again halted, fired from the saddle, and came slowly on. Scarlett was the first man in, closely followed by his A.D.C., Lieutenant A. Elliot, his trumpeter, and Private Shegog, his orderly, all of the 5th D.Gs. The Inniskilling squadron moved almost simultaneously with The Greys, followed in quick succession by the leading squadron 5th D.Gs. and the second squadrons of The Greys and 5th D.Gs. Next the detached squadron Inniskillings, keeping perfect dressing, tore in at a great pace on to the Russian left flank, and took them on their bridle hands with great effect. The going was good and slightly uphill and as the six squadrons drove deep into the solid mass of Russians, numbers of the latter on foot and some loose horses appeared making off to their left. The two squadrons 4th D.Gs. now came up level with the Russian right flank, wheeled into line and charged, followed immediately by both squadrons of the Royals, who came in against the overlapping right front. The Russians, tormented beyond endurance and utterly unable to make head against their aggressors, broke away to their left and tried to rally. They were spread over acres of ground. At once Brandling advanced, broke them up with the fire of his guns, and they retreated over the ridge. In eight minutes all was over and a few minutes afterwards the Heavies looked as quiet and formidable as if they had never been engaged.'

A survivor of the charge (Major Thornhill) describing it in after years said: 'It was just like a *mêlée* coming in or out of a crowded theatre, jostling horse against horse, violent language, hacking and pushing, till suddenly the Russians gave way'.

The much less successful charge of the Light Brigade, which took place the same day, has become far the better known of the two. Out of ten people who have heard of the action by the Light Brigade it may be doubted whether one has heard of the brilliant success of the Heavies.

The order which launched the Light Brigade on what is probably regarded as the most famous charge in history is still in existence and is the property of the Royal United Service

Plate XXII   TROOPER, REVIEW ORDER, 9TH LANCERS, 1841.

(By kind permission of the Colonel of the 9th Queen's Royal Lancers, from the oil-painting by J. Loder.)

The crossed lances badge of the regiment can be seen on the shabracque below the Royal Cipher.

Institution. It is a short note in pencil, which was scribbled in the saddle with a sabretache as a writing desk by General Airey, Quarter-Master General to Lord Raglan, the Commander-in-Chief. It reads as follows:

'Lord Raglan wishes the cavalry to advance rapidly to the front, follow the enemy & try to prevent the enemy carrying away the guns. Troop horse artillery may accompany. French cavalry is on your left. Immediate. R. Airey.'

The order was hardly a model of clarity. It did not say which of the two cavalry brigades was to attack or whether both were intended; nor did it specify which were the guns referred to.

Captain Nolan of the C.-in-C.'s staff, the author of the work on cavalry already referred to, was directed to carry the order. He was already at a gallop when Lord Raglan called after him, 'Tell Lord Lucan that the cavalry should attack immediately'.

Lord Lucan, commanding the Cavalry Division, was puzzled. He could see no enemy and no guns, for he was too far down in the valley to have the same view of the battlefield as had Lord Raglan. He accordingly asked Nolan for further information. A short time later Nolan was dead, but according to Lucan he replied, 'There, my Lord, is the enemy; there are your guns'.

Lucan thereupon despatched Nolan with his message to Lord Cardigan commanding the Light Brigade. The commander of the Cavalry Division did not immediately amplify the instruction; for between him and his subordinate (who was also his brother-in-law) there was, unfortunately, a bitter enmity. The two commanders, widely different in character, were only alike in two respects. Both were outstandingly gallant in action. Both were unfitted to command any cavalry unit larger than a squadron.

Having delivered his message, Nolan joined his friend, Captain Morris, commanding the *17th Lancers*, and asked his permission to accompany the regiment in the charge.

In the meantime Lucan rode over to Cardigan and told him that the order implied that he was to advance to the end of the valley, and that he would support him with the Heavy Brigade. Cardigan saluted with his sword and pointed out that he had no knowledge of the Russian strength nor of the enemy's tactical dispositions. Lord Lucan replied, 'I know, but Lord Raglan will have it'. Cardigan saluted again and rode over to his second-in-command, Lord George Paget, with the remark, 'Well, here goes the last of the Brudenells'. (Brudenell was Cardigan's family name.)

Cardigan drew up the Brigade in two lines. In the first were the *13th Light Dragoons* (Colonel Charles Edmund Doherty), the *11th Hussars* (*Prince Albert's Own*) (Colonel John Douglas), and the *17th Lancers* (Captain Morris); and in the second line the *4th Light Dragoons* (Lord George Augustus Frederick Paget) and the *8th Hussars* (*King's Royal Irish*) (Colonel Frederick George Shewell). The last regiment, however, was weak in numbers as it provided a large detachment as escort to Lord Raglan. The above order was altered slightly by Lucan, who ordered the *11th Hussars* to take up a position behind the *13th* and *17th*, thus altering the formation to three lines.

Cardigan took post in front of the Brigade. His second-in-command, Paget, was in front of the centre of the third line. The latter has related in his journal an amusing preliminary to the charge.

'After we had mounted and just before we commenced our advance, Colonel Shewell, commanding the 8th Hussars, happened to rest his eye on one of his men with a pipe in his mouth, which so excited his military ire that he holloaed to him that he was disgracing his regiment by smoking in the presence of the enemy—a grave view of the question which certainly I (his commanding officer) did not, or at least had not, up to that time reciprocated, inasmuch as I at this very moment was enjoying a remarkably good cigar. The question then arose in my mind, am I to set this bad example? (in the Colonel's opinion at least) or should I throw away a good cigar?—no such common article in these days, be it remembered. Well, the cigar carried the day, and it lasted me till we got to the guns —with shame do I say it.'

Cardigan gave the order to advance at the trot. The Brigade had about a mile and a quarter to cover before reaching the

Russian position at the end of the valley. Here were drawn up the squadrons which had been beaten by the Heavy Brigade, supported by a dozen guns. Flanking the advance to the north, however, were eight battalions of Russian infantry, four squadrons of cavalry and fourteen guns; and on the south flank of the line of advance, eleven battalions of infantry with thirty guns. The Light Brigade was, in fact, moving rapidly into a zone which could be swept by a mass of fire from both artillery and small arms. Some 700 horsemen were on the point of charging an unbroken army in a defensive position.

Something of the horrified astonishment with which our French allies watched this incredible manœuvre is echoed in the comments of General Canrobert, as recorded by Rousset:

'History has sometimes witnessed the generous sacrifice of a cavalry which has immolated itself to save an army, or even the noble despair of men who do not wish to survive a defeat. But here there was nothing of that kind; neither defeat nor peril threatened the English Army.'

Soon after the advance began there was a peculiar and tragic incident. Captain Nolan suddenly left his place in the line and galloped across the front of the Brigade waving his sword, only to be killed instantly by one of the first shells fired by the enemy guns. Cardigan appears to have regarded Nolan's action as an inexcusable affront, without considering whether there was any reason for it. It seems probable, however, that Nolan, knowing the Commander-in-Chief's intention, suddenly realized the ghastly mistake which was being made and attempted to stop it.

The shot which killed Nolan was the precursor of a terrific blast of fire which swept away men and horses, tearing great gaps in the advancing lines. The pace started to quicken, but the imperturbable Cardigan was holding his command in hand for the decisive clash. 'Steady, steady, the 17th Lancers! Close in to your centre; look to your dressing!' Watching this steady and orderly advance towards apparent annihilation, the French General Bosquet exclaimed, '*C'est magnifique mais ce n'est pas la guerre*'.

In his diary Lord George Paget says, 'Ere we had advanced

half our distance, bewildered horses from the first line, rider-less, rushed in upon our ranks, in every state of mutilation, intermingled soon with riders who had been unhorsed. . . . The smoke, the noise, the cheers, the groans, the *ping, ping* whizzing past one's head; the *whirr* of the fragments of shells; the well-known *slush* of that unwelcome intruder on one's ears! What a sublime confusion it was. The *din of battle*!'

As the Light Brigade, at a gallop now, hurled themselves at the Russian guns, these fired a last salvo which wrought havoc in the first line and dislocated the second. Cardigan was the first through the gun line, and after him some twenty sur-vivors of the *17th Lancers*. The Russian cavalry attempted a counter-attack, with the 1st and 53rd Regiments of the Cos-sacks of the Don. But the rear line of the Light Brigade was now up, and Colonel Shewell led the *8th Hussars* straight into the Cossacks and drove them back.

The final stage of the attack is narrated by Lord George Paget. He says, 'We had got beyond the guns at the entrance of a sort of widish gorge, when finding it useless to proceed, our fellows turned round to go back, and about we went. At this moment, however, seeing a lot of their cavalry coming on us, within fifteen yards, I holloaed to them to *Front*, which they right gallantly did, when a cry arose, "They are coming down on us in our rear, my lord"; and to our consternation we saw a regiment of lancers formed up in our rear, between us and our retreat. The case was now desperate. Of course, to retain the guns was out of the question. We went about again and had to cut a way through this regiment, which had skilfully formed so as to attack us in flank. I holloaed "Left shoulder forward!" but my voice was drowned, and I hesitate not to say that had that regiment behaved with common bravery not one of us would have returned. . . . Well, having got by them, we had to ride back a mile, through the murderous fire we had come through, of guns, shells, and minie rifles from the hills of brushwood on each side; and all I can say is, that here I am, but how any of us got back I don't know. . . . At one time we were between four fires, or rather four attacks—right and left,

Plate XXIII

THE 12TH ROYAL LANCERS, 1844

(By kind permission of the Commanding Officer, 9th/12th Royal Lancers (Prince of Wales's).)

front and rear. That is a heavy fire from right and left and cavalry in front and rear.'

To echo Lord George Paget, it was rather astonishing how many survivors there were. Out of 673 all ranks who went into action, 303 became casualties, and 460 horses were lost.

In September of the following year the *10th Hussars* were given the opportunity of showing what they could do with their much admired Arabs. A squadron of the regiment was included in the reinforcements to an expedition which had been sent to the Sea of Azoff. On 21st September the squadron was given a reconnaissance task, and one of the troops was despatched to a place called Seit Ali. The following morning the troop encountered a Cossack unit, which it charged and dispersed. In following the Russians up, however, the Hussars ran into a body of about 300 Cossacks, who were in the process of forming up. The subsequent action of the troop is narrated by Liddell in his *Memoirs of the Tenth Royal Hussars*, 1891. The troop retreated, checking the advance of the enemy cavalry, but after going about a mile, 'we heard a shout, and saw a strong body of the enemy forming across our line of retreat. There was no other course open but to penetrate this newly arrived force, so drawing in his scouts, Captain Clarke wheeled about and charged through their centre. The Cossacks met this charge with a volley (mounted) which was quite harmless. The troop of the Tenth had thus the advantage of encountering the enemy at the halt, and, after cutting its way through, it made good its retreat.'

In May, 1856, when the *10th Hussars* finally left for England, the Arab horses, to the distress of all ranks, had to be handed over to the Turkish government.

The *10th* was distinguished from the other regiments of Hussars by a special pattern of shako which it had adopted in India in place of the busby; no doubt as being more suitable for a hot climate.

Sir Walter Gilbey, in his book *Small Horses in Warfare*, notes the superiority of the smaller type of horse for the conditions of the Crimea. He was located for a short time at Abydos in

Asia Minor in close contact with the mounted troops provided by the Bashi Bazouks and the Armenians. The horses had been brought with the troops from the islands of the Archipelago, and were only 14 to 14·3 hands in height, with a strong strain of Arab blood. They stood up to conditions which Sir Walter Gilbey considered would have broken down the best English charger in the British Army; yet their feed consisted only of chopped straw, with the addition of a small daily ration of barley when the grain was procurable. This, he adds, was not always the case.

The Crimean war was probably the last occasion when British horse soldiers went into action in all the gorgeous panoply of full dress. The tight-fitting and brilliant uniforms were quite unsuitable for a prolonged campaign under contemporary conditions, and, as the war progressed, various relaxations of dress were permitted. In the Indian mutiny, which followed very closely on the Crimean war, authorized uniform was largely discarded. The action taken by the *14th Light Dragoons*, as related by G. C. Stent in *Scraps from my Sabretache*, is typical of many mounted regiments:

'As it was anticipated we might have some rough work to do before we came back, the authorities sensibly permitted us to wear our turbans instead of the awkward shakos; for which we felt very thankful, the puggrie having been our headdress ever since the regiment had been in India, on all occasions, except in full-dress, when we wore the shako. I believe the 14th was the only regiment in India who wore the puggrie, till the Mutiny broke out. On account of this we were always styled by the natives the Puggrie Wallahs. We also discontinued wearing stocks and gloves. . . . We, therefore, for fear of future accidents, in the shape of being ordered to wear them again, played football for a short time with the shakos, and threw both stocks and gloves away as useless and only so much superfluous baggage.'

The Crimean war also marked another change in the history of mounted troops, though this was not apparent at the time, nor, indeed, for many years afterwards. It was probably the

Plate XXIV

THE ROYAL DRAGOONS, 1848

(By kind permission, from the original oil painting by John Ferneley, Jnr., now in the possession of Brigadier-General Sir Ernest Makins.)

Throughout most of the nineteenth century the trumpeter of the Royal Dragoons was mounted on a grey horse.

last major war in which sword and lance were the paramount weapons of cavalry and the knee-to-knee charge the ideal method of using them. As the power and range of firearms increased, so the rôle of cavalry approached more and more to that of the original Dragoons; that is, mounted infantry.

In 1842 the percussion firearms known as Pattern 1842 were approved for the Army. The cavalry weapon was of musket bore for the Heavy Cavalry and carbine bore for the Light Cavalry; though, as already stated, the practical difference between the two arms of mounted troops had practically disappeared. The musket-bore carbine had a 26-inch barrel and the carbine bore one of 21-inch. Lancers, however, still carried no carbines. They were the only regiments in which pistols were retained for all ranks when they were withdrawn from the rest of the cavalry in 1840. Carbines were of little practical use in the Crimea, however, for the men were too tightly uniformed to be used for dismounted work. In some regiments, in fact, their overalls were so tight that they found difficulty in mounting their horses.

In 1851 the revolver was introduced from America where it had become extremely popular as a weapon for mounted use. It was immediately adopted by mounted officers in India and South Africa, and most officers carried it in the Crimea.

During the Indian mutiny a rifled muzzle-loading pistol made its appearance as a cavalry weapon, and at least two regiments of irregular cavalry were armed with revolvers.

About 1848 a new type of sword was introduced for Heavy Cavalry which was a great improvement on the previous pattern. The blade was 36 inches long and slightly curved. It was soon superseded, however, for, in 1853, there appeared a sword which was common to all types of cavalry. It had a straight 36-inch blade and was suitable for both cutting and thrusting. The regulations laid down, however, that it was primarily intended for thrusting. This sword had not been generally issued at the time of the Crimean war, and many of the cavalry regiments were still armed with the older models.

As one might expect, horse casualties in the Crimea were very heavy. Over a period of six months the loss of transport horses amounted to 38 per cent, and the 5048 cavalry and artillery horses with which the Army started the campaign were reduced by the first winter to a strength of 2258.

CHAPTER XIII

THE END OF AN ERA

During the latter part of the nineteenth century the universal adoption of the rifle, and the consequent increase in the range and accuracy of firearms, effected a revolution in uniform, equipment and tactics as great as that caused when the smooth-bore musket replaced the bow and arrow. The serried ranks of attackers were gradually replaced by formations in open order; brilliant uniforms gave way to battlefield clothing in neutral tints, to conceal movement and dispositions; and the new weapons demanded a high standard of individual marksmanship rather than the rigid drill of the short-range and largely unaimed volley.

As regards mounted troops opportunities for shock tactics became fewer and more fleeting, and proficiency in dismounted action with firearms consequently assumed greater and greater importance. It was a long time, however, before the tremendous power of the rifle was appreciated.

In 1867 the British cavalry were issued with the breech-loading instead of the muzzle-loading rifled carbine, and officers were equipped with revolvers or pistols which took the same cartridge. The old carbine had been carried in a short bucket under the wallet from which it could be easily removed and slung on the man. The new Snider, however, was carried in a deep bucket behind the leg.

In 1871 the Martini-Henry carbine was approved, and this was in general issue shortly before the Afghan war of 1878–9. At the same time Indian cavalry were armed with the Snider. Thirty rounds were carried by each man.

On the whole carbines were not received enthusiastically by the cavalry, particularly the regiments of Lancers which had been equipped with no firearm other than pistols. It is recorded, indeed, that one Lancer regiment when it first received carbines loaded them all on to stable barrows and wheeled them to a manure heap.

During the Afghan war of 1878–9 some commanding officers found jack-boots and slung swords hampered the troopers so much for dismounted work that they generally 'stayed on their horses and let the carbines be'. In his *Forty-One Years in India* Lord Roberts comments adversely on the cavalry's method of wearing its weapons. Referring to mounted troops fighting on foot in the operations round Kabul, he says that they were 'much impeded by their long boots and their swords dangling between their legs, the sight, indeed, of Cavalry soldiers trying to defend themselves on foot without a firearm confirmed the opinion I had formed during the Mutiny, as to the desirability for the carbine being slung on the man's back when going into action. Lieutenant-Colonel Bushman . . . curiously enough had brought with him from England a sling which admitted of this being done, and also of the carbine being carried in the bucket on all ordinary occasions. This pattern was adopted, and during the remainder of the campaign the men of the 9th Lancers placed their carbines on their backs whenever the enemy were reported to be in sight. At the same time I authorised the adoption of an arrangement also brought to my notice by Colonel Bushman, by which the sword was fastened to the saddle instead of round the man's body. This mode of wearing the sword was for some time strenuously opposed in this country, but its utility could not fail to be recognised, and in 1891 an order was issued sanctioning its adoption by all mounted troops.'

The *5th Punjab Cavalry* were trained in using their carbines from the saddle, and on at least one occasion they fired them in this fashion against swordsmen lying down in positions where they could not get at them with the sabre. But in general, however, there was little enthusiasm for training in musketry in those regiments which had not come under Roberts' influence, and the breech-loading carbine was as little used as had been the muzzle-loader.

Plate XXV 1ST MIDDLESEX LIGHT HORSE (METROPOLITAN LIGHT HORSE), 1861-67.

(By kind permission, from the original water-colour drawing by G. Laporte, in the possession of Mr. Godfrey Brennan)

The green uniform of this Yeomanry Hussar regiment will be noted.

Lord Roberts, one of the greatest horse soldiers of all time, was also mounted on one of the most famous chargers. This was his grey Arab 'Vonolel'. 'Vonolel' was bought by Roberts, then a Lieutenant-Colonel, after the Lushai campaign in Assam. It was named after a Lushai warrior chief whose son had succeeded him at the time of the campaign. The objective of the force was still called by the inhabitants 'Vonolel's country'. 'Vonolel' carried his master through the Afghan campaign, including the famous march from Kabul to Kandahar; and when Roberts came home he brought his charger with him. In 1896 Queen Victoria presented 'Vonolel' with the Kabul–Kandahar medal and the Afghan War Medal with four clasps: Peiwar Kotal, Charasia, Kabul and Kandahar. 'Vonolel's' last appearance in public was at Queen Victoria's Diamond Jubilee in 1897, when Roberts rode him at the head of the Colonial contingent. This great horse died in 1899 and was buried in a corner of the grounds of the Royal Hospital.

At the end of the Afghan war Roberts' health broke down and he was forced to return home. In *Forty-One Years in India* he has left a picture of his last sight of the Kabul–Kandahar Field Force as he passed it on 'Vonolel':

'Riding through the Bolan Pass I overtook most of the regiments of the Kabul–Kandahar Field Force marching towards Sibi, thence to disperse to their respective destinations. As I parted with each corps in turn its band played "Auld Lang Syne", and I have never since heard that memory-stirring air without its bringing before my mind's eye the last view I had of the Kabul–Kandahar Field Force. I hear the martial beat of drums and plaintive music of the pipes; and I see Riflemen and Gurkhas, Highlanders and Sikhs, guns and horses, camels and mules, with the endless following of an Indian army winding through the narrow gorges, or over the interminable boulders which make the passage of the Bolan so difficult to man and beast.'

In March, 1869, an unpopular reorganization was introduced into the cavalry. This was the formation of cavalry regiments into four squadrons for administrative as well as tactical purposes, instead of the old organization of eight troops directly under regimental headquarters. Since this entailed the loss of their separate troop commands by the four junior captains, there was great opposition to it.

The value of the small local horse in overseas campaigns was again demonstrated in the Sudan in 1884.

In 1873 the *10th Hussars* had returned to India after a long spell of service in England. During that time they had become used to the typical British cavalry mount. Their Colonel had selected horses for the regiment which had as much breeding as possible, believing, as he did, that this was of far greater importance for hard continuous work than an emphasis on size or imposing appearance. It was something of a shock, therefore, when, on arrival in India, the *10th* were given an assortment of countrybreds, Persians and Walers. By 1881 some sort of standardization had been achieved. Most of the troop horses were Walers, whilst the officers were largely mounted on Arabs.

In 1884 the *10th Hussars* embarked once more for England. Meanwhile, however, the Egyptian campaign had started, and the regiment was diverted to Suakim for active service. They arrived, of course, without any mounts. At Suakim, however, General Valentine Baker, an old commanding officer, came on board and offered the horses of his three regiments of Egyptian Gendarmerie. The offer was gratefully accepted, but the horses when they appeared seemed to the horrified regiment to be well below even the Indian standard. They were small Syrian Arab ponies with very rough saddles, mostly of an old French cavalry pattern.

However, their appearance was misleading; for, throughout the operations which followed, they proved exceedingly tough, and showed no sign of fatigue after twenty-four hours without water. On the other hand, Colonel Liddell, the new commanding officer, thought that their lack of size, weight and pace militated against the really effective use of the regiment as cavalry.

The *19th Hussars*, who were also engaged in this war, were

Plate XXVI

Stable jacket   Frock-coat.   Field Day Order.   Review Order.   Frock-coat.   Stable jacket.

OFFICERS OF 11TH HUSSARS, *circa* 1865.

By kind permission of the Colonel of the 11th Hussars. From the water-colour by O. Norie.)

mounted on the same type of local horse. In their case, however, for the 1885 campaign, it was a deliberate choice owing to the proved unsuitability of English horses to stand up to hard work under tropical conditions with little water and desert fare. The regiment therefore left Cairo dismounted and took over the Syrian Arabs at Wady Halfa. They were all stallions of an average age of eight to nine years, and standing about 14 hands. About half of them had already been with the *19th* during the campaign of the previous year, and had been very exhausted at the end of it.

From Wady Halfa the *19th* marched to Korti, some 360 miles, at an average of sixteen miles per day, excluding two halts, one of one day and one of two days. As feed they were given 6 pounds of barley or dhoora (a local form of millet) and 10 pounds of dhoora stalk daily. The subsequent march of 336 miles across the desert to Gubat was covered at an average daily rate of nearly twenty-six miles, on a daily diet during the first ten days of from 5 to 6 pounds of grain and 2 gallons of water. Finally, during the advance to the Nile the horses went fifty-five hours with no water at all and only 1 pound of grain, and this had been preceded by only one ration of grain of 6 pounds during the month's halt at Gubat, given them two days before the last advance started.

It was some thirteen years after these events, however, that there took place in the Sudan a cavalry affair which ranks among the great mounted actions of the British Army.

For the final advance up the Nile, which was to end in the decisive battle of Omdurman, various British reinforcements were despatched to join Kitchener's army. Amongst them were the *21st Lancers*, the only British cavalry regiment in the force. The remaining mounted troops consisted of the Camel Corps of eight companies, nine squadrons of Egyptian cavalry, and one Egyptian horse artillery battery.

Attached to the *21st Lancers* as a troop leader was Sir Winston Churchill, then a Lieutenant in the *4th Queen's Own Hussars*; and in his own matchless prose he has described the great charge in which he took part. This gallant episode in the history of the *21st Lancers* began with the repulse of the Dervish onslaught on Kitchener's position, which ended the first stage of the battle of Omdurman.

Sir Winston Churchill's account, which is taken from his book *The River War*, is as follows:

'As the fusillade slackened, the Lancers stood to their horses. Then General Gatacre, with Captain Brooke and the rest of his Staff, came galloping along the rear of the line of infantry and guns, and shouted for Colonel Martin. There was a brief conversation—an outstretched arm pointing at the ridge—an order, and we were all scrambling into our saddles and straightening the ranks in high expectation. We started at a trot, two or three patrols galloping out in front, towards the high ground, while the regiment followed in a mass—a great square block of ungainly brown figures and little horses, hung all over with water-bottles, saddle-bags, picketing-gear, tins of bully beef, all jolting and jangling together; the polish of peace gone; soldiers without glitter; horsemen without grace; but still a regiment of light cavalry in active operation against the enemy.

'The crest of the ridge was only half a mile away. It was found unoccupied. The rocky mass of Surgham obstructed the view and concealed the great reserve collected around the Black Flag. But southward, between us and Omdurman, the whole plain was exposed. It was infested with small parties of Dervishes, moving about, mounted and on foot, in tens and twenties. Three miles away a broad stream of fugitives, of wounded, and of deserters flowed from the Khalifa's army to the city. The mirages blurred and distorted the picture, so that some of the routed Arabs walked in air and some through water, and all were misty and unreal. But the sight was sufficient to excite the fiercest instincts of cavalry. Only the scattered parties on the plain appeared to prevent a glorious pursuit. The signalling officer was sent to heliograph back to the Sirdar that the ridge was unoccupied and that several thousand Dervishes could be seen flying into Omdurman. Pending an answer, we waited; and looking back northwards,

Plate XXVII

THE BAND OF THE ROYAL DRAGOONS, 1890.

(From a water-colour drawing by Richard Simkin, now in the possession of Brigadier-General Sir Ernest Makins.)

The Eagle badge on the drum banner commemorates the regiment's capture of a French Eagle at Waterloo.

across the front of the *zeriba*, where the first attack had been stopped, perceived a greyish-white smudge, perhaps a mile long. The glass disclosed details—hundreds of tiny white figures heaped or scattered; dozens hopping, crawling, staggering away; a few horses standing stolidly among the corpses; a few unwounded men dragging off their comrades. The skirmishers among the rocks of Surgham soon began to fire at the regiment, and we sheltered among the mounds of sand, while a couple of troops replied with their carbines. Then the heliograph in the *zeriba* began to talk in flashes of light that opened and shut capriciously. The actual order is important. "Advance," said the helio, "and clear the left flank, and use every effort to prevent the enemy re-entering Omdurman." That was all, but it was sufficient. In the distance the enemy could be seen re-entering Omdurman in hundreds. There was no room for doubt. They must be stopped, and incidentally these small parties in the plain might be brushed away. We remounted; the ground looked smooth and unbroken; yet it was desirable to reconnoitre. Two patrols were sent out. The small parties of Dervishes who were scattered all over the plain and the slopes of the hill prevented anything less than a squadron moving, except at their peril. The first patrol struck out towards Omdurman, and began to push in between the scattered Dervishes, who fired their rifles and showed great excitement. The other patrol, under Lieutenant Grenfell, were sent to see what the ground looked like from further along the ridge and on the lower slopes of Surgham. The riflemen among the rocks turned their fire from the regiment to these nearer objects. The five brown figures cantered over the rough ground, presenting difficult targets, but under continual fire, and disappeared round the spur. However, in two or three minutes they re-appeared, the riflemen on the hill making a regular rattle of musketry, amid which the Lancers galloped safely back, followed last of all by their officer. He said that the plain looked as safe from the other side of the hill as from where we were. At this moment the other patrol returned. They, too, had had good fortune in their adventurous ride.

Their information was exact. They reported that in a shallow and apparently practicable *khor* about three-quarters of a mile to the south-west, and between the regiment and the fugitives, there was drawn up a formed body of Dervishes about 1,000 strong. Colonel Martin decided on this information to advance and attack this force, which alone interposed between him and the Arab line of retreat. Then we started.

'But all this time the enemy had been busy. At the beginning of the battle the Khalifa had posted a small force of 700 men on his extreme right, to prevent his line of retreat to Omdurman being harassed. This detachment was composed entirely of the Hadendoa tribesmen of Osman Digna's flag, and was commanded by one of his subordinate Emirs, who selected a suitable position in the shallow *khor*. As soon as the 21st Lancers left the *zeriba* the Dervish scouts on the top of Surgham carried the news to the Khalifa. It was said that the English cavalry were coming to cut him off from Omdurman. Abdullah thereupon determined to strengthen his extreme right; and he immediately ordered four regiments, each 500 strong drawn from the force around the Black Flag and under the Emir Ibrahim Khalil, to reinforce the Hadendoa in the *khor*. While we were waiting for orders on the ridge these men were hurrying southwards along the depression, and concealed by a spur of Surgham Hill. The Lancer patrol reconnoitred the *khor*, at the imminent risk of their lives, while it was only occupied by the original 700 Hadendoa. Galloping back, they reported that it was held by about 1,000 men. Before they reached the regiment this number was increased to 2,700. This, however, we had no means of knowing. The Khalifa, having despatched his reinforcement, rode on his donkey with a scanty escort nearly half a mile from the Black Flag towards the *khor*, in order to watch the event, and in consequence he was within 500 yards of the scene.

'As the 21st Lancers left the ridge, the fire of the Arab riflemen on the hill ceased. We advanced at a walk in mass for about 300 yards. The scattered parties of Dervishes fell back and melted away, and only one straggling line of men in dark blue waited motionless a quarter of a mile to the left front. They were scarcely a hundred strong. The regiment formed into line of squadron columns, and continued at a walk until within 300 yards of this small body of Dervishes. The firing behind the ridges had stopped. There was complete silence, intensified by the recent tumult. Far beyond the thin blue row of Dervishes the fugitives were visible streaming into Omdurman. And should these few devoted men impede a regiment? Yet it were wiser to examine their position from the other flank before slipping a squadron into them. The heads of the squadrons wheeled slowly to the left, and the Lancers, breaking into a trot, began to cross the Dervish front in column of troops. Thereupon and with one accord the blue-clad men dropped on their knees, and there burst out a loud, crackling fire of musketry. It was hardly possible to miss such a target at such a range. Horses and men fell at once. The only course was plain. The Colonel, nearer than his regiment, already saw what lay behind the skirmishers. He ordered "Right wheel into line" to be sounded. The trumpet jerked a shrill note, heard faintly above the trampling of the horses and the noise of the rifles. On the instant all the sixteen troops swung round and locked up into a long galloping line, and the 21st Lancers were committed to their first charge in war.

'Two hundred and fifty yards away the dark-blue men were firing madly in a thin film of light-blue smoke. Their bullets struck the hard gravel into the air, and the troopers, to shield their faces from the stinging dust, bowed their helmets forward like the Cuirassiers at Waterloo. The pace was fast and the distance short. Yet, before it was half covered, the whole aspect of the affair changed. A deep crease in the ground—a dry watercourse, a *khor*—appeared where all had seemed smooth, level plain; and from it there sprang, with the suddenness of a pantomime effect and a high-pitched yell, a dense white mass of men nearly as long as our front and about twelve deep. A score of horsemen and a dozen bright flags rose as if by magic from the earth. Eager warriors sprang forward to anticipate the shock. The rest stood firm to meet it. The Lancers acknowledged the apparition only by an increase in pace. Each man wanted sufficient momentum to drive through such a solid line. The flank troops, seeing that they overlapped, curved inwards like the horns of a moon. But the whole event was a matter of seconds. The riflemen, firing bravely to the last, were swept head over heels into the *khor* and jumping down with them, at full gallop and in the closest order, the British squadrons struck the fierce brigade with one loud furious shout. The collision was prodigious. Nearly thirty Lancers, men and horses, and at least two hundred Arabs were overthrown. The shock was stunning to both sides, and for perhaps ten wonderful seconds no man heeded his enemy. Terrified horses wedged in the crowd, bruised and shaken men, sprawling in heaps, struggled, dazed and stupid, to their feet, panted, and looked about them. Several fallen Lancers had even time to remount. Meanwhile the impetus of the cavalry carried them on. As a rider tears through a bullfinch, the officers forced their way through the press; and as an iron rake might be drawn through a heap of shingle, so the regiment followed. They shattered the Dervish array, and, their pace reduced to a walk, scrambled out of the *khor* on the further side, leaving a score of troopers behind them, and dragging on with the charge more than a thousand Arabs. Then, and not till then, the killing began; and thereafter each man saw the world along his lance, under his guard, or through the back-sight of his pistol; and each had his own strange tale to tell.

'Stubborn and unshaken infantry hardly ever meet stubborn and unshaken cavalry. Either the infantry run away and are cut down in flight, or they keep their heads and destroy nearly all the horsemen by their musketry. On this occasion two living walls had actually crashed together. The Dervishes fought manfully. They tried to hamstring the horses. They fired their rifles, pressing the muzzles into the very bodies of their opponents. They cut reins and stirrup leathers. They flung their throwing spears with great dexterity. They tried every device of cool determined men practised in war and familiar with cavalry; and besides, they swung sharp, heavy swords

222

which bit deep. The hand-to-hand fighting on the further side of the *khor* lasted for perhaps one minute. Then the horses got into their stride again, the pace increased, and the Lancers drew out from among their antagonists. Within two minutes of the collision every living man was clear of the Dervish mass. All who had fallen were cut at with swords till they stopped quivering, but no artistic mutilations were attempted.

'Two hundred yards away the regiment halted, rallied, faced about, and in less than five minutes were re-formed and ready for a second charge. The men were anxious to cut their way back through their enemies. We were alone together—the cavalry regiment and the Dervish brigade. The ridge hung like a curtain between us and the army. The general battle was forgotten, as it was unseen. This was a private quarrel. The other might have been a massacre; but here the fight was fair, for we too fought with sword and spear. Indeed the advantage of ground and numbers lay with them. All prepared to settle the debate at once and for ever. But some realisation of the cost of our wild ride began to come to those who were responsible. Riderless horses galloped across the plain. Men, clinging to their saddles, lurched helplessly about, covered with blood from perhaps a dozen wounds. Horses streaming from tremendous gashes, limped and staggered with their riders. In 120 seconds five officers, 65 men, and 119 horses out of fewer than 400 had been killed or wounded.

'The Dervish line, broken by the charge, began to re-form at once. They closed up, shook themselves together, and prepared with constancy and courage for another shock. But on military considerations it was desirable to turn them out of the *khor* first and thus deprive them of their vantage ground. The regiment again drawn up, three squadrons in line and the fourth in column, now wheeled to the right, and galloping round the Dervish flank, dismounted and opened a heavy fire with their magazine carbines. Under the pressure of this fire the enemy changed front to meet the new attack, so that both sides were formed at right angles to their original lines. When the Dervish change of front was completed, they began to advance against the dismounted men. But the fire was accurate, and there can be little doubt that the moral effect of the charge had been very great, and that these brave enemies were no longer unshaken. Be this as it may, the fact remains that they retreated swiftly, though in good order, towards the ridge of Surgham Hill, where the Khalifa's Black Flag still waved, and the 21st Lancers remained in possession of the ground—and of their dead.'

In the early 'seventies mounted infantry made their appearance in the British Army, and in the Zulu war of 1879 they played a very important part in the later operations. After the disaster of Isandhlwana several infantry regiments contributed detachments of men who could ride to form mounted infantry. At Helpmakaar, for instance, the *4th (King's Own)*, *13th*, *80th* and *90th Regiments* provided 25 men each to form No. 1 Squadron. At first little change was made in the infantry uniform, but later on a more practicable and comfortable dress was introduced. It consisted of a broad-brimmed felt hat with a coloured pagri, brown breeches, a patrol jacket of mimosa colour with a large number of pockets, thigh-length brown canvas laced gaiters, and a coloured shirt of flannel open at the neck. The weapon first issued was the sabre, but this was soon replaced by a rifle slung on the back. The saddle was provided with wallets in front in which were packed a flannel shirt, two pairs of socks, a towel and toilet kit. The other equipment carried on the horse embraced a blanket, a tin mug, knife, fork and spoon, flint and steel, and a revolver. Anything extra required for distant expeditions was carried in saddle-bags.

After the end of the Zulu war the use of mounted infantry lapsed; but the Boer war of 1881 and the campaigns in Egypt led to a recognition of the importance of the mobility which mounted troops conferred. In consequence small units of mounted infantry were formed in the late 'eighties and training schools were established at Aldershot and the Curragh. About 1898 a manual on mounted infantry was issued. The establishment of a battalion was laid down as consisting of four companies each of 141 all ranks, divided into four troops, and a machine-gun section on battalion headquarters. Every battalion on foreign service was to include one mounted infantry company, and two companies were to be attached to each cavalry brigade. By the start of the Boer war, therefore, the machinery existed for a vast increase in the mounted strength of the Army.

At this period when there was such an increasing demand for mobility in the Army, the civilian use of the horse had vastly decreased. The rapid spread of the railways over the country had put an end to the demand for coach horses and roadsters, and, furthermore, the comparative ease of rail travel resulted in a much lesser use of the saddle horse. The position as regards potential reserves of horses for the Army was so deplorable that, in 1873, a Committee under Lord Rosebery was appointed 'To Enquire into the Condition of the Country with regard to Horses, and its Capabilities of Supplying any Present or Future Demands for them'. The evidence produced before this Committee showed that there was no shortage of thoroughbreds, as might be expected since the race course and the hunting field were a source of continuing demand. Other breeds, however, showed a marked decrease. There were far fewer agricultural horses and Cleveland Bays, whilst the old-fashioned Hackneys or Roadsters, which, with the Cleveland Bays, were the most valuable of harness horses for the Army, were practically unobtainable.

In spite of the Committee's work the position was to become far worse. In the ten years ending in 1873, the year the Committee was appointed, the number of horses imported was 29,000. In the following ten years this figure rose to nearly 200,000!

The Norfolk Hackney had a great history. The county had a reputation for its roadsters as far back as the seventeenth century. Marshall, in his *Rural Economy of Norfolk* of 1795, says that the farmers of the county bred an active horse, which could trot and gallop, before the reign of Queen Anne; and he gives the following description of races between teams of five of these horses harnessed to empty waggons:

'A team followed another upon a common broke into a gallop, and, unmindful of the ruts, hollow cavities and rugged ways, contended strenuously for the lead, whilst the foremost team strove as eagerly to keep it. Both were going at full gallop, as fast indeed as horses in harness could go for a considerable distance, the drivers standing upright in their respective wagons.' In the middle of the eighteenth century a descendant of the famous Darley Arabian of 1706 was mated with a mare of this Norfolk stock to produce the sire of practically all the Hackneys of to-day.

The enormous continental demand for these Hackneys was shown in evidence before the Rosebery Committee. The representative of one firm said that the number of stallions which they sent out of the country every year amounted to 'from thirty to forty . . . to France and Italy and different countries'. And another firm reported of the French agents that: 'They buy the very best and they get mares; you cannot get them to buy a bad mare'. The mares which were purchased were not confined to any particular class, but they were mated by their new owners with the Hackney stallions. One of these French agents said that he had bought from twenty to thirty Hackney stallions a year for twenty-three years, and that they were used to procure Artillery horses, because 'they do not want to canter, and they improve the courage of the native mares'.

A large number of the Cleveland Bays were also exported; and the result of this wholesale disposal of harness stallions was that requirements for high-class carriage horses had to be met by importation from the Continent.

The history of the Cleveland Bay is particularly interesting. The type originated in a Yorkshire pack horse of mediaeval times, bred particularly in the district of Cleveland, clean of leg and bay in colour. When the first coaches appeared the strong and active Clevelands were in great demand to pull them over the shocking roads. As in the case of the Hackney, in order to increase the pace of the Cleveland Bay, Arab blood was introduced, and in the middle of the eighteenth century Cleveland Bay mares were mated with sires descended from the Darley and Godolphin Arabians. The result was an outstanding harness horse. In the middle of the nineteenth century, after the disappearance from the roads of the stage and mail coaches, large thoroughbred stallions were mated with Cleveland Bay mares to produce a big horse for private and state carriages. The result of this union was the Yorkshire Coach Horse, a beautiful animal which stood at about 17 hands, and was in great demand. Apart from their expense, however, the Yorkshire Coach Horses were not as suitable for Army needs as the original Cleveland Bays. The latter were, and are, probably the finest all-round carriage horses that have ever been produced.

The advent of the Boer war resulted in a great demand for horses for the Army; a demand which, owing to casualties and the raising of new units, increased as the war went on. In 1900, for instance, fifty-four batteries of artillery were raised, requiring a total of 7074 horses. Ultimately £22 million was spent on horses for the Army in South Africa, or about one-tenth of the cost of the war.

The Boer war confronted the Army with a problem which it had not encountered before. The great wide open country was ideally suited to the mobile and hard-hitting enemy commandos. The Boer army was, in fact, a force of mounted infantry. On mobilization each man reported to the headquarters of his commando with horse, rifle, ammunition, 'biltong' (dried meat) and biscuits. The horses were small sturdy beasts, rarely exceeding $14\frac{1}{2}$ hands and accustomed to covering from thirty-five to forty miles a day without loss of condition. The Boer commandos divided their marches into stages of six miles, each of which they covered in the hour. A stage was followed by a halt of ten minutes, during which the horses were off-saddled, and turned loose under the care of a few sentries to roll and graze. When the horses were too tired to roll at the end of a stage, it was normal to halt for the night.

As far as possible the horses were fed by grazing, and this was supplemented by oat straw. Oats were a universal crop on Boer farms, and for fodder they were cut just before ripening

227

and tied into 6-pound bundles, each bundle being one day's ration for a horse.

The commandos nearly always fought dismounted. Their horses were essentially a means of transport, and were left out of the firing line when their riders went into action. Furthermore, the Boers had managed to avoid the enormous waste of strength incurred by providing horse-holders. All their horses were taught to stand still when the reins were thrown over their heads and left hanging to the ground.

The success of the Boer tactics and the early disasters of the war resulted in a recognition of the need for much greater mobility, and a consequent expansion of the Army's mounted forces. As a first step it was decided to use the Yeomanry overseas for the first time in their history. Commanding officers of Yeomanry regiments were authorized to enrol men into their units who had had previous service and who could ride and shoot efficiently. From the augmented regiments volunteer contingents were grouped to form a large body of mounted infantry called the Imperial Yeomanry. Each regimental contingent of 116 men constituted a company, and four companies were formed into a composite battalion. Altogether there were nineteen of these battalions. In addition to those formed from the Yeomanry, many mounted infantry units were raised from contingents furnished by regular infantry regiments. These comprised both battalions grouped in separate mounted infantry formations, and independent units serving as infantry divisional mounted troops.

All mounted infantrymen had the same equipment. They had 150 rounds of ammunition carried in three leather bandoliers; one of which was worn round each shoulder and the third, which also supported a bayonet, round the waist. A waterbottle and haversack were carried on the man, and a rolled cavalry greatcoat, a canteen and nose-bags filled with corn on the saddle.

The need for mounted infantry was appreciated immediately by Lord Roberts when he assumed the appointment of Commander-in-Chief. Shortly after he arrived in South Africa the 6th and 7th Divisions disembarked at Cape Town. Roberts directed them to provide one company of mounted infantry from each infantry battalion. This produced another 3000 mounted troops (though their value was somewhat limited until they had mastered their new method of locomotion). Two new regiments were also raised named *Roberts'* and *Kitchener's Horse*, after the Commander-in-Chief and his Chief of Staff.

The horses themselves presented something of a problem. Many of them were not given sufficient time to acclimatize themselves after disembarkation before being required for service. The result was a high percentage of horse casualties from sickness. The only horses apparently tough enough to stand up to these conditions were those sent out by the London bus companies.

In his book, *Our Cavalry* of 1912, Major-General M. F. Rimington has some interesting comments on the horses used in South Africa. According to General Rimington the natural height of a horse is from 14 to 15 hands at the most; and all horses larger than this are in the nature of forced growths obtained by selection and good food for mares and foals. At the same time he held that stamina has not grown in proportion. The best horse, he considered, to carry a moderately heavy man, weighing about 17 stone together with saddlery and equipment, was an Irish one of about 15·2 hands; but such an animal would have to be carefully fed and watered and not overdone. A lighter man, he thought, was best mounted on a polo pony type of horse of about 15 hands and as near a thoroughbred as possible. Although he thought 15·2 hands the biggest horse which should be used in a campaign, he found it difficult to state what the smallest size should be. Chest measurement was, however, the best test of stamina, and he quoted a good judge as saying that: 'A 13·2 hands pony sixty-four inches round will do double the work of a 14·2 hands pony of equal girth'. At the same time, General Rimington pointed out, a squadron mounted on 15·2 hands horses will, in a charge, easily defeat one mounted on 14·2 hands horses; even so, the 15·2 hands horses will be more difficult to keep in condition and their food will cost more.

General Rimington showed how widely we departed from a sound horse policy for the Boer war. Instead of collecting little Boer or Basuto ponies of 14 to 14·2 hands for remounting the cavalry, we obtained much larger animals from unsuitable sources. The enemy benefited considerably; for the ponies which we neglected to make use of became the Boers' reserve of remounts. Rimington maintained that the horse of the country is always the most suitable for use in that country. It is indeed probable that, before the end of the war, many of those mounted on the standard chargers of the British Army would have been glad to exchange them for Basuto ponies.

The British Cavalry in the Boer war, magnificent regiments though they were, were handicapped in their performance by their training. The power of modern firearms had already made the cavalry charge in mass a thing of the past. But this had not been really appreciated, for there had been few opportunities of observing the effects of rapid rifle and artillery fire against serried ranks of charging horsemen. The result was that commanders tended to reserve their horses for the decisive moment of the traditional charge, and the tremendous value of cavalry in mobile rôles was not available to the Commander-in-Chief to the extent that it should have been. As we shall see in the next chapter, opportunities for well-organized cavalry charges still remained. But the charge was no longer cavalry's primary function; it was a subsidiary weapon to be used against such fleeting or other suitable targets as presented themselves. Lord Roberts had prophesied ten years earlier that the cavalry of the future would have to be employed far more as mounted infantry, but his words had been largely unheeded.

The unfortunate result of this erroneous emphasis in cavalry training was that the Commander-in-Chief relied increasingly on his large force of mounted infantry for the more important mobile tasks. Lord Roberts' disappointment in the performance of his cavalry is shown in a letter which he wrote to Erskine Childers, in connection with the latter's book *War and*

[By kind permission of the Parker Gallery

THE CHARGE OF GENERAL FRENCH'S CAVALRY DIVISION AT KLIP DRIFT.

The Boer War uniform and equipment can be clearly seen.

the Arme Blanche. In reference to his operations against the Boers, Roberts says, 'I hoped that by turning their flanks the mounted portions of the force would have fallen upon them as they were retreating. But in this, as you have pointed out, I was invariably disappointed owing to quite small parties of Boers being able to keep off whole Brigades of Cavalry, and to the Cavalry themselves never having been taught to fight under the altered conditions of modern warfare.'

The employment of the mounted infantry in South Africa foreshadowed the use of cavalry in the First World War. And the mounted infantry did on occasions charge, although they were not specifically trained to do so, which proved that there were occasions when shock action was the most effective use of horsemen. General Rimington states that the *Royal Artillery Mounted Rifles* were seen charging on horseback with fixed bayonets a few days after they had joined a South African column; and he adds that in doing so they were imitating the Australian contingent in the column who made a practice of it.

The cavalry were not helped by their weapons in the Boer war. In the same month as the war broke out a new sword was introduced which was suitable neither for cutting nor for thrusting, being an unsuccessful compromise at proficiency at both. Furthermore, the cavalry magazine carbine was out-ranged by the Boer Mauser; with the result that the cavalry had to be rearmed with the infantry rifle.

CHAPTER XIV

THE LAST OF THE HORSE SOLDIER

At the close of the Boer war it is probable that the horse was held of greater importance in the British Army than at any other period of its long history; or at any rate since the end of the thirteenth century. Few subalterns then serving can have imagined that there were some amongst them who, before they retired, would see the virtual disappearance of the horse from the Army. For forty years later, except for those in the mounted squadrons of the Household Cavalry and a few minor establishments, none were left. The internal-combustion engine had eliminated the horse from the battlefield.

Again, few could have predicted that the years 1902–14 were the last in which would be seen the gorgeous pageantry of all the mounted units of the Army in the full-dress trappings of man and horse. In 1914 full dress disappeared with the outbreak of the war, and it never came back.

The First World War reversed the trend of the Boer war. Although in at least one theatre the horse soldier was to play a greater part than ever before, the siege conditions of the Western Front restricted the rôle which mounted troops could perform and led to many units being dismounted and reorganized as infantry or cyclists. The feeling of one of these unfortunate units is shown by a tombstone which was erected by *The Westmorland and Cumberland Yeomanry* in a field at Rungally Farm, about a mile from Cupar in Fife. It bore the following inscription:

SACRED TO THE MEMORY OF SPURS

Born 30-11-14   Departed 4-7-16

Stranger pause and shed a tear;
A Regiment's heart is buried here,

233

> Sickened and died through no disorder,
> But broken by a staggering order.
> Our hearts were warm. Theirs cold as icicles
> To take our horses and give us bicycles.
> For cavalry, they said, there was no room,
> So we buried our spurs in this blasted tomb.
>
> The Ordnance gave, The Ordnance hath taken away.
> RETURN IF POSSIBLE

Cavalry action on the Western Front was practically limited to the period of the retreat from Mons in 1914. Here the cavalry played an important part in delaying the advance of the German forces. Opportunities for mounted action were infrequent, but in his book *1914* Field-Marshal Lord French particularly mentions the affair at Moncel, on the morning of 7th September, as a fine example of shock action.

On this occasion the 2nd Cavalry Brigade was left-flank guard to the Cavalry Division, with the *9th Lancers* as its vanguard. On reaching the village of Moncel, the leading troop found that it was already occupied by a German cavalry patrol. The *9th Lancers* troop promptly charged at the gallop and drove the Germans out. Another one and a half troops of the *9th Lancers* moved up to a position on the left of the village. With them went the regimental headquarters, including the Commanding Officer, Lieutenant-Colonel Campbell, and the Second-in-Command, Major Beale-Browne. The Germans, however, had not finished with the village. The *1st Garde Dragoner Regiment* arrived before it and the two leading squadrons drove out the troop of the *9th Lancers*. In the meantime the third squadron of this German regiment came up to the north of the village in support. Seizing his opportunity, Colonel Campbell led the one and a half troops of the *9th Lancers* straight at the flank of this third squadron. The Germans changed front to meet the charge and were advancing at a canter when Campbell's troopers crashed into them at full gallop, pierced them and, swinging round, rallied to the south of the village. The discomfited Germans now came under rapid fire from the *18th Hussars*, who had been sent up by the

234

Plate XXIX   *[By kind permission of the Imperial War Museum*

A TROOPER OF THE 17TH LANCERS, 1918.

Note the small signal flag and the gas mask worn on the back.

Brigade Commander in support. Badly mauled, the *1st Garde Dragoners* withdrew.

It was in Palestine, however, that mounted troops really came into their own; and for the last time cavalry filled that decisive rôle which in the Second World War fell to the Armoured Forces. To the cavalryman of the time it must have seemed as the fulfilment of all his hopes, rather than the swan-song which, in fact, it was.

From a cavalry point of view the interesting part of the campaign started with the advance towards Beersheba in the late summer of 1917.

The administrative arrangements are worth recounting. No blankets or greatcoats were carried by the mounted troops, as it was hoped that the operations would be concluded before the onset of the winter rains. Each trooper was equipped with a pair of officer's pattern saddle wallets, in which were packed three days' rations (including the emergency ration) comprising bully beef, biscuit and groceries. Necessary articles of clothing were also carried in these wallets. Two nose-bags were attached to the saddle, in each of which was one day's forage, consisting of 9½ pounds of grain. A third day's forage was carried in limbered G.S. waggons, of which there were three to each regiment. Regimental technical stores, cooking utensils, etc., were loaded in a fourth limbered G.S. waggon. Entrenching tools were carried on pack animals. Cavalry divisions were thus completely self-supporting for three days. The divisional trains of horsed transport did not accompany their divisions. Instead the corps lorry column established advanced supply dumps each day, and the divisional trains replenished at these dumps and carried forward the next day's supplies to their formations.

In the course of the first month's operations there were a number of interesting mounted actions. The following illustrations are chosen to show different methods of attack.

The first example is of horses being used to get to close contact, whilst the final assault is carried out on foot.

On 31st October, 1917, Brigadier-General Cox, commanding

the 1st Australian Light Horse Brigade, was ordered to co-operate in the attack on Tel el Saba, in the neighbourhood of Beersheba, by assaulting it from the south. General Cox decided to carry out the attack with two regiments, the *2nd* and *3rd Australian Light Horse*. The first he directed on two block-houses and the second on Tel el Saba itself. A recon-naissance by the regimental commanders revealed no covered approach to the enemy positions; and they accordingly decided to get forward as far as they could in a rapid mounted advance, and then to continue the attack on foot.

The two regiments were under cover in a wadi. Beyond this was a long stretch of open country in full view of the enemy and covered by the Turkish artillery. The Australian Light Horse swept out of the wadi, and, in a long line of troop columns at wide intervals, galloped towards the enemy position. A mass of Turkish artillery fire was directed at the charging troopers, but the advance was so rapid that the gunners were unable to pick up the range, and there were few casualties. As they approached closer to the Turks the Australians were engaged by machine guns, but at such a fast-moving target the range was apparently too great for Turkish accuracy and the fire was comparatively ineffective. At 1500 yards from the enemy position the regiments rode into a depression which gave them cover from Turkish observation. Here they dis-mounted, re-formed and continued the advance on foot.

In this same battle another cavalry attack was carried out, one of the most remarkable of its kind, in which the regiments rode over the enemy infantry before dismounting to complete their capture of the position.

The 4th Australian Light Horse Brigade had not been in action all day and did not expect to be called on. One regiment was on outpost duty and horses had been off-saddled. One hour of daylight remained when the Brigade received an order to get close enough to the town of Beersheba to make a dismounted attack before dark. Owing to the short time at his disposal, Brigadier-General Grant, commanding the Brigade, collected the two regiments he had with him, the *4th* and *12th Australian*

Light Horse, and moved forward at a trot. The third regiment, *11th Australian Light Horse*, he ordered to follow in reserve. It was then 4.30 P.M. General Grant formed up his two regiments in some dead ground which was about 3000 yards from the enemy trenches at the south-east of the town. In front of him the ground fell in a long slight slope towards the enemy, and was completely open. The Turkish trenches had been located in air photographs, but they did not appear to be wired.

Owing to the little daylight that now remained, Grant considered that there was insufficient time to make a dismounted attack. He therefore decided to take the position by a charge. He accordingly sent a message to the two nearest batteries, *A Battery H.A.C.* and the *Nottinghamshire Battery R.H.A.*, and requested them to support his attack. The batteries galloped forward into action in the open at a range of 2500 yards and opened fire on the Turkish trenches and on their supporting artillery and machine guns.

As soon as the artillery was in action Grant advanced to the attack. The *4th Light Horse* was on the right and the *12th* on the left; each regiment moving in column of squadrons in line with 300 yards' distance between squadrons, and four to five paces' interval between each man.

The Brigade was not armed with swords, but as they galloped straight at the Turkish trenches the troopers held their bayonets extended in front of them like swords.

As soon as they saw the horsemen the Turks opened fire; but the speed of the charging cavalry and their loose formation was too much for the Turks. They were too bewildered even to alter their sights, with the result that in the earlier part of the advance there were only a few casualties, and in the last few hundred yards practically none at all.

It was growing dark as the leading squadrons reached the Turkish trenches. They leaped over two lines of these, and then dismounting on the far side went into the trenches with the bayonet. Succeeding squadrons galloped straight through into Beersheba, overtaking and routing retreating Turks, and overrunning the enemy's transport and guns. The Turkish position and Beersheba had been captured within ten minutes of the charge starting.

The total casualties in the Brigade amounted to only 32 killed and 32 wounded, and the majority of these occurred in the hand-to-hand fighting in the trenches.

The charge was a most gallant affair. It had taken place over unknown country in the gathering dusk, and without even the certainty that there was no wire in front of the Turkish trenches. The moral results were almost as important as the material. In common with most other soldiers, the Turks had not considered a frontal attack by cavalry on infantry in trenches to be a practicable proposition; and the rapid success which such an attack had achieved not only shook the nerves of the infantry but undermined the confidence of the Turkish command.

A week after the action at Beersheba there was another cavalry charge, but this time executed with the sword. On 8th November, 1917, the 60th Division was following up the Turkish withdrawal over open, rolling country, when its right flank came suddenly under heavy fire in the neighbourhood of Huj. The enemy force was a Turkish rearguard consisting of two battalions of infantry supported by several batteries of artillery. Owing to the lack of cover there were a large number of casualties amongst the British infantry.

Colonel Gray-Cheape, commanding the *Warwickshire Yeomanry*, was at the Divisional Headquarters, and the Divisional Commander, Major-General Shea, requested him to charge the enemy guns immediately. The *Warwickshire Yeomanry* was somewhat dispersed and Colonel Gray-Cheape only had a few troops under his immediate control. However, he also managed to collect some troops of the *Worcestershire Yeomanry* and led this composite force of ten troops to a slightly covered approach to the east of the enemy position. This cover enabled him to get forward unseen to within 800 yards of the Turks. He was now on the flank of the enemy gun position, which comprised one field battery and one mountain battery, with a section of machine guns on a slight rise between these two batteries, and behind these a third battery of heavy howitzers.

Deploying his force into three waves, Colonel Gray-Cheape gave the order to charge; and the cavalry swept out from the cover and straight at the guns. The Turks hastily swung the guns round to engage the charging horsemen, and the escort of Turkish infantry jumped on to the limbers and opened rapid fire.

The leading wave rode into the field guns, the nearest battery, whilst the troops in the second wave wheeled right-handed into the howitzers, and then swung round to take the mountain guns in the rear. The third wave passed through the field battery and rode down the machine gunners. In a few minutes it was all over, and the Turkish guns stood silent amidst their dead crews. But the cost had been heavy. Of the 170 of all ranks who took part in the charge 75 had been killed or wounded. The casualties in horses (as in all other charges of the campaign) had been considerably heavier.

This was the first occasion in the campaign when the troopers had had a chance to use the 1908 pattern sword, and it proved itself a remarkably fine weapon. It had a straight narrow blade of 35 inches which was not well adapted for cutting, though the point could be so used to a limited extent. But, for thrusting, it was probably the best sword that has ever been in the hands of mounted troops.

There was one other cavalry attack of this period of particular interest, and this again took place one week later. In this case some of the cavalry carried out the final attack mounted and others on foot.

On 13th November, 1917, an infantry brigade of the 52nd Infantry Division advancing up a slope towards the village of El Mughar was engaged by heavy enemy machine gun and rifle fire from positions around the village and by artillery fire from field guns to the north of it. The ground was very open and the brigade was unable to make any progress. The Divisional Commander thereupon sent a message to Major-General Barrow, commanding the Yeomanry Division, asking if he could relieve the situation by attacking El Mughar from the west. The 6th Mounted Brigade was conveniently placed for such attack; and in anticipation of orders to carry it out, Brigadier-General Godwin, commanding the Brigade, had already ordered a reconnaissance as to the best line of approach, and had moved the *Buckinghamshire Yeomanry* forward to a suitable forming-up area in a wadi. General Barrow confirmed General Godwin's intention and the attack was ordered.

Reconnaissance reports showed that the country between the Brigade and the enemy was very open and devoid of cover, and the distance from the forming-up area in the wadi to the Turkish position was about two miles. On this Godwin decided that the only course open to him was a mounted charge. He accordingly issued his orders for an attack on a two-regiment front: the *Buckinghamshire Yeomanry* on the right and the *Dorsetshire Yeomanry* on the left. The third regiment, the *Berkshire Yeomanry*, was to be held in reserve.

The *Dorsetshire Yeomanry* was first galloped up in small parties to the wadi, and then the two regiments trotted forward, well opened out and in column of squadrons at a distance of 200 yards. The Brigade's Horse Artillery and machine guns gave covering fire.

As soon as the Turks saw the advancing horsemen they opened a very heavy fire. Nevertheless the two regiments trotted steadily until they reached a distance of about half a mile from the enemy position. The pace was then increased to a canter. The final approach was up a rocky slope to the Turkish infantry on the crest. A hundred yards from the enemy position the *Buckinghamshire Yeomanry* were ordered to charge. In successive waves the three squadrons rode over the Turks, who were broken and demoralized by the speed and violence of the attack. The regiment then rallied rapidly and consolidated the position.

The *Dorsetshire Yeomanry* were faced with a more difficult final approach. The ground was rocky and broken, and the leading squadron dismounted and completed the attack on foot with the bayonet. However, the two other squadrons remained mounted and managed to reach the top and overcome the enemy opposition before the dismounted squadron arrived. The effect on the accuracy of rifle fire by charging horsemen is demonstrated by the far heavier casualties both in men and in horses which were suffered by the dismounted squadron. This was probably due, though, more to shaken morale than to the speed of the attack.

Following the success of the two leading regiments, the reserve, the *Berkshire Yeomanry*, was then directed through them to the village beyond, from which the Turks were still firing. Galloping up to the verge of the village, the *Berkshires* then dismounted and cleared it with the bayonet.

The cavalry actions so far described were, however, on a comparatively small scale. It was General Allenby's great offensive in 1918 which provided the only opportunity in the war, and probably the last in the history of war, for the complete destruction of an army by the rapid advance of a mass of horsemen. A door was, as it were, forced open in the enemy's lines; and, as the door was pushed back on its hinges, through the gap poured a torrent of mounted troops. In six weeks they swept over 400 miles of enemy territory.

Owing to the demands of the Western Front occasioned by the German offensive of March, 1918, many of the regiments which had taken part in the earlier part of the Palestine campaign had been sent to France. But the Desert Mounted Corps, with its four cavalry divisions, constituted one of the largest bodies of horse ever to operate tactically under one command. It consisted of the Anzac Mounted Division of nine regiments of Australian Light Horse and New Zealand Mounted Rifles, the Australian Mounted Division of nine regiments of Australian Light Horse and one regiment of French *Chasseurs d'Afrique*, and the 4th and 5th Cavalry Divisions comprising five British Yeomanry regiments and thirteen regiments of Indian Cavalry (the latter including three regiments of Imperial Service Lancers).

General Allenby's Force Order No. 68 started: 'The Commander-in-Chief intends to take the offensive. The Army pivoting on its positions in the Jordan valley will attack on the front between the high ground east of El Mughar and the sea with the object of inflicting a decisive defeat on the enemy. . . .'

The main attack was in the coastal sector where the infantry advance was to roll back the Turkish forces towards the east, clearing a path for the cavalry to go through.

The Anzac Mounted Division had been left in the Jordan valley, and one Australian Light Horse Brigade had been placed under the command of the attacking infantry corps. The whole of the rest of the cavalry, however, was available for the break through.

The attack started at 4.30 A.M. on 19th September, 1918. W. T. Massey, the war correspondent, in his book *Allenby's Final Triumph*, describes the tension of waiting for zero hour. He tells how the last few minutes of nerve-strung silence were suddenly broken by a beautiful horse in a signal section champing at its bit and becoming playful. And then 300 guns opened up with a shattering roar; and a racing enthusiast next to Massey said, 'They're off!'

Allenby's weeks of careful preparation and deception were rewarded by complete surprise, and so rapid was the infantry advance that the way was open for the cavalry before sunrise.

By 9 A.M. the 5th Cavalry Division on the left was over the first obstacle, the Nahr Falik, and away on its dash to the north. Before noon the 4th Cavalry Division on the right was also clear. Behind the 4th came the Australian Mounted Division.

By 11 A.M. the 13th Cavalry Brigade of the 5th Division had reached Hudeira, more than twenty miles from their starting-point, and had captured some 250 prisoners and four guns. In the latter part of the advance the wheeled vehicles had found some difficulty with the soft going. The Divisional Commander accordingly decided to make a rapid move on Nazareth with his 13th and 14th Brigades, leaving the 15th Brigade to come on behind escorting the guns and the fighting echelon of the wheeled transport. The 13th Brigade reached Nazareth at dawn the following morning, having covered some sixty miles in twenty-two hours. After overcoming an improvised

Plate XXX   [By kind permission of the Imperial War Museum

THE GLOUCESTER YEOMANRY, 1918.

This photograph was taken during General Chauvel's march
through Damascus, 2nd October, 1918.

Plate XXXI   [By kind permission of the Imperial War Museum

CAVALRY IN RESERVE, 17TH SEPTEMBER, 1918.

Halted to water the horses in the River Authie, Aux le Chateau.

but stubborn resistance, the Brigade collected some 2000 prisoners, amongst whom were some of the staff of the German commander-in-chief, General Liman von Sanders, still wearing the pyjamas in which they had been so rudely awakened.

On the right of the advance the leading Brigade, the 10th, of the 4th Cavalry Division reached the Plain of Armageddon on the 20th at 5.30 A.M., and its advanced guard surprised a battalion of infantry on the march. Two squadrons of the *2nd Indian Lancers* deployed immediately and charged. Forty-six Turks were killed with the lance and the remainder of the battalion surrendered.

The Brigade continued to Afuleh, where it captured eight railway locomotives and two trains which were waiting to lift retreating Turkish units northwards. From Afuleh, the 4th Division advanced along the valley of Jezreel and captured Beisan, having covered eighty-five miles in thirty-four hours.

In the meantime the Australian Mounted Division which had followed in Corps Reserve was directed on Jenin, ten miles south of Afuleh and on the enemy's main escape route. On the afternoon of the 20th it was seized by the 3rd Light Horse Brigade in a mounted attack. This Brigade had recently undergone a technical change from mounted infantry to cavalry, the practical effect of which was to arm it with swords. With these the Australians charged the Turkish trenches and overwhelmed the defence. The village together with some thousands of prisoners and a mass of war material fell into their hands.

This brilliant advance of the Desert Mounted Corps sealed the fate of the Turkish Army. It disintegrated, and those portions which managed to escape to the north were no longer a fighting force.

Ten days later Damascus fell, and this finale to the campaign is recorded in a report by Brigadier-General Wilson, commanding the 3rd Australian Light Horse Brigade. He says:

'On the night of Sept 30–Oct 1 this brigade bivouacked on the hills overlooking the village of Dumar about four miles north-west of Damascus on the Beyrout road. The road was during the night covered by six machine guns, and heavy casualties were inflicted on the enemy trying to escape by that road, and the balance of them were turned back into the City. The Beyrout road was thus closed to the enemy from sunset on the 30th September. At 5 A.M. on October 1 the brigade descended to the main road at Dumar and marched along that road south-easterly into Damascus. The 10th Light Horse regiment formed the advanced guard, Major Olden being in charge of the vanguard. On entering the north-western suburbs a good deal of rifle shooting was indulged in by the inhabitants, some shooting or sniping at the column. In a few cases the snipers were observed and their fire was returned. To discourage the sniping Major Olden moved the vanguard at the gallop until in front of the Town Hall where he halted. The time was now between 6.30 and 7 o'clock. Major Olden then asked for the Civil Governor and was told he was up-stairs. Major Olden dismounted and went into the Town Hall, where he found a large assembly of notables and people in uniforms as if arranged for a public function. Emir Said was sitting in the municipal chair, and when Major Olden asked for the Civil Governor, Emir Said rose and came forward as such and shook hands. Through an interpreter Emir Said said, "In the name of the civil population of Damascus I welcome the British Army".'

Experience with horses in this campaign is of interest. Most of those in the Desert Mounted Corps were Walers, which made first-class cavalry mounts. They had, of course, been known in the British Army for many years; particularly in India. Walers were the produce of thoroughbred stallions, bought cheap in England, and the local Australian mares. The horses bred from this union were rather light but extremely tough, and proved themselves better able than any other breed to stand up to the rigours of active service. The Australians rightly believed them to be far superior for army purposes to the half-bred weight-carrying hunters, so popular in the British Army. In the Palestine campaign the Walers could carry about 21 stone on less than half the normal ration and, if required, they could manage with only one drink every thirty-six hours.

Plate XXXII   [*By kind permission of the President of the Headquarters Mess, Royal Signals*

ROYAL SIGNALS CABLE LAYING IN THE FIELD.

The waggon was pulled by a six-horse team. The mounted figure in the background is the detachment commander. The well-known blue and white arm band of the Royal Signals will be noted. The cable is being guided by a mounted linesman with a crookstick.

Many of the draught horses brought out from England were far too heavy. The virtual disappearance of the excellent light draught horses which had hauled coaches and buses has already been mentioned, and it had been erroneously thought that heavy cart horses could take their place. These, however, could not keep up with cavalry on long marches of fifty miles and more, which were quite common in this campaign; and if they were forced to do so they died. The Australian draught horses were animals of only about 15 to 15·2 hands, with short backs and a good deal of thoroughbred in their make-up. They were well able to do all that was required of them.

Shortly after the end of the war, in 1920, there was formed the last mounted arm of the British Army. This was *The Royal Corps of Signals*. It was not, however, entirely new. The Signal Service of *The Corps of Royal Engineers* had, for all practical purposes, been an entirely separate entity even before the outbreak of the First World War, and its transformation into the *Royal Signals* entailed nothing more than a change of badge. The most picturesque as well as the best-known feature of the *Royal Signals* was the horse-drawn cable waggon. This consisted of the waggon itself, on which were four great drums of cable and a stack of black and white poles, and a limber to which the waggon was attached. Limber and waggon were drawn by a six-horse team. In addition there was a L.G.S. waggon, with a pair of horses, which carried extra cable, spares and rations. The personnel of the detachment consisted of a mounted N.C.O. in command; Nos. 1 and 2, who rode on the limber and had a buzzer telephone for communication to the signal office; No. 3, who rode at the rear of the waggon and paid out the cable or controlled its reeling in; No. 4, who rode on the front seat of the waggon with his back to the limber and controlled the brakes and watched out for any difficulties with the cable; No. 5, very much of a spare number and mounted on the other seat at the rear of the waggon; No. 6, a mounted man who rode behind the waggon with a crookstick through which ran the cable both in reeling out and reeling in, and by means of which in laying

No. 6 could place the cable in a safe lie; No. 7, another mounted man who rode behind the detachment, dismounting when necessary to make the cable safe; and No. 8, who normally remained at the base signal office to keep communication with the waggon. In addition there were three mounted drivers with the six-horse team, and one driver on the L.G.S. waggon.

It is probable that for many past, and a few present, officers and other ranks of the *Royal Signals* the cable waggon remains the fondest memory of their soldiering days. For many the mention of the horse cable detachment will recall a clear brisk morning on the Yorkshire moors beyond Catterick Camp, with the steam rising from the horses and the sharp ring of their hoofs on the hard surface. There would be two short blasts on the commander's whistle, and the detachment would break into a trot; and the green insulated cable would go singing away through No. 6's crookstick as No. 3 pulled hard with his gloved hand to keep its speed up with the team. And then, with luck, soft going, and the thrill of a well-drilled team laying fast cable amidst the thunder of hoofs. There would be break for lunch, perhaps, in the neighbourhood of one of those incomparable Yorkshire inns; and never since surely has a pint of draught beer ever tasted so good.

The 1930's witnessed the rapid advance of mechanization throughout the Army, and by 1937 the *Royal Signals*, in common with many others, had lost its horses. But the strange thing is that it has not yet been possible to devise any mechanical system which will lay or recover cable with the efficiency and speed of the old cable waggon.

When the Second World War started there were few horse soldiers left in the British Army. The entire British Expeditionary Force was mechanized, and the only mounted units were in the Middle East. Of these the last horsed cavalry regiments of the Regular Army were mechanized in 1940, and there remained the 5th Cavalry Brigade of three Yeomanry regiments, the *Cheshire Yeomanry*, the *North Somerset Yeomanry* and the *Yorkshire Dragoons*.

In the month of June, 1941, British forces had the un-

Plate XXXVIII.

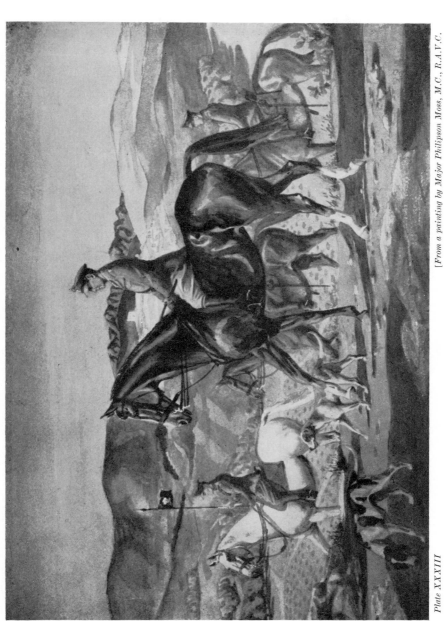

[From a painting by Major Philipson Moss, M.C., R.A.V.C.

THE CHESHIRE YEOMANRY IN PALESTINE, 1941.

Lt.-Col. Williams, the Commanding Officer, with his groom (L./Cpl. Edge) and his galloper (Tpr. C Johnson).

welcome task of taking the field against their former allies in
Syria serving under the French Vichy Government. Of the
5th Cavalry Brigade two regiments, the *Cheshire*, or *Earl of
Chester's*, *Yeomanry* and the *Queen's Own Yorkshire Dragoons*
had the distinction of serving right through the Syrian
campaign as horse cavalry regiments. They are therefore
the last mounted units of the British Army to have served in
action as such.

The *Cheshire Yeomanry* went out from England to the
Middle East under the command of Lieutenant-Colonel
D. E. Williams, M.B.E., T.D., who commanded the regiment
throughout the campaign. They were armed with swords
and rifles, and had one Hotchkiss machine gun section in
each troop, and a Vickers machine gun troop on regimental
headquarters. Practically all the horses were commandeered
hunters. The *Yorkshire Dragoons* were commanded by Lieutenant-Colonel H. F. B. Stephenson.

For the advance into Syria the *Cheshire Yeomanry*, less B
Squadron, were under the command of the 21st Australian
Brigade. (B Squadron was detached under the command of the
25th Australian Brigade.) The regiment crossed the frontier
at 5 A.M. on 8th June, 1941, about two miles inland from the
Mediterranean coast. The *Cheshire Yeomanry* then moved in
an easterly direction for about ten miles, before turning north
to cross the Litani River. The day's march was about forty-
five miles.

At dawn on the following morning Colonel Williams sent
forward two troops to reconnoitre the crossings over the
Litani. The troop on the right found an undefended bridge
by which it crossed the river. The left troop also got across but
were held up by machine gun fire from a village north of the
Litani. Colonel Williams decided to attack the village and
ordered Major W. B. Hutchinson, commanding C Squadron,
to cross the bridge and carry the enemy position. The Vickers
machine gun troop would give covering fire from a position
on the high ground south of the Litani. The threat of shock
action by mounted troops resulted in the enemy evacuating
the village, which C Squadron entered unopposed.

247

Near to the coast the advance of the Australians had been held up with heavy casualties. Colonel Williams was accordingly ordered to attack the left flank of the defending Vichy forces on the morning of 10th June. This last chance of a cavalry charge was again thwarted by the enemy withdrawing. That it was the threat of a cavalry attack that caused the enemy retreat is beyond doubt, for Colonel Williams says that: 'I later heard from Vichy French officers who were held as hostages in Jerusalem that the reason for their withdrawal was information that large numbers of cavalry were menacing their left flank—in point of fact the Cheshire Yeomanry less one squadron.'

In these same operations a troop of C Squadron of the Yorkshire Dragoons was engaged in a skirmish which may have been the last mounted engagement.

After these first three days and until the end of the campaign the two regiments were engaged in providing mounted patrols.

After the Syrian campaign was over the Cheshire Yeomanry lost its horses and in due course was reorganized as a unit of the *Royal Signals*. The Yorkshire Dragoons kept its horses until March 1942 and then became a unit of the Royal Armoured Corps.

The last words on the subject may fittingly be said by Colonel Williams, for they sum up the whole spirit of the horse soldier:

'There was no actual farewell mounted parade but the whole regiment, all ranks, had a mounted cross-country race of 4 miles which finished with swimming the Jordan. I cannot find out who was the winner as this seems rather obscure; however it was very much enjoyed by all.'

INDEX

Abercorn's Regiment of Horse, 78
Afghan War, 1878–9, 214
Agincourt, campaign of, 29, 30
Airey, General, 205
*Albermarle's Troop of Horse Guards,
    Duke of*, 59
Alfonso of Spain, 19
Allenby, General, 241
Almanza, battle of, 87, 90, 91
Almenara, battle of, 90
Andrews, Lieutenant John, 191
Angelo, Domenick, 115
Anne, Queen, 83, 225
Anzac Mounted Division, 241
Archers, mounted, 24, 26, 35
Argyll, Duke of, 95
Armour, 19, 20, 21, 22, 27
Arran's Regiment of Horse, Duke of, 82
Arthur, King, 17
Artillery, 64
Auberoche, battle of, 26
Audley, Thomas, 35
Australian Cavalry, 236-44
Australian Mounted Division, 241-3

'Backs and Breasts', 67
Baggot, Major, 109
Baker, General Valentine, 216
Bakewell, 82
Balaclava, charges at, 203-4
Balmerino, Lord, 109, 110
Barbaro, Daniel, report in 1551 by, 41
Baron, 24
Barrow, Major-General, 239
Bascinet, 27
Bayeux Tapestry, 18
Bayonets, 68
    Withdrawal from cavalry, 193
Beale-Browne, Major, 234
Bealson, Robert, 183
Beau Brummel, 157-8
Beauvoir, Peter de, 54-5
Beersheba:
    Administrative arrangements for
        advance to, 235
    Attack on, 236-7
Belesme, Robert de, 20
Benson, Captain George, 84
Berkshire Yeomanry, 240-1
Berwick, Duke of, 78, 87, 110

*Berwick's Troop of Irish Life Guards,
    Duke of*, 76-8
Blandeville, Thomas, book of, 43
Blathwayt, William, 66
Boer Army, 227
Boer War, 227-8
Boer War of 1881, 224
Bonnivert, Gédéon, diary of, 69-76
Bore of firearms, 49
Bosquet, General, 207
Boulogne, siege of, 37
Bourn, Daniel, 185
Boyne, battle of, 76, 78
Brooks, Nathaniel, 64
'Brown Bess', 102
Brown, Cornet Philip, letters of, 102,
    107-8
Brown, Sir Anthony, 39
Buchan, Earl of, 31
Buckinghamshire Yeomanry, 240
Bulstrode, Sir Richard, 50
Bunker Hill, battle of, 137
Burgoyne, Major-General, 135
Busaco, battle of, 172
Busby, history of the, 161-2
Butler, Colonel, 78

Cable waggon, 245-6
Cadogan, Lord, 85, 87
Caerlaverock:
    Poem of, 24-6
    Siege of, 24
Cambrensis, Giraldus, 20
Campbell, Lieutenant-Colonel, 235
Campbell, Lieutenant-Colonel James, 86
Canrobert, General, 207
Canterbury, Archbishop of, 28
Carbine:
    Board of General Officers, recommenda-
        tions as to, 136
    'Brown Bess' pattern, 102
    Civil War, 49
    Heavy Cavalry, 1796, 163
    James II series, 68
    Light Dragoons:
        Regiments, 1759, 123
        Troops, 1756, 117
    Martini-Henry, 213
    'Paget', 163
    Pattern of 1770, 135

Index

Carbine—*contd.*
  Percussion, of 1842, 211
  Queen Anne issue, 92
  Rifled, of 1803, 164
  Snider, 213
  Trial patterns of 1786, 135-6
Cardigan, Lord, 205, 206, 208
Cathcart, James, 86
Cathcart, Lord Charles, 84, 95
Cavalry:
  In the Boer War, 230
  In the Napoleonic wars, 168
  Police duties, eighteenth and nine-
    teenth centuries, 113
  Reorganization of 1869, 215
  Unit of Elizabeth I's wars, 44
Cavalry Division, 4th, 241-3
Cavalry Division, 5th, 241-2
Cavalry Regiments:
  Abercorn's Regiment of Horse, 78
  Albemarle's Troop of Horse Guards,
    Duke of, 59
  Arran's Regiment of Horse, Duke of, 82
  2nd Australian Light Horse, 236
  3rd Australian Light Horse, 236
  4th Australian Light Horse, 236-7
  10th Australian Light Horse, 244
  11th Australian Light Horse, 237
  12th Australian Light Horse, 236-7
  Berkshire Yeomanry, 240-1
  Berwick's Troop of Irish Life Guards,
    Duke of, 76-8
  Buckinghamshire Yeomanry, 240
  Butler's Troop of Horse Grenadiers, 78
  Cheshire Yeomanry, 246-8
  Cumberland's Light Dragoons, Duke of,
    111-12, 117
  Dorsetshire Yeomanry, 240
  2nd Dragoon Guards, 113
  3rd Dragoon Guards, 84, 86, 157,
    170, 192
  4th Dragoon Guards, 150, 203
  5th Dragoon Guards, 84, 157, 203
  6th Dragoon Guards, 84
  7th Dragoon Guards, 84, 87
  3rd Dragoons (later 3rd Hussars), 104
  4th Dragoons (later 4th Hussars), 87,
    96, 107, 170
  8th Dragoons (later 8th Hussars), 91, 92
  9th Dragoons (later 9th Lancers), 172
  11th Dragoons (later 11th Hussars), 123
  13th Dragoons (later 13th Hussars), 170,
    172
  Duke of Albemarle's Troop of Horse
    Guards, 59
  Duke of Berwick's Troop of the Irish Life
    Guards, 76-8
  Duke of Cumberland's Light Dragoons,
    111, 112, 117

  Duke of York's Troop of Horse Guards,
    59, 60
  Earl of Arran's Regiment of Horse, 82
  FitzJames's Regiment of Irish Horse,
    110, 136
  Galmoy's Regiment of Horse, 78
  Horse Grenadiers, 63, 113
  Horse Guards (later the Life Guards),
    59, 60, 61, 63, 80, 113
  Horse Guards (Jacobite), 109
  Horse Guards, 3rd Troop, 102
  4th Queen's Own Hussars, 217
  7th Hussars, 81
  8th Hussars, 206, 208
  10th Hussars, 93, 157, 161, 162, 167,
    173-4, 181, 199-203, 209, 216
  11th Hussars, 206
  15th Hussars, 162-3, 166, 174
  15th/19th Hussars, 132
  18th Hussars, 174, 234
  19th Hussars, 216-17
  Imperial Yeomanry, 228
  2nd Indian Lancers, 243
  Inniskilling Dragoons, 79, 148, 203
  Inniskilling Regiment of Horse, 77
  Kenmure's Horse, 109
  King's Dragoon Guards, The, 82, 84,
    86, 129, 157, 182
  King's Own Dragoons (later 3rd
    Hussars), 133, 161
  King's Own Regiment of Horse (later
    King's Dragoon Guards), 102
  King's Own Royal Regiment of Dragoons
    (later the Royal Dragoons), 64
  King's Troop of Horse Guards, 59, 60
  Kingston's Light Horse, 110
  Kitchener's Horse, 229
  9th Lancers, 234
  17th Lancers, 205, 206, 208
  21st Lancers, 217, 224
  Life Guards, 59, 176, 178, 182
  Life Guards, 1st Troop (Jacobite), 109
  Life Guards, 2nd Troop (Jacobite), 109
  4th Light Dragoons (later 4th Hussars),
    206
  10th Light Dragoons (later 10th
    Hussars), 132
  11th Light Dragoons (later 11th
    Hussars), 135, 192
  13th Light Dragoons (later 13th
    Hussars), 206
  14th Light Dragoons (later 14th
    Hussars), 165, 210
  15th Light Dragoons (later 15th
    Hussars), 121, 125, 132, 161
  16th Light Dragoons (later 16th
    Lancers), 121, 137, 157
  17th Light Dragoons (later 17th
    Lancers), 121, 137

Index

Cavalry Regiments—contd.
18th Light Dragoons (later *18th Hussars*), 121
19th Light Dragoons (later *19th Hussars*), 121
20th Light Dragoons (later *20th Hussars*), 160
London and Westminster Light Horse, 137, 147
Lord Churchill's Regiment (later the *Royal Dragoons*), 64
Lord Oxford's Regiment (later the *Royal Horse Guards*), 60
Luttrell's Regiment of Horse, 78
North Somerset Yeomanry, 246
Parker's Regiment of Horse, 76, 78
Pearce's Dragoons, 90-1
Prince of Wales's Dragoon Guards (3rd Dragoon Guards), 138
Prince of Wales's Own Dragoons, 94
Prince of Wales's Regiment of Horse, 50, 52
5th Punjab Cavalry, 214
Purcell's Regiment of Horse, 78
Queen's Bays, 90
Queen's Dragoons, 137
Queen's Regiment of Horse (later the *King's Dragoon Guards*), 82
Queen's Troop of Horse Guards, 60
Roberts' Horse, 229
Rochford's Dragoons, 90-1
Ross's Dragoons, 80
Royal Dragoons, 1st The, 64-5, 84, 91, 137, 157, 159, 172, 179, 180, 193
Royal Foresters, 121, 123
Royal Horse Guards, 59, 92, 97, 157, 178, 182
5th Royal Irish Lancers, 84-5
Royal Regiment of Horse (later the *Royal Horse Guards*), 59, 60
Royal Regiment of Horse Guards (later the *Royal Horse Guards*), 64
Royal Scots Greys, 63, 67, 81, 84-7, 95, 129, 155, 160, 179, 193, 203
Rutland Light Dragoons, 145
Sarsfield's Regiment of Horse, 78
Sarsfield's Troop of the Irish Life Guards, 78
Scottish Troop of Horse Guards, 61
Somerset Yeomanry, 146
South Notts Yeomanry, 148
Sutherland's Regiment of Horse, 76, 78
Tangiers Horse (later *1st The Royal Dragoons*), 64
Trimburn's Horse, 87
Tyrconnel's Regiment of Horse, 76, 78
Unton Crook's Regiment (later the *Royal Horse Guards*), 60
Warwickshire Yeomanry, 238
Westmorland and Cumberland Yeomanry, 233
Wiltshire Yeomanry, 191
Worcestershire Yeomanry, 238
Yorkshire Dragoons, 246
York's Troop of Horse Guards, 56, 60
Cent Lances Écossaises, 31
Challoner, Sir Thomas, 42
Charles I, King, importation of horses under, 48
Charles II, King, 65
Cheshire Yeomanry, 246-8
Chevaux-légers, 31
Childers, Erskine, 230
Chivalry, Order of, 19
Churchill, Colonel Charles, 94
Churchill, Sir Winston, 217
Churchill's Regiment, Lord, 64
Civil War, the, 49
Clothing Regulations, 1729, 100
Coach and Harness Makers, Company of, 66
Coach, Mail, 184, 186-7
Coach, Stage, 57, 65, 183, 186-7, 189
Coif, 27
Combermere, Lord, 168
Compagnies d'Ordonnance, 31
Conway, General, 135
Corps of Staff Guides, 175
Coutilier, 31, 35
Cowdray House paintings, 39
Cox, Brigadier-General, 235
Craig, Sir James, expedition to Naples under, in 1805, 159
Crimean War:
    Dress in, 210-11
    Horse casualties in, 212
Cromwell, Oliver, 57
Cuirasses, 67
Cuirassiers, 57
Cuirbouilli, 21
Culloden, battle of, 110-11
Cumberland, Duke of, 101, 111-12, 117, 127
Cunningham, Sir Albert, 79
Curragh, the, 68
Custrell, 35, 63

Dallas, Lieutenant-General Sir Thomas, 133-4
Dalrymple, Lieutenant-Colonel, essay by, 133
Damascus, fall of, 243-4
Davies, Private Sam, letters of, 104-7
Demi-lance, 35, 44
Derby, Earl of, 26
Desert Mounted Corps, 241
Dettingen, battle of, 104
Devonshire, Duchess of, 158

Index

Docking of horses, 43, 115, 148
  Army Order prohibiting, 116
  Army Order re-introducing, 149
Doherty, Colonel Charles Edmund, 206
Dorsetshire Yeomanry, 240
Douglas, Colonel John, 206
Drag, Jerry, 189
Dragoon Guards, formation of, 112
Dragoons (*for individual regiments see under* Cavalry Regiments):
  Dress and equipment in the reign of James II, 68
  Function in early years and later development, 63-4
  General Kane's opinion on, 84
  In the Civil War, 49, 57
  In the Peninsula, 166
  New regiment in the reign of James II, 93
  Order affecting, by Duke of Cumberland, 101
  Pay in the reign of George I, 94
  Raising of the first units, 63
  Standing orders by the Duke of Cumberland, 127

Edgehill, battle of, 50
Edward I, King, 22, 24
  Army of, 24
Edward II, King, 23, 28
  Improvement of horses under, 28
Edward III, King, 24
Egerton, Major-General, 60
Elcho, Lord, 109
Elizabeth I, Queen, 43, 44
  Improvement of horses under, 42
  Irish cavalry in the reign of, 44
  Unit of cavalry under, 44
Elliot, Lieutenant-General, 135
El Mughar, action at, 239
Erle, Lieutenant-General, 87
Eugene, Prince, 86

Fairfax, Sir Thomas, 52-3
Ferdinand of Brunswick, 136
Firearms, new series in the reign of James II, 68
Firelocks in the Civil War, 49
First World War, the, 233
Fishing, horse's hairs for, 129, 132
FitzJames's Regiment of Irish Horse, 110, 136
Flintlocks in the reign of James II, 68
Fontenoy, battle of, 108, 110
French, Field-Marshal Lord, 234

Galmoy's Regiment of Horse, 78
Garran, 44
Gatacre, General, 218

Gauls, 17
Genappe, action at, 176, 178
Gendarmes, 31
Gentlemen-at-Arms, 34
Gentlemen Pensioners, 34
George I, King, 93
George II, King, 86, 115
George III, King, 143
George IV, King, as Prince of Wales, 158
Godwin, Brigadier-General, 240
Gore, Brigadier-General Humphrey, 93
Graham, James, 81
Graham, Sir Thomas, 174
Granby, Marquess of, 117, 136
Grant, Brigadier-General Colquhoun, 173-4
Gray-Cheape, Colonel, 238
Grenades, 68
Gronow, Captain, 157
Guidon, 138
  Ceremonies of 'fetching' and 'lodging', 140-1, 143
  Light Dragoons, 140

H.A.C., A Battery, 237
Hainault, Count of, 28
Hamilton, Lieutenant A. J., 179
Hammer-hatchets, 68
Harwood, Sir Edward, 48
Hauberk, 18, 21
Hawley, General, 87, 98-9
Heavy Brigade at Balaclava, 203
Helm, 18, 21
  Barrel, 21
  Great, 22
Henry I, King, 20
Henry II, King, 20
Henry V, King, army of, 29
Henry VII, King, Act of 1495, 33
Henry VIII, King, 35
  Law concerning stature of horses, 42
  March from Calais, 37
  Protection of horses under, 33
  Royal review in 1550, 39-40
Henry the Fowler, 19
Heraldry, 21
'Highflyer' Coach, 189
Hinde, Captain R., 99, 110, 123, 125, 133, 140, 155
Hobelar, 23, 26, 29, 43
Hoff, William, 198
Holmes, Colonel George, 192
Hombourgh, action of, 125
Honeywood, Major Philip, 104
Horse Artillery, 166
Horse Guards & Grenadiers, *see* Cavalry Regiments
Horse management, 125

Horse, regiments of, dress and equipment under James II, 68

Horses:
Armenians and Bashi Bazouks, of, 210
Civil War, in the, 49, 57
Coach, number required to work a, 188
Crimea, in the, 209
Fast coaches, influence on, 187
Furniture, Norman, 18
Routine for a long journey, 190
Troop, in 1792, 82

Horses, breeds and types of:
Arab, 20, 57, 200-2, 209, 226
Barb, 20, 57
Brabançon, 21
Cape, 198, 200-1
Cleveland Bay, 225-6
'Cloth Sek', 34
Clydesdale, 61
Cob, 57
Connemara, 23
Courser, 28
Curtal, 34
Darley Arabian, 226
Dextrarius, 21
Flemish, 21, 61
Gentle, 34
Godolphin Arabian, 227
Great, 21, 28, 34, 42, 43, 57, 84
Great Trotting, 34
Hackney, 28
Hengest, 28
Hobin, 23, 28
Lanarkshire, 61
Lombardy, 28
'Male', 34
Nag, 28
Norfolk Hackney, 225-6
Norman, 19
'Old English Black', 82
Palfrey, 28
Persian, 201, 216
Powys, 20
Saxon, 19
Shire, 22, 84
Somer, 28
Spanish, 19, 20
Spanish Jennet, 20, 28
Syrian Arab, 216-17
Trotter, 28
Trotting 'Gambaldyn', 34
Waler, 198, 216, 244
Yorkshire Coach Horse, 227
Huj, action at, 238
Hundred Years War, 31
Huntingdon, Earl of, 31
Hussars, 138, 173 (see also under Cavalry Regiments)
Expenses of a subaltern in, 162

Hutchinson, Major W. B., 247

Indian Mutiny, dress in, 210
Infantry Regiments:
Coldstream Regiment (later the Coldstream Guards), 56
Dutch Guards, 77
4th (King's Own) Foot (later The King's Own Royal Regiment), 224
11th Foot or The Devonshire Regiment, 88
13th Foot or The Somerset Light Infantry, 90, 224
80th Foot (later the 2nd Battalion The South Staffordshire Regiment), 224
90th Foot (later the 2nd Battalion The Cameronians), 224
Ingilby, Lieutenant, 176
Inniskilling cavalry regiments, 78
Inns, billeting at, 159
Irish Brigade, the, 110
Irish cavalry, 43-4
Irish Commissariat Corps, 165

Jackson, Colonel Basil, 175
Jacobite cavalry, 76
Jacobite rising of 1715, 95
James I, King, 48
James II, King, 66, 76, 78
Expansion of the Army in the reign of, 66
James, Hugh, 81
Javelin, 18
Jenin, charge at, 243
John, King, 21
Jones, Lieutenant Charles, 173

Kabul–Kandahar Field Force, 215
Kabul, operations at, 214
Kabul to Kandahar march, 215
Kane, Brigadier-General Richard, 84
Kelly, Captain Edward, 176
Kilmarnock, Lord, 109
Kingston, Duke of, 110
Letter from the Secretary at War, 111
Light Horse, 110
King's Troop of Horse Guards, 59, 60
Kitchener's Horse, 229
Knight-Bachelor, 24
Knight-Banneret, 24
Knight's Fee, 24

Lance, 18
Lance organization, 31, 35
Lanier, Major-General, 79
Liddell, Colonel R. S., 174, 216
Life Guards, see Cavalry Regiments
Light Brigade at Balaclava, 204

Light Dragoons, 98 (*see also under* Cavalry Regiments)
Accoutrements and weapons, 1756, 117
Establishment of troops in 1756, 117
Horses, 1756, 120
In the Peninsula, 166
Provision of Royal escort by, 143
Regiments, arms in, 1759
Regiments, raising of, 1759
Replacement of drums by trumpets, 133
Training, 120, 121
Troops, disbandment of, 1763, 123
Uniform in 1756, 119
Light Horse Brigade, charge by *3rd*, 243
Lindsay, Captain William, 123
Litani River, operations at, 247
London and Westminster Light Horse, 137, 147
Long, General R. B., 157, 168
Loudoun, Earl of, 95
Loy Smith, Sergeant-Major G., 192
Lucan, Lord, 203, 205-6
Lumley, General, 170
Lushai campaign, 215
Luttrell, Narcissus, 81
Luttrell's Regiment of Horse, 78

McAdam, 183
Method of road-making, 185
MacCarthy, Lieutenant-General Justin, Lord Mountcashel, 79
McGuffie, J. H., 157, 169
Mail, chain, 22
Mail, single, 21
Man-at-arms, 24, 44
Mangan, Henry, 79
Manners, Lieutenant-Colonel Lord Robert, 181
Markham, Gervase, 44
Markham, veterinary writer, 43
Marlborough, Duke of, 84-6
'Marquess of Huntly' coach, 189
Marsden, Commissariat officer, 174
Marshall, 225
Marston Moor, battle of, 53
Martin, Colonel, 218, 220
Massey, W. T., 242
Men of Arms, 34
Michele, Giovanni, report in 1557 by, 41
Micklethwayt, Captain, 54
Milne, S. M., 132
Minden, campaign of, 129
Monk, General, 56, 60
Monmouth rebellion, 66
Moodkee, battle of, 198
Morris, Captain, 205
Mount Badon, battle of, 17

Mounted infantry, 224-5, 228, 231
Musketoon, 49, 102

Napoleonic wars, cavalry in the, 168
Nazareth, capture of, 242
Nolan, Captain L. E., 134, 196, 205, 207
Norman Army, 17-18
Norman soldier, dress and equipment, 18
North Somerset Yeomanry, 246
Northumberland, Earl of, 33
Horses of, 34
Nottinghamshire Battery *R.H.A.*, 237

Olden, Major, 244
Omdurman, battle of, 217
Order of the Garter, Statutes of, 34-5
Ormonde, Duke of, 80, 92
Oudenarde, battle of, 85
Oxford's Regiment, Lord, 60

Paget, Lord, 166
Paget, Lord George, 206-9
Parker's Regiment of Horse, 76, 78
Pearce's Dragoons, 90-1
Pembroke, Earl of, 115, 148
Peninsular War, 166
Pennon, 18
Percussion firearms, 211
Pert, Major-General, 52
Pettit, Lieutenant and Adjutant, 191
Pistols:
'Brown Bess' type, 102
Civil War, 49
Heavy cavalry, 1796, 63
James II series, 68
Light Dragoons:
Regiments, 1759, 123
Troops, 1756, 117
'Paget', 163
Queen Anne issue, 92
Police duties of cavalry, eighteenth and nineteenth centuries, 113
Ponsonby, General Sir William, 179, 180
'Pots', 67
Poultney, Colonel, 80
Prince of Wales's Dragoon Guards, 138
Own Dragoons, 94
Regiment of Horse, 50, 52
Puckering, Major H., 50-2
Punjab Cavalry, 5th, 214
Purcell's Regiment of Horse, 78
Putney Heath, review of 1684 on, 64

Queen's Bays, 90
Queen's Dragoons, 137
Queen's Regiment of Horse, 82
Queen's Troop of Horse Guards, 60
Quentin, Lieutenant-Colonel, 181
'Quicksilver' Mail, 188

Raglan, Lord, 205
Raine, James, 54
Red coat:
In King James's Army, 67
Introduction of, 57
'Red Rover' coach, 189
Revolver, 211
Richmond, Duke of, 97
Rich, Sir Robert, 107
Rifle, 213
Issue of infantry pattern to cavalry, 231
Rimington, Major-General, M. F.,
Comments on horses in South Africa, 229-30
Roads in seventeenth century, 57
Roberts, Field-Marshal Lord, 214-15, 228, 230-1
Roberts's Horse, 229
Rochford's Dragoons, 90-1
Roman Army, 17
Roman de Rou, 17-18
Roses, wars of, 31, 33
Ross, Colonel, 80
Ross's Dragoons, 80
Royal Artillery, 162, 203
Royal Artillery Mounted Rifles, 231
Royal Engineers, 162
Royal Foresters, 121, 123
Royal Horse Artillery, 166, 176, 198, 203
Nottinghamshire Battery, 237
Royal Horse Guards, 59, 92, 97, 157, 178, 182 (*see also under* Cavalry Regiments)
Royal Irish Lancers, 5*th*, 84, 85
Royal 'Plates', 83
Royal Scots Greys, see Cavalry Regiments
Royal Signals, 162, 175, 245, 246, 248
Royal Staff Corps, 175
Royal United Service Institution, 204
Royal Waggon Train, 158
Rupert, Prince, 50, 58
Rutland Light Dragoons, 145
Ryswick, Treaty of, 80

Sahagun, action at, 162, 166
St. Pierre, Colonel, 91
Salamanca, battle of, 168
Sanders, General Liman von, 243
Sarsfield, Major-General Patrick, Earl of Lucan, 78
Regiment of House, 78
Troop of Irish Life Guards, 78
Scarlett, General, 203
Schomberg, Duke, 77
Scottish Troop of Horse Guards, 61
Seit Ali, action at, 209
Severne, General, 91

Shea, Major-General, 238
Shee, Captain, 110
Sheldon, Major-General Dominick, 77, 84
Shewell, Colonel Frederick George, 206
Shield, 18
Sinclair, Master of, 96
Slade, Brigadier-General, 167
Smithers, Private James, 172, 180
Snaphance, 68
Somerset, Lord E., 182
Somerset Yeomanry, 146
South Notts Yeomanry, 148
Speres, 34
Sprigge, Joshua, 50
Spurs, prick, 18
Stage-coach, 57, 65, 183
Stage-waggon, 57, 65
Stair, Lord, 84, 86, 114
Standards, 138
Stanhope, Lord, 90
Staremberg, Marshal, 92
Stephanides, William, 20
Steuart, A. Francis, 96
Stuart, Prince Charles, 108, 110
Surcoat, 21
Surtees Society, 54
Sutherland's Regiment of Horse, 76, 78
Swedish-feather, 57
Swine-feather, 57
Swords:
Cavalry:
1853, 211
1908, 239
Dragoon:
At the Boyne, 79
In Queen Anne's wars, 91
Heavy cavalry, 1848, 211
Horse and Dragoons:
Eighteenth century, 102
In the reign of Charles II, 65
Horse, in Civil War, 49
Light Dragoon:
Regiments in 1759, 123
Troops in 1756, 117
Norman, 18
Royal Warrant of 1796, 151

Tangiers Horse, 64
'Tantivy Trot, the', 189
Tel el Saba, attack on, 236
Telford, 183
Thornhill, Major, 204
Tremamondo, Anthony Angelo, 116-17
Trimburn's Horse, 87
Trumpet calls, cavalry, in 1635, 44
Tyrconnell, Duke of, 77
Tyrconnell's Regiment of Horse, 76, 78

Index

Uffenbach, Zacharias Conrad von, 92
Union Brigade, the, 179
Unton Crook's Regiment, 60
Usagre, action at, 169
Uxbridge, Lord, 178

Venetian Ambassador, report by, 1519, 33
Victoria, Queen, 215
Villers-en-Cauchies, action of, 157
Vimiero operations, shortage of horses in, 165
Voluntary mounted corps, 137
'Vonolel', 215

Wace, Robert, 17-18
Warde, Lieutenant-General, 150
Wardrobe accounts, 28
Warwickshire Yeomanry, 238
Waterloo, battle of, 176, 179, 180
Wellington, Duke of, 168, 174, 177-8, 181
Westmorland and Cumberland Yeomanry, 233
Wheel-lock, in the Civil War, 49
'Widdowsmen', 94
Wilhelmsthal, battle of, 136
William the Conqueror, 17-20

William of Orange (King William III), 66-7, 69, 76-8, 80
William Rufus, 20
Williams, Lieutenant-Colonel D. E., 247-8
Wilson, Brigadier-General, 243
Wilson, Cornet W. H. B. J., 192
Wiltshire Yeomanry, 191
Winchester, Statute of, 22, 24
Wood, Anthony à, 61
Wood, Captain Charles, 181
Worcester, Marquess of, 174
Worcestershire Yeomanry, 238
Wyck, John, 60

Yeomanry (*for individual regiments see* Cavalry Regiments):
  Boer War, in, 228
  Civil Power, in aid of, 148, 190-1
  First World War, 238-41
  Raising in 1794 of, 145
  Second World War, 246-8
Yeomen of the Crown, 33
Yorkshire Dragoons, 246
York's Troop of Horse Guards, Duke of, 56, 60

Zulu War, 224

Printed by Lithography in Great Britain by Jarrold & Sons Ltd., Norwich